Presidents from
Hoover through Truman,
1929–1953

D0169107

Recent Titles in
The President's Position: Debating the Issues

Presidents from Washington through Monroe, 1789–1825
Amy H. Sturgis

Presidents from Theodore Roosevelt through Coolidge, 1901–1929
Francine Sanders Romero

PRESIDENTS FROM HOOVER THROUGH TRUMAN, 1929–1953

Debating the Issues in Pro and Con Primary Documents

JOHN E. MOSER

WARNER MEMORIAL LIBRARY
EASTERN UNIVERSITY
ST. DAVIDS, 19087-3696

The President's Position: Debating the Issues
Mark Byrnes, Series Editor

GREENWOOD PRESS
Westport, Connecticut • London

2-5-13

E 176.1 .P9214 2002

Presidents from Hoover

Library of Congress Cataloging-in-Publication Data

Presidents from Hoover through Truman, 1929–1953 : debating the issues in pro and con primary documents / [compiled by] John E. Moser.
     p. cm.—(The president's position : debating the issues)
    Includes bibliographical references and index.
    ISBN 0–313–31441–1 (alk. paper)
    1. Presidents—United States—History—20th century—Sources. 2. United States—Politics and government—1929–1933—Sources. 3. United States—Politics and government—1933–1953—Sources. 4. Hoover, Herbert, 1874–1964—Political and social views. 5. Roosevelt, Franklin D. (Franklin Delano), 1882–1945—Political and social views. 6. Truman, Harry S., 1884–1972—Political and social views. I. Moser, John E., 1966– II. Series.
    E176.1.P9214   2002
    320'.6'097309041—dc21   2001023333

British Library Cataloguing in Publication Data is available.

Copyright © 2002 by John E. Moser

All rights reserved. No portion of this book may be reproduced, by any process or technique, without the express written consent of the publisher.

Library of Congress Catalog Card Number: 2001023333
ISBN: 0–313–31441–1

First published in 2002

Greenwood Press, 88 Post Road West, Westport, CT 06881
An imprint of Greenwood Publishing Group, Inc.
www.greenwood.com

Printed in the United States of America

The paper used in this book complies with the Permanent Paper Standard issued by the National Information Standards Organization (Z39.48–1984).

10 9 8 7 6 5 4 3 2 1

Copyright Acknowledgments

The author and publisher are grateful to the following for granting permission to reprint from their materials:

G. Garet, "Farm Relief So Far," *Saturday Evening Post* 202:52 (June 28, 1930), courtesy of *Saturday Evening Post*.

"The Muscle Shoals Veto" by Nation Editor reprinted with permission from the March 18, 1931 issue of *The Nation*.

Felix Morley, "The Return to Nothingness," *Human Events* 2:35 (August 29, 1945), courtesy of Eagle Publishing, Inc.

Cover art: Hoover: Library of Congress; Roosevelt: Franklin D. Roosevelt Library; Truman: U.S. Army, courtesy of Harry S. Truman Library.

CONTENTS

Series Foreword		vii
Acknowledgments		xi
Timeline		xiii
Introduction		1
1	Herbert Hoover (1929–1933)	11
	The Agricultural Marketing Act (1929)	15
	The London Naval Treaty (1930)	19
	The Hawley-Smoot Tariff (1930)	24
	The Wickersham Commission (1931)	29
	The Veterans' Bonus Bill (1931)	34
	The Muscle Shoals Joint Resolution (1931)	38
	The War Debt Moratorium (1931)	42
	The Reconstruction Finance Corporation (1932)	46
	The Emergency Relief Bill (1932)	50
	Recommended Readings	54
2	Franklin Delano Roosevelt (1933–1945)	57
	The Agricultural Adjustment Act (1933)	64
	The Civilian Conservation Corps (1933)	68
	The National Industrial Recovery Act (1933)	72
	The Social Security Act (1935)	78

The National Labor Relations Act (1935)   84

The Wealth Tax (1935)   89

Supreme Court Reorganization (1937)   94

Executive Reorganization (1937–1938)   99

The Ludlow Amendment (1938)   104

The Fair Labor Standards Act (1938)   109

The Neutrality Revision (1939)   115

The Selective Service Act (1940)   120

Lend-Lease (1941)   125

The War Labor Disputes Act (1943)   132

Recommended Readings   136

3   Harry S. Truman (1945–1953)   139

The Dropping of the Atomic Bomb (1945)   144

Price Controls (1946)   150

The Truman Doctrine (1947)   155

The Taft-Hartley Act (1947)   160

Truman's Loyalty Program (1947)   166

The Marshall Plan (1948)   171

Civil Rights (1948)   177

The Housing Act (1949)   182

The North Atlantic Treaty (1949)   187

National Health Insurance (1949)   193

Point Four (1949)   199

Intervention in Korea (1950)   205

McCarthyism (1950)   211

The Dismissal of General Douglas MacArthur (1951)   217

Recommended Readings   223

Bibliography   225

Index   229

SERIES FOREWORD

When he was running for president in 1932, Franklin D. Roosevelt declared that America needed "bold, persistent experimentation" in its public policy. "It is common sense to take a method and try it," FDR said. "If it fails, admit it frankly and try another. But above all, try something." At President Roosevelt's instigation, the nation did indeed take a number of steps to combat the Great Depression. In the process, the president emerged as the clear leader of American public policy. Most scholars see FDR's administration as the birth of the "modern presidency," in which the president dominates both domestic and foreign policy.

Even before FDR, however, presidents played a vital role in the making of public policy. Policy changes advocated by the presidents—often great changes—have always influenced the course of events, and have always sparked debate from the presidents' opponents. The outcomes of this process have had tremendous effects on the lives of Americans. The President's Position: Debating the Issues examines the stands the presidents have taken on the major political, social, and economic issues of their times as well as the stands taken by their opponents. The series combines description and analysis of those issues with excerpts from primary documents that illustrate the position of the presidents and their opponents. The result is an informative, accessible, and comprehensive look at the crucial connection between presidents and policy. These volumes will assist students doing historical research, preparing for debates, or fulfilling critical thinking assignments. The general reader interested in American history and politics will also find the series interesting and helpful.

Several important themes about the president's role in policy making emerge from the series. First, and perhaps most important, is how greatly the president's involvement in policy has expanded over the years. This has happened because the range of areas in which the national government acts has grown dramatically and because modern presidents—unlike most of their predecessors—see taking the lead in policy making as part of their job. Second, certain issues have confronted most presidents over history; tax and tariff policy, for example, was important for both George Washington and Bill Clinton, and for most of the presidents in between. Third, the emergence of the United States as a world power around the beginning of the twentieth century made foreign policy issues more numerous and more pressing. Finally, in the American system, presidents cannot form policy through decrees; they must persuade members of Congress, other politicians, and the general public to follow their lead. This key fact makes the policy debates between presidents and their opponents vitally important.

This series comprises nine volumes, organized chronologically, each of which covers the presidents who governed during that particular time period. Volume one looks at the presidents from George Washington through James Monroe; volume two, John Quincy Adams through James K. Polk; volume three, Zachary Taylor through Ulysses Grant; volume four, Rutherford B. Hayes through William McKinley; volume five, Theodore Roosevelt through Calvin Coolidge; volume six, Herbert Hoover through Harry Truman; volume seven, Dwight Eisenhower through Lyndon Johnson; volume eight, Richard Nixon through Jimmy Carter; and volume nine, Ronald Reagan through Bill Clinton. Each president from Washington through Clinton is covered, although the number of issues discussed under each president varies according to how long they served in office and how actively they pursued policy goals. Volumes six through nine—which cover the modern presidency—examine three presidencies each, while the earlier volumes include between five and seven presidencies each.

Every volume begins with a general introduction to the period it covers, providing an overview of the presidents who served and the issues they confronted. The section on each president opens with a detailed overview of the president's position on the relevant issues he confronted and the initiatives he took, and closes with a list of suggested readings. Up to fifteen issues are covered per presidency. The discussion of each issue features an introduction, the positions taken by the president and his opponents, how the issue was resolved, and the long-term effects of the issue. This is followed by excerpts from two primary documents, one representing the president's position and the other representing his opponents' position. Also included in each volume is a timeline of significant events of the era and a general bibliography of sources for students and others interested in further research.

As the most prominent individual in American politics, the president receives enormous attention from the media and the public. The statements, actions, travels, and even the personal lives of presidents are constantly scrutinized. Yet it is the presidents' work on public policy that most directly affects American citizens—a fact that is sometimes overlooked. This series is presented, in part, as a reminder of the importance of the president's position.

Mark Byrnes

ACKNOWLEDGMENTS

Most of the actual work on this book was done during the summer of 2000 when I was a visiting scholar at the Social Philosophy & Policy Center at Bowling Green State University in Ohio. I owe a tremendous debt of gratitude to the directors and staff of that institution, which provided me with the financial resources and support necessary for the completion of the project. Special thanks to Travis Cook and Carrie-Ann Biondi, who took care of the logistics, and to Mahesh Ananth, the center's research assistant, for locating many of the most important sources. Gary Dean Best, of the University of Hawaii at Hilo, was a fellow scholar at the center, and our extensive discussions about the interwar period played a significant role in the shaping of this volume.

Quite a few of the primary source documents included herein were obtained during my brief research trip to the Herbert Hoover Presidential Library in West Branch, Iowa. I would also like to extend my appreciation to the staff there, particularly Dale Mayer.

I would further like to thank my editors, both Barbara Rader at Greenwood Press and Mark Byrnes of Middle Tennessee State University, for their helpful comments and suggestions.

My wife, Monica, also deserves considerable gratitude, for tolerating a summer spent apart while I completed the manuscript 600 miles away from home.

TIMELINE

1928

June 14
Herbert Hoover nominated for president at the Republican National Convention in Kansas City, Missouri.

November 6
Hoover elected president of the United States, defeating Democratic candidate Alfred E. Smith; Franklin D. Roosevelt elected governor of New York in a close race.

1929

March 4
Hoover inaugurated as thirty-first president.

April 16
Hoover sends message to Congress calling for creation of Federal Farm Board.

June 15
Hoover signs Agricultural Marketing Act establishing Federal Farm Board, a $500 million fund for low-interest loans to farming cooperatives.

October 7
Hoover meets with British prime minister Ramsay MacDonald at a retreat in Rapidan, Virginia.

October 29
The stock market crashes, with more than sixteen million shares sold. The Great Depression begins.

1930

May 1
Hoover sends London Naval Treaty to the Senate for ratification.

June 16
Hoover signs Hawley-Smoot Tariff Bill, raising import duties to their highest levels ever.

November 4
Democrats win control of the House of Representatives and virtual control of the Senate in midterm elections.

December 31
Hoover announces the Senate's ratification of the London Naval Treaty.

1931

January 20   Hoover releases the report of the Wickersham Commission on the enforcement of the Prohibition laws.

February 26   Hoover vetoes the Veterans' Bonus Bill, which would have extended cash advances to veterans; Congress passes the bill over Hoover's veto the very next day.

March 3   Hoover vetoes the Muscle Shoals joint resolution, which would have created a corporation to operate government dams and power plants in Alabama.

June 20   Hoover proposes moratorium on war reparations and debts.

December 7   Hoover asks Congress to establish the Reconstruction Finance Corporation (RFC) to aid economic recovery; Hoover signs moratorium on war reparations and debts.

1932

January 22   Hoover signs the Reconstruction Finance Corporation Bill.

June 16   Hoover renominated for president at Republican National Convention in Chicago.

June 28   Federal troops forcibly evict the Veterans' Bonus Army from Washington, D.C.

July 11   Hoover vetoes the Emergency Relief Bill.

November 8   Roosevelt elected president of the United States, defeating Hoover; Democrats win control of both houses of Congress.

1933

March 4   Roosevelt inaugurated as thirty-second president of the United States; the first "Hundred Days" begins, during which Roosevelt signs dozens of bills, including legislation to create the National Recovery Administration, the Agricultural Adjustment Administration, and the Civilian Conservation Corps.

1934

November 6   Democrats score major gains in the midterm congressional elections. Harry S. Truman defeats incumbent Republican Roscoe C. Patterson to become U.S. senator from Missouri.

1935

May 27   The Supreme Court, in *Schechter v. United States*, declares the National Industrial Recovery Act unconstitutional.

June–August   The "Second Hundred Days" sees the passage of (among other bills) the Social Security Act, the National Labor Relations Act, and the so-called "Wealth Tax."

1936

January 6   The Supreme Court, in *United States v. Butler*, declares key parts of the Agricultural Adjustment Act unconstitutional.

| November 3 | Roosevelt reelected in a landslide over Kansas governor Alfred Landon; Democrats gain still more seats in Congress. |

1937

January 20	Roosevelt inaugurated for this second term as president.
February 5	Roosevelt proposes the Judicial Procedures Reform Act, which would add six new justices to the Supreme Court. Critics immediately denounce the bill as an attempt to "pack" the Court with Roosevelt loyalists.
July 14	Congress kills Roosevelt's "court-packing" plan.
October 19	A severe economic downturn begins; soon called the "Roosevelt Recession," it lasts until June 1938.

1938

April 8	Congress kills Roosevelt's plan for reorganization of the executive branch.
April 14	Roosevelt asks Congress to approve a large-scale spending program to revive the economy.
June 25	Roosevelt signs the Fair Labor Standards Act, which sets minimum wages and maximum hours of work.
June–August	Roosevelt actively campaigns against conservative Democrats in primary elections; opponents accuse him of attempting a "purge" of the party.
November 8	Midterm congressional elections give Republicans major gains in both the House and the Senate.

1939

| September 1 | German troops invade Poland; World War II begins. |
| November 4 | Roosevelt signs legislation revising the neutrality laws to allow trade with belligerent nations on a "cash-and-carry" basis. |

1940

June 21	France surrenders to Germany.
July 26	Roosevelt orders an embargo on scrap iron and aviation fuel to Japan.
September 2	Roosevelt authorizes the transfer of fifty old destroyers to Great Britain.
September 16	Congress passes the Selective Service Act, establishing the country's first peacetime draft.
November 5	Roosevelt reelected president, defeating Wendell Willkie; Truman wins reelection to the U.S. Senate.

1941

| March 1 | Senate votes to create Special Committee to Investigate the National Defense Program, headed by Truman. |
| March 11 | Roosevelt signs the Lend-Lease Act, authorizing the transfer of millions of dollars in supplies and weapons to Great Britain. |

June 22   German troops invade the Soviet Union; lend-lease aid is extended to that country as well.

July 21   Japanese forces occupy French Indochina.

July 26   Roosevelt orders the freezing of all Japanese assets in the United States.

August 9–12   Roosevelt meets British Prime Minister Winston Churchill at Placentia Bay, in Newfoundland.

December 7   Japanese aircraft attack U.S. Pacific Fleet at Pearl Harbor; United States declares war on Japan the following day; Germany and Italy declare war on the United States three days later.

1942

February 19   Roosevelt authorizes internment of Japanese Americans living on the West Coast.

June 4   Four Japanese aircraft carriers sunk by American planes at the battle of Midway.

August 7   U.S. Marines land on Guadalcanal in the South Pacific.

November 8   U.S. forces land in North Africa.

1943

June 20–21   Race riot in Detroit leaves thirty-four dead and roughly seven hundred injured.

June 28   Congress passes the Smith-Connally War Labor Disputes Act over Roosevelt's veto.

July 10   Allied troops land on Sicily.

September 9   Allied troops invade Italy.

November 28   Roosevelt meets with Churchill and the Soviet leader, Joseph Stalin, at Teheran, in Iran.

1944

June 6   D day: Allied forces land on the northern coast of France in the largest naval invasion in history.

July 21   Truman is nominated for the office of vice president at the Democratic National Convention in Chicago.

November 7   Roosevelt reelected to a fourth term as president, defeating Thomas E. Dewey; Truman is elected vice president.

1945

February 4–12   Roosevelt meets with Churchill and Stalin at Yalta in the Soviet Union.

April 12   Roosevelt dies of a cerebral hemorrhage in Warm Springs, Georgia; Truman sworn in as thirty-third president of the United States.

May 8   Germany surrenders; Truman announces the end of World War II in Europe.

June 29   Truman vetoes price control bill.

August 6   First atomic bomb dropped on Hiroshima; 40,000 Japanese die instantly.

August 9	Second atomic bomb dropped on Nagasaki.
August 15	Japan surrenders to the Allies.

1946

November 5	Midterm elections give Republicans control of both houses of Congress.
November 9	Truman orders an end to all wage and price controls except on rents, sugar, and rice.

1947

March 12	Truman unveils what would become known as the "Truman Doctrine"; asks Congress for $400 million to help the governments of Greece and Turkey resist communist pressure.
March 21	Truman institutes loyalty-security program for federal employees.
June 20	Truman vetoes the Taft-Hartley Act, charging that it is unfair to labor; Congress overrides Truman's veto three days later.

1948

April 3	Truman signs the Foreign Assistance Act of 1948, which implements the Marshall Plan for U.S. aid to Europe.
May 14	Truman announces U.S. recognition of the state of Israel.
June 26	Truman orders that food and supplies be airlifted into West Berlin in contravention of a Soviet blockade of the city.
July 15	Truman is renominated for president at the Democratic National Convention in Philadelphia.
November 3	Truman wins reelection in an upset victory over Thomas E. Dewey, governor of New York. Democrats regain control of both the House and the Senate.

1949

January 5	Truman announces his plan for a new round of liberal reforms, which he calls the "Fair Deal."
January 20	Truman is inaugurated for second term; calls for a "bold new program" to alleviate poverty in the developing world (Point Four Program).
April 4	Ten European nations, plus the United States and Canada, sign the North Atlantic Treaty, which establishes the North Atlantic Treaty Organization (NATO).
July 15	Truman signs the Housing Act, which provides for federal aid to slum clearance programs and public housing projects.
September 23	Truman announces there is evidence that the Soviet Union has successfully detonated an atomic bomb.
October 1	Mao Tse-tung proclaims that China is now a communist "People's Republic."

1950

February 9	Wisconsin senator Joseph McCarthy alleges that communist agents have infiltrated the State Department.

June 25   North Korean troops invade South Korea; Truman orders U.S. forces to Korea on the following day.

September 23   Congress passes the McCarran Internal Security Act, which requires that Communist organizations register with the government, over Truman's veto.

November 6   Chinese troops enter North Korea, marking full-scale Chinese involvement in the Korean War.

1951

April 11   Truman relieves Douglas MacArthur of command of U.S. forces in Asia for criticizing administration policy in the Korean War.

1952

March 29   Truman announces that he will not run for reelection.

November 4   Dwight David Eisenhower is elected thirty-fourth president of the United States, defeating Democratic candidate Adlai Stevenson.

INTRODUCTION

The average young man graduating high school in the spring of 1929 would probably be looking forward to a stable, reasonably high-paying job in the nation's booming industrial sector. He might become a factory worker, or perhaps a salesman or a clerk in an office. If he took a job with a large corporation, he could be expected to receive annual stock bonuses and profit-sharing plans, life insurance policies, and even old-age pensions. If he had a little money to spare, he might invest in the stock market, which for the past three years had been booming like never before. For millions of American men, a job with a major corporation was the ticket to prosperity; the stock market the key to a fortune. It appeared that Americans had never had it so good.

A young woman graduating in 1929 had fewer options, but the future still would have seemed bright. Most likely she would marry within the next several years; in the meantime, she might take a job as a nurse, a schoolteacher, or a maid in the home of a wealthy family. Once married, she would have enjoyed a level of equality with her husband that had never been seen in American history. Moreover, as soon as she reached the age of twenty-one she would have a right that her mother most likely had not enjoyed at her age—the right to vote. Finally, she would also benefit from the booming economy. During her time of employment she would earn more than most women in history, and although she would typically leave her job when she got married, her husband's salary would enable her to purchase a wide range of household appliances that would help her with her daily chores.

Indeed, the major theme of the late 1920s was optimism, and no one expressed this optimism more openly than President Herbert Hoover.

Even before he became president, Hoover was one of the most respected men in the country, if not the world. After receiving an engineering degree from Stanford University, he began a career in mining, developing successful mining operations in Australia, Asia, Africa, and Latin America. During and after World War I he organized a massive relief effort to feed starving people in war-torn Europe, and became an international celebrity in the process. Later, as secretary of commerce under Presidents Harding and Coolidge, he inaugurated the policy—which continues to this day—of collecting statistical data on unemployment. He sincerely believed that American individualism, supported by a dynamic federal government, could end the nation's problems. As he put it in a speech in 1928, the country had "come nearer to the abolition of poverty, to the abolition of fear of want, than humanity has ever reached before."[1]

Hoover had two priorities upon becoming president. The first was to relieve the plight of farmers, driven deep into debt by low prices for farm products and the increased use of new machinery (particularly gasoline-powered tractors) in agriculture. In June 1929, Congress passed the Agricultural Marketing Act, which created a Federal Farm Board with the power to make loans to farming cooperatives. The second was naval disarmament; he hoped to prevent an arms race that appeared to be developing among the United States, Great Britain, and Japan. To this end he made preparations for a naval conference to be held in London in 1930 to limit the construction of new warships.

But perceptive observers saw trouble on the horizon. To be sure, farmers were by and large not benefiting from the economic boom. Even more ominous was the growing indebtedness of all Americans, not just farmers. Ordinary workers and middle-class people took advantage of "installment buying," which allowed them to purchase automobiles and other consumer products without having the money up front. Meanwhile, many of those who invested in the stock market did so "on margin," meaning that they could buy stocks for a fraction of their face value, on the promise that they would pay the rest at some unspecified future point. Thousands of investors entered the market in this way, and the result was a dramatic increase in stock values—even in the stocks of companies that were failing to show a profit.

On October 24, 1929—only seven months after Hoover took office—the boom came to a quick end. The stock market crashed, and the thousands of investors who had purchased stock on margin were asked to make good on their promise to pay. When they could not, they were forced to sell their stocks, so that stock prices continued to plummet over the next two weeks. For ten years thereafter, the country would continue to struggle through the worst economic crisis of its history—the Great Depression. Cut off from their sources of capital, businesses scaled back their activities, and laid off millions of workers. This in turn made the situation worse, since unemployed people could not buy the sort of consumer goods—radios, washing machines, vacuum cleaners, and most importantly automobiles—that had sustained the economic growth of the 1920s. Throughout Hoover's presidency, therefore, the economy continued to deteriorate.

Hoover believed that the severity of the crisis required a strong response by the federal government. Capital, he argued, had to be pumped into the economy so that business confidence could be restored and the unemployed put back to work. It was in this spirit that he established, with congressional approval, the Reconstruction Finance Corporation (RFC). The RFC extended loans to banks and major corporations in the hope that they would hire more employees, place orders with other firms, and make investments in new enterprises. At the same time, Hoover recognized the international scope of the crisis, and called for a temporary suspension of payments on the debts incurred by European countries during World War I (see War Debt Moratorium of 1931).

There were, however, certain measures that Hoover refused to take. He opposed the idea of making direct payments to individuals and families, fearing that this would make them dependent on the federal government and unwilling to work. He therefore vetoed legislation such as the Veterans' Bonus Bill (1931) and the Emergency Relief Bill (1932). Moreover, he did not believe that the government should compete with private business, which led him to veto a congressional resolution to bring electricity to parts of the rural South (the Muscle Shoals joint resolution of 1931). Finally, Hoover was concerned that large budget deficits might make the depression worse, so he tried to keep federal spending low through measures like the Economy Act (1932).

Despite Hoover's best efforts, the economy continued to slump. By late 1932 American banks were collapsing at an alarming rate, and some were beginning to call for the adoption of fascist or communist forms of government, such as those already in existence in Italy and the Soviet Union. Nevertheless, Hoover stood again as the Republican presidential nominee. Very few people expected him to win; in fact, many people had come to believe that Hoover was simply not interested in trying to end the depression. On election day, therefore, the voters turned overwhelmingly to the Democratic candidate, Franklin Delano Roosevelt.

Unlike Hoover, Franklin D. Roosevelt had been in politics all his life. He had served in the New York state legislature, served as assistant secretary of the navy under Woodrow Wilson, had run for vice president on the Democratic ticket in 1920, and was elected governor of New York in 1928. During the 1932 presidential campaign he promised "a new deal for the American people," but remained vague as to what this might mean. Ultimately his victory was due to a combination of Hoover's extreme unpopularity and Roosevelt's cheery, optimistic style. As one Supreme Court justice put it, he was a "second-class intellect," but he had a "first-class temperament."[2]

In his inaugural address, Roosevelt promised quick and dramatic action, and he was as good as his word. Within the first hundred days of his administration Congress passed an amazing series of bills that the president favored. In an attempt to increase the supply of money, the dollar was taken off the gold standard. An Agricultural Adjustment Act promised aid to farmers, but only on the condition that they reduced the amount of food they produced so that prices would rise. A public works bill spent millions of dollars to put the unemployed to work. Another bill created the Tennessee Valley Authority, which brought the federal government into the provision of electricity to rural areas; still another set up the National Recovery Administration, which had the power to set wages and prices in particular industries. A few of the measures enacted during the first "Hundred Days" were extensions of Hoover's own program; most, however, went far beyond, involving the federal government in areas that Hoover had insisted should remain within the scope of the private sector.

But although Roosevelt's New Deal was wildly popular, it immediately drew fire from both the Right and the Left. Conservatives in both the Republican and Democratic parties claimed that the president was violating the Constitution, and some feared that he was trying to set himself up as a dictator. Radicals, meanwhile, complained that Roosevelt was not doing enough to destroy the power of large banks and major corporations. Many on the Left demanded the establishment of a full-scale welfare system similar to those which had already been established in some European countries.

When the early legislation of the New Deal failed to bring about economic recovery, Roosevelt veered sharply to the Left in 1935, unveiling a series of new, more radical measures. These included nearly $1 billion in new spending on public works projects, a heavy new tax on the wealthiest Americans, and a system of old-age insurance called Social Security. The National Labor Relations Act gave a tremendous boost to labor unions, by guaranteeing the right of workers to organize and requiring employers to bargain with union representatives. Many on the Left applauded these moves, while conservatives complained that Roosevelt was turning America into a socialist country.

Although the promised economic recovery never came, most Americans gave the New Deal their enthusiastic support. At least, they reasoned, Roosevelt seemed to be doing something on their behalf. Moreover, he was succeeding in creating a new coalition of reliably Democratic voters. Union workers in the Northeast joined with small farmers from the South and Midwest, while African Americans abandoned their traditional support for the Republican Party. When he stood for reelection in 1936 against Alf Landon, the Republican governor of Kansas, the voters returned him to office in a landslide.

Roosevelt's second term, however, would bring disappointment. His attempt to add more justices to the Supreme Court was interpreted as an attack on the Constitution, and Congress handed the president his first serious political defeat. Moreover, the economy took a sudden downturn in 1937, underscoring Roosevelt's failure to bring the country out of the depression. The president's attempt to drive more conservative members of his own party from Congress by campaigning for their opponents in the 1938 primaries met with disaster. Not only did most of the conservatives survive the challenge, but they returned to Washington vowing revenge against the president who had tried to unseat them. The general elections compounded the president's problems, as Republicans made major gains for the first time in ten years. Thereafter, Republicans would be able to join with conservative Democrats to block further presidential initiatives. By 1939 the New Deal was effectively at an end.

However, by that time international affairs had increasingly occupied Roosevelt's mind. Americans had remained aloof from foreign commitments since the end of World War I. Many believed that the depression had come about at least in part as the result of that war, and almost all Americans agreed that if another war broke out in Europe, the United States had to stay out. To ensure that this would be the case, a series of Neutrality Acts passed in the mid-1930s, placing severe restrictions on arms sales and loans to countries that were at war. Arms sales and loans, many believed, would cause the U.S. government to favor one side over another, thus making it more likely that America would be drawn into future conflicts. In addition, a constitutional amendment to require a national referendum for a declaration of war came close to passing Congress in early 1938.

Yet just as Americans were trying to insulate themselves from foreign wars, the leaders of Germany, Italy, and Japan were building up their armed forces and embarking on aggressive new foreign policies aimed at conquering new territories. By late 1939 Germany had absorbed Austria and Czechoslovakia, Italy had seized Ethiopia and Albania, and Japan was engaged in a full-scale invasion of China. When in September German troops invaded Poland, France and Britain declared war on Germany. World War II had begun.

Although nearly all Americans supported the cause of Britain and France, very few actually wanted to go to war. Roosevelt realized this, but favored aiding Germany's opponents. Almost immediately after the outbreak of the war in Europe, he pushed Congress to pass new legislation modifying the neutrality acts and permitting certain arms sales to Britain and France. In 1940, after the German army defeated France, he authorized the transfer of fifty old destroyers to the British navy, and backed the country's first peacetime draft.

The foreign crisis had one positive effect for Roosevelt—it rejuvenated public support for him at the end of what had been a difficult second term. In 1940 he decided to run for an unprecedented third term as president, this time against Indiana lawyer Wendell Willkie. Although Willkie conducted a far more spirited and effective campaign than Landon had in 1936, the threat of war convinced many Americans that they were better off sticking with the tried and true Roosevelt. He won reelection with nearly 55 percent of the vote.

Safely elected to a third term, the president chose to put forward his most daring foreign policy initiative to date. By the end of 1940 Great Britain was running out of money to buy American weapons and supplies, and Roosevelt feared that if something were not done quickly the island nation might be forced to surrender to Germany. After weeks of intense presidential lobbying, in early 1941, Congress passed the Lend-Lease Act, which allowed the transfer of ships, aircraft, tanks, and other implements of war to Great Britain. When the German army invaded the Soviet Union in June 1941, lend-lease aid was extended to that country as well.

While this was going on, Japan continued its war against China, and took advantage of the defeat of France to occupy the French colony of Indochina (what is today Vietnam, Kampuchea, and Laos). The Japanese further outraged American opinion by joining Germany and Italy in the Axis alliance. Roosevelt responded to these provocations with a series of trade sanctions that he thought would curb Japanese aggression. However, these sanctions, particularly restrictions on the export of oil, threatened to cripple Japan's economy. By late 1941 Japan was facing a desperate situation, and the country's leaders decided that a quick war might encourage the United States to change its policies. On December 7, therefore, Japanese carrier-based aircraft launched a surprise attack on the U.S. Pacific Fleet at Pearl Harbor in Hawaii.

The bombing of Pearl Harbor shocked and outraged American opinion, and Roosevelt quickly got a declaration of war from Congress. Several days later Germany and Italy declared war on the United States, making the conflict truly global in scope. For the next three and a half years America found itself fighting the Axis powers alongside Great Britain and the Soviet Union, and the U.S. armed forces would be engaged in fighting on six of the world's seven continents. Slowly, the German and Italian armies were driven back in North Africa and Europe, while the Japanese were forced on the defensive in Asia and the South Pacific. By the summer of 1945 Germany and Italy had surrendered, and the Japanese islands were under daily bombardment.

American involvement in World War II had far-reaching effects on the country's economy and society. The need for millions of soldiers and sailors virtually eliminated unemployment, which had been the most disturbing feature of the depression. Indeed, by 1943 labor was actually becoming scarce, giving workers a new degree of leverage in their relations with management. To check the growing power of labor unions, Congress passed, over Roosevelt's veto, the War Labor Disputes Act, which threatened striking workers with conscription if they failed to return to work.

The war also had a tremendous impact on women and African Americans. Women entered the workforce in huge numbers, as secretaries and even factory workers, to replace the men who had gone to war. Thousands of blacks, meanwhile, left the South for cities in the Northeast, where they took jobs in the booming industrial sector. As they gained economic clout, African Americans began to speak out more strongly against discrimination and other evils that affected them. The social changes of World War II would, in fact, spark the emergence of the movements for civil rights and women's liberation that would come into full bloom in the late 1950s and 1960s.

In April 1945, only six months after his reelection to a fourth term as president, Franklin Roosevelt died of a cerebral hemorrhage. His successor was Harry S. Truman, who just a few months earlier had been a fairly obscure senator from Missouri. In fact, he had not even been informed of the biggest American research project of the war—the so-called "Manhattan Project," which sought to develop an atomic bomb. A team of scientists successfully detonated such a weapon in July, and, when the Japanese government refused to surrender, an American bomber dropped an atomic bomb on the city of Hiroshima on August 6. Forty thousand people were killed in the initial blast; 100,000 more died within days of burns and radiation. Three days later a second bomb was dropped on Nagasaki, killing another 70,000. The Japanese government announced its surrender soon thereafter.

The end of the war left a dramatically changed international landscape. The defeated Axis nations lay in ruins, and even some of the victorious Allies—namely, Britain and France—would never regain their status as great powers. Only two countries were more powerful in 1945 than they had been in 1939—the United States and the Soviet Union. Although they had been allies during the war, there was a legacy of mutual distrust that ran deep. The Soviet leader, Joseph Stalin, presided over a government that many Americans felt was little better than the Axis regimes that they had just helped to defeat. Stalin, for his part, spoke of renewing the struggle against the capitalist world—of which, by this time, the United States was the undisputed leader.

Over the next five years, a whole series of incidents arose that convinced Truman—and the American people—that the United States had to take an active role in preventing the expansion of Soviet communism. In 1947 Congress endorsed the so-called "Truman Doctrine" by voting to send economic and military aid to Greece and Turkey, then believed to be under Soviet pressure. The following year Congress approved the Marshall Plan, which spent millions of dollars in an effort to rebuild the shattered economies of European countries. Finally, in 1949 the United States joined the North Atlantic Pact, thus guaranteeing that American forces would be used to defend Western Europe against any Soviet attack. These steps mark the start of the cold war, a period of tension between the Soviets and Americans that would last through the 1980s.

But while Truman's foreign policy met with considerable success, the president ran into some serious problems when it came to domestic affairs. In 1946 voters elected a Republican majority to Congress for the first time since the Hoover administration, and the new Congress immediately set about to repeal what they saw as the worst excesses of the New Deal. In 1947 they passed a constitutional amendment to prevent any president from serving more than two terms—a belated slap at Franklin Roosevelt. Their most important accomplishment, however, was the passage (over the president's veto) of the Taft-Hartley Act, which sought to curb the power of labor unions.

Contrary to predictions, Truman managed to win reelection in a race against New York governor Thomas Dewey in 1948. Yet despite the fact that the Democrats regained majorities in both houses of Congress, Truman's domestic agenda met with little more success in the second term than it had in the first. Although he managed to win congressional support for a new foreign aid program (Point Four) and public housing, a working alliance of Republicans and southern Democrats blocked his proposals for national health insurance and civil rights for African Americans.

Foreign affairs brought further crisis, as communism appeared to be triumphing almost everywhere. The Soviet Union successfully detonated an atomic bomb in August 1949. During that same month a communist government took control of China, prompting many in Congress and the public to ask why the administration had not done more to protect its friends in Asia. The following year troops from Soviet-backed North Korea invaded South Korea. Truman quickly ordered U.S. forces to help turn back the offensive, but the result was a costly and unpopular war that seemed to drag on endlessly. Back home, Wisconsin senator Joseph McCarthy was getting headlines by accusing the administration of harboring communists and communist sympathizers in the State Department. Finally, the president's public standing hit an all-time low in 1951, when he dismissed the popular General Douglas MacArthur from command of American forces in Asia. As the 1952 presidential election approached, Truman announced that he would not be a candidate.

By 1952 the United States was a very different place than it had been in 1929. The experience of the depression had fundamentally changed most Americans' ideas of the role of the federal government. When Herbert Hoover entered office Washington was little more than a sleepy little southern town on the Potomac River, and few looked to it for anything more than the bare minimum needs of national defense. In 1952 Washington was booming, the central nervous system of an enormous military establishment and thousands of federal agencies. Americans now looked to the federal government not only to protect their constitutional rights, but also to maintain economic growth, to provide a "safety net" for those who lost their jobs, and to care for them in old age.

Just as important was the changing view of Americans regarding their place in the world. In 1929 few believed that the United States had vital interests beyond the nation's borders. Most saw other countries—particularly European countries—as hopelessly corrupt and prone to violence. America's best policy, they believed, was to remain uninvolved, except perhaps through trade and missionary work. Yet World War II and the emerging cold war changed their minds. Americans now concluded that the world was a dangerous place, and that a foreign policy of nonentanglement no longer served the country's needs. In 1941 the government had decided that national security depended on the ability of Great Britain and the Soviet Union to defend themselves against Germany; only nine years later, Truman decided that it also depended on the defense of South Korea. As Truman left office, it seemed that no part of the world was too remote in the struggle against communism.

Yet there was one powerful aspect of similarity between America in 1929 and 1952, and that was a sense of boundless optimism. Americans in 1929 looked forward to a future of material prosperity never before seen in human history. Like Hoover, they saw a partnership between private enterprise and government as the key to eliminating lingering problems such as the farm crisis. Although the depression frustrated these hopes over the next ten years, they emerged again in the wake of World War II. Once again the economy was booming, and Americans were enjoying living standards higher than anywhere else in the world. Moreover, the victory over the Axis powers gave them a sense of confidence about their country's power. As they saw it, they had faced evil and had triumphed once; they would triumph again against the evil of Soviet communism.

One sign of this renewed sense of confidence was the birth rate. Beginning immediately after World War II, and continuing through the 1950s, America experienced what became known as the "baby boom." The birth rate in the late 1940s reached an all-time high—twenty-five births for every 1,000 people—and well over 4 million children were being born each year. The "baby boom" generation would itself have a tremendous impact on American politics, culture, and society from the 1960s onward.

As was the case in 1929, this sense of confidence sometimes blinded Americans to real problems within their borders. Extreme poverty reigned in certain parts of the country, particularly in the rural South. African Americans, aware of their newly found economic power, had already begun to demand that they no longer be treated as second-class citizens; soon women and other groups would do the same. Finally, the same spirit that led the United States to come to the defense of Great Britain in 1941, and South Korea in 1950, would drive the country toward a longer, more frustrating struggle in Vietnam. Future presidents would have plenty to occupy their attention.

NOTES

1. Michael E. Parrish, *Anxious Decades: America in Prosperity and Depression, 1920–1941* (New York: W. W. Norton, 1992), 208.

2. David M. Kennedy, *Freedom from Fear: The American People in Depression and War* (New York: Oxford University Press, 1999), 100.

1

HERBERT HOOVER

(1929–1933)

Perhaps no president has entered office as popular, and left the White House as hated, as Herbert Hoover. Since his much-publicized campaign to feed Europe in the wake of World War I, he had been an international celebrity; even his future nemesis, Franklin Roosevelt, expressed hope that he would run for president of the United States in 1920. When President Warren G. Harding chose him as secretary of commerce, both the Republican and Democratic parties applauded the move. He served in that capacity throughout the Harding and Coolidge administrations—Harding called him "the smartest gink I know"[1]—and under his leadership the Commerce Department was the only cabinet department to grow, both in number of employees and in the size of its budget. When Coolidge announced that he would not seek another term as president, Hoover was the natural choice of the Republican Party in 1928.

On the campaign trail, Hoover promised voters "a chicken for every pot and a car for every garage"; in other words, he pledged to make the benefits of free enterprise available to all sectors of the population. He won by a landslide, and it is clear that from the beginning the American people expected a lot from him. Citing his background in engineering, newspapers across the country referred to him as "the Great Engineer," who would make the engine of capitalism run more smoothly and effectively. "They have a conviction that I am a sort of superman," Hoover wrote to a trusted associate, "and that no problem is beyond my capacity."[2]

For Hoover, who grew up in rural Iowa, the first priority was dealing with the agricultural situation. Overproduction forced farm prices lower and lower during the 1920s, so that many farmers were facing bankruptcy. Less than a month after his inauguration, he asked Congress to create a Federal Farm Board with the power to extend low-interest loans to farmers. These loans would allow farmers to withhold their products from the market until prices increased. Congress did as he asked, and Hoover signed the Agricultural Marketing Act into law in June 1929.

The president also hoped to advance the cause of disarmament. In 1928 Congress had voted for a significant expansion in the size of the navy, designed to match building programs already in progress in Japan and Great Britain. Hoover feared that a serious arms race would develop if some kind of agreement were not reached, and to that end he invited Ramsay MacDonald to be the first sitting British prime minister to visit the United States. The 1929 visit led to a new round of negotiations, and eventually to an international conference at London the following year that placed limits on further naval construction.

But the true test of Hoover's leadership would come in October 1929, when the booming economy of the 1920s came to a dramatic halt. The stock market began to falter in late October, and then plummeted on Tuesday, October 29. Over the next several years the economy was in free-fall. The stocks of such major corporations as U.S. Steel and General Motors lost 90 percent of their value, and businesses across the country struggled to stay afloat by canceling orders and laying off workers.

Hoover's response to the "Great Depression" was to use all the resources at the government's command in order to cope with the crisis. His main concern was to ensure that wages remained high. As long as ordinary people could afford to buy things, he reasoned, the economy would have to improve. To that end, he held a series of conferences with corporate leaders who promised that they would not reduce wages. Moreover, he pushed through Congress legislation creating the Reconstruction Finance Corporation (RFC), which was authorized to make emergency loans to struggling banks and corporations. The result was an unprecedented growth in government spending, and a federal deficit that reached $2.2 billion by 1931.

The president believed that the depression had originated in Europe. In an effort to protect American businesses from falling global prices, he signed the Hawley-Smoot Act, which increased import duties to their highest rate in U.S. history. He also believed that the international system of war debts and reparations, which had been a feature of the global economy since the end of World War I, was partially to blame for the economic crisis. He therefore proposed a one-year moratorium on all such payments.

In spite of this unprecedented activity, the economy continued its downward spiral. By March 1933 industrial production was less than half what it had been in August 1929. The Hawley-Smoot Tariff effectively destroyed American exports, as foreign countries retaliated by raising their own tariff rates. The crisis quickly spread to the banking system; in 1931 and 1932 more than 5,000 banks closed their doors, and by the end of Hoover's presidency, American banking was in ruins. And although real wages actually increased thanks to Hoover's agreements with business leaders, this made little difference to the millions of Americans who were unemployed—roughly one in four by 1933.

Hoover would later be remembered less for what he did to fight the depression than for what he refused to do. In the midterm elections of 1930 Democrats regained control of the House of Representatives for the first time in ten years, and made considerable gains in the Senate as well. The new Congress passed a great deal of legislation, much of which Hoover vetoed. This included the Emergency Relief Bill, which sought to channel $300 million in federal funds to the unemployed, the Veterans' Bonus Bill, which would have made cash payments to World War I veterans, and the Muscle Shoals joint resolution, which would have involved the government in the provision of cheap electricity to thousands of households in the South. In the first two cases, Hoover insisted that such expenditures would unbalance the budget and would have little effect on the economy. As for Muscle Shoals, the president argued that while the federal government should do all it could to aid private corporations in promoting recovery, it should not set itself up in competition with private power companies.

Because of his opposition to such congressional initiatives, Hoover was often accused of being a "do-nothing" president who was content to let the economy—and the American people—fend for themselves. In fact, this was anything but the case. Hoover was the first president who believed that the government had a responsibility to maintain a healthy economy. He boasted in October 1932 that his administration had embarked upon "the most gigantic program of economic defense and counter-attack ever involved in the history of the Republic."[3] By the time he left office he had spent billions in federal funds in an attempt to end the depression. In many ways the policies of his successor, Franklin D. Roosevelt, would be modeled on Hoover's efforts.

However, this is not the image that most Americans had of Herbert Hoover in the early 1930s. His opponents in both parties managed even to use his positive accomplishments against him, such as the war debt moratorium and the Reconstruction Finance Corporation. Hoover, they claimed, was more concerned in bailing out foreign countries and big banks and corporations than he was in relieving the distress of ordinary people.

By 1932, the president had become one of the least popular figures in the country. Empty pockets turned inside out were being called "Hoover flags." Newspapers used by homeless people to cover their bodies were "Hoover blankets." Shantytowns that popped up on the edges of many

American cities were called "Hoovervilles." In Washington, Hoover's colleagues noted the "ever-present feeling of gloom" that pervaded the White House. As one of his cabinet members put it, "I don't remember there has ever been a joke cracked in a single meeting in the last year-and-a-half."[4]

Although the Republican Party dutifully nominated Hoover to a second term in the summer of 1932, there was little enthusiasm for his candidacy. During that same summer, 20,000 army veterans descended on Washington and set up a massive "Hooverville" in the middle of the city. Hoover ordered them to disperse in late July, and when they refused the U.S. Army forcibly evicted them. For weeks, newsreels and journalistic accounts told stories, often greatly exaggerated, of helpless and unarmed men, women, and children being brutalized by soldiers allegedly acting under the president's orders. Hoover's public image, already tarnished in the eyes of most Americans, fell to a new low. The November elections would establish what everyone already knew was true—that Hoover had lost the confidence of the American people. Franklin D. Roosevelt won in a landslide even greater than the one that had brought Hoover to office four years earlier.

After his retirement from politics Hoover continued to make public statements. He was a persistent and severe critic of Roosevelt's "New Deal" policies, and would later question the foreign policies of Roosevelt and Harry Truman. Yet he did more than criticize; he remained an important advisor to the Republican Party well into the 1950s. After World War II he addressed the daunting question of feeding postwar Europe, thus returning to the issue that had first brought him to prominence a generation earlier. Later, President Truman appointed Hoover to form a commission to examine the organization of the executive branch.

Hoover lived his final years in the Waldorf-Astoria Towers in New York City. From 1940 on he wrote no less than nineteen books, many of which were collections of his own essays and speeches. He remained active in Republican politics, giving speeches at every Republican National Convention through 1960. He continued to correspond with friends and well-wishers until his own death in October 1964. He was ninety years old.

NOTES

1. Robert K. Murray, *The Harding Era: Warren G. Harding and His Administration* (Minneapolis: American Political Biography Press, 1969), 195.

2. Martin Fausold and George Mazuzan, *The Hoover Presidency: A Reappraisal* (Albany: State University of New York, 1974), 52–53.

3. Murray Rothbard, *America's Great Depression* (New York: Sheed and Ward, 1963), 187.

4. Fausold and Mazuzan, *The Hoover Presidency*, 91–92.

THE AGRICULTURAL MARKETING ACT (1929)

The crisis of American farmers stood out in sharp contrast to the prosperity being enjoyed by most other sectors of the American economy in the 1920s. The problem was simple—new technology made it possible for individual farmers to grow more than ever before, and as a result prices for agricultural products were dropping steadily. While this was good news for most Americans, who were paying less for food and clothing as a result, it also meant that millions of farm families were seeing their annual incomes decline.

By the 1920s farmers found themselves locked into a vicious cycle. To earn more, they tried to grow more, often investing in expensive mechanized equipment (particularly tractors) in the process. However, this only drove prices lower, as supply increased and demand remained relatively stable. As a result, farmers' incomes not only failed to increase, but actually fell, and farm families increasingly found themselves in debt. The result was often foreclosure and the loss of farms that had been owned by particular families for generations.

As early as the 1870s agricultural reformers had begun calling on farmers to withhold their products from the market until such time as they could fetch a higher price. Yet this was more easily said than done. Family budgets were generally stretched about as far as they could go by harvest time, so most farmers had to get their crops to market as soon as they could. The problem was that most of them were trying to sell their products during precisely the same months, and as a result farm prices dropped every year at harvest time.

The Agricultural Marketing Act was the federal government's first major step toward dealing with the farm crisis. Its main feature was the establishment of the Federal Farm Board, which was authorized to make up to $500 million in low-interest loans to agricultural cooperatives. These cooperatives were simply groups of farmers who promised to sell their products as a group, rather than individually. Loans from the Federal Farm Board would relieve the farmers who belonged to these cooperatives from the need to sell their crops as soon as they were harvested. Instead the cooperatives would purchase farm commodities at above-market prices, then store them until such time as prices increased.

This was precisely the sort of plan that Herbert Hoover liked. Having grown up in rural Iowa, he recognized the problems faced by farmers. At the same time, he opposed most of the solutions that had been suggested for ending the farm crisis, which generally involved having the government artificially inflate the price of farm commodities. The Federal Farm Board would encourage farmers to work together to solve their problems, and would offer the support of the federal government without actually involving the government in the fixing of prices. One of Hoover's first acts upon becoming president, therefore, was to ask Congress to pass legislation that would call it into existence. The House and Senate swiftly obliged, and Hoover signed the Agricultural Marketing Act into law on June 15, 1929.

Not everyone believed that the Federal Farm Board could deliver on its promises. Opponents argued that it would do nothing to solve the fundamental problem of overproduction; in fact, they claimed that having cooperatives pay above-market prices would actually encourage farmers to produce more, and would drive rural America deeper into debt. As it turned out, they were largely correct. In early 1930 the international market was swamped with grain from the United States, Argentina, Canada, and the Soviet Union. The price of wheat actually fell at a time when the cooperatives had predicted it would rise. By the summer of 1931 the federal government owned nearly 300 million bushels of wheat for which it had paid more than twice the market price. As one observer put it, the Federal Farm Board had provided "a first-class way of throwing good money into a bottomless pit."[1] Foreclosures on farms continued, and farmers began to demand more radical measures to relieve their situation.

The first document in this section is Hoover's initial message to Congress asking for passage of the Agricultural Marketing Act. The counterpoint is a critical 1930 article from the *Saturday Evening Post* by the noted journalist Garet Garrett.

NOTE

1. Michael E. Parrish, *Anxious Decades: America in Prosperity and Depression, 1920–1941* (New York: W. W. Norton, 1992), 246.

HOOVER CALLS FOR THE CREATION OF A FEDERAL FARM BOARD

[. . .] I have long held that the multiplicity of causes of agricultural depression could only be met by the creation of a great instrumentality clothed with sufficient authority and resources to assist our farmers to meet these problems, each upon its own merits. The creation of such an agency would at once transfer the agricultural question from the field of politics into the realm of economics and would result in constructive action. The administration is pledged to create an instrumentality that will investigate the causes, find sound remedies, and have the authority and resources to apply those remedies.

The pledged purpose of such a Federal farm board is the reorganization of the market of the marketing system on sounder and more stable and more economic lines. To do this the board will require funds to assist in creating and sustaining farmer-owned and farmer-controlled agencies for a variety of purposes, such as marketing; adequate working capital to be advanced against commodities lodged for storage; necessary and prudent advances to corporations created and owned by farmers' marketing organizations for the purchase and orderly marketing of surpluses occasioned by climatic variations or by harvest congestion; to authorize the creation and support of clearing houses, especially for perishable products, through which, under producers' approval, cooperation can be established with distributors and processors to more orderly marketing of commodities and for the elimination of many wastes in distribution; and to provide for licensing of handlers of some perishable products so as to eliminate unfair practices. Every penny of waste between farmer and consumer that we can eliminate, whether it arises from methods of distribution or from hazard or speculation, will be a gain to both farmer and consumer. . . .

Certain safeguards must naturally surround these activities and the instrumentalities that are created. Certain vital principles must be adhered to in order that we may not undermine the freedom of our farmers and of our people as a whole by bureaucratic and governmental domination and interference. We must not undermine initiative. There should be no fee or tax imposed upon the farmer. No governmental agency should engage in the buying and selling and price fixing of products, for such courses can lead only to bureaucracy and domination. Government funds should not be loaned or facilities duplicated where other services of credit and facilities are available at reasonable rates. No activities should be set in motion that will result in increasing the surplus production, as such will defeat any plans of relief.

The most progressive movement in all agriculture has been the upbuilding of the farmer's own marketing organizations, which now embrace nearly 2,000,000 farmers in membership and annually distribute nearly $2,500,000,000 worth of farm products. These organizations have acquired experience in virtually every branch of their industry, and furnish a substantial basis upon which to build further organization. Not all these marketing organizations are of the same type, but the test of them is whether or not they are farmer owned or farmer controlled. In order to strengthen and not to undermine them, all proposals for government assistance should originate with such organizations and be the result of their application. Moreover by such bases of organization the Government will be removed from engaging in the business of agriculture.

The difficulties of agriculture can not be cured in a day; they can not all be cured by legislation; they can not be cured by the Federal Government alone. But farmers and their organizations can be assisted to overcome these inequalities. Every effort of this character is an experiment, and we shall find from our experience the way to further advance. We must make a start. With the creation of a great instrumentality of this character, of a strength and importance equal to that of those which we have created for transportation and banking, we give immediate assurance of the determined purpose of the Government to meet the difficulties of which we are now aware, and to create an agency through which constructive action for the future will be assured.

In this treatment of this problem we recognize the responsibility of the people as a whole, and we shall lay the foundations for a new day in agriculture, from which we shall preserve to the Nation the great values of its individuality and strengthen our whole national fabric. . . .

Congressional Record. 71st Cong., 1st sess., vol. 71, pt. 1 (April 16, 1929): 42–43.

JOURNALIST GARET GARRETT EVALUATES THE AGRICULTURAL MARKETING ACT

. . . The Federal Farm Board, in January, made a large loan to the Land o' Lakes Creameries, Inc., of Minneapolis, which is one of the successful old cooperative associations in the country. Now, as to this loan, one is bound to ask certain questions. If the Federal Farm Board is in the business of assisting distressed agriculture, certainly it could have found many farmer organizations more in need of aid than the Land o' Lakes Creameries, Inc.; for as a solvent association, with a long record of profit and sound management, it could get any reasonable accommodation of credit at the bank.

The answer is that, of course, it could borrow on reasonable terms at the bank for all normal commercial purposes. But it could not borrow money at the bank for the purpose of protecting the market price of butter. That was the trouble. The price of butter was falling. It had fallen below thirty cents a pound, and nobody knew where it might stop. What the Land o' Lakes Creameries needed was a large sum of money not only for the purpose of holding its own butter off the market but also to buy and store the butter of other associations, because they were all pressing it for sale on a falling market. The only source of money for that purpose was the Federal Farm Board. It loaned the money, the Land o' Lakes Creameries bought up surplus butter and put it away, and with what result? The price of butter advanced to thirty-six cents a pound— which was a fair price—and then everything was all right again.

One must ask, for whom was everything all right again? Is it not very strange that the Government should lend money to butter makers for the immediate purpose of advancing the price six cents a pound, when there are 3,000,000 butter eaters unemployed? How is such use of government money to be justified?

The answer is that if there had been a panic in agricultural-commodity prices the number of unemployed might have become 6,000,000. And butter is an agricultural commodity? There again is a matter of opinion. If the opinion is sound, you may say the end justifies the means, and pass on; though not without wonder still that it lies in the wisdom of a board at Washington to say what price people shall pay for butter in order that unemployment shall not increase; nor without wonder at the seeming contradiction that, as it lends money to the Land o' Lakes Creameries, Inc., to buy and remove surplus butter from the national market, the Federal Farm Board at the same time issues a warning against the overproduction of butter, exhorts farmers to eat more of it and sell less, and then, with the other hand, lends money to the Lower Columbia Cooperative Dairy Association for the purpose of increasing its plant. . . .

This use of government money, if it continues, is bound to increase by extension, for such is the natural law of political benefit. If it increases, with no positive control of production, there is disaster in sight for the United States Treasury. On the other hand, positive control of production by the Government entails such interference in his affairs as no farmer would tolerate. That enigma lies in any scheme of subsidy, bonus, guaranty or price protection whereby a surplus-producing industry will be made more profitable than it already is. The more profitable you make it the greater the temptation will be to produce a surplus. That is what the Federal Farm Board is facing without power.

Garet Garrett, "Farm Relief So Far," *Saturday Evening Post* 202:52 (June 28, 1930): 6–7, 109–10, 115.

THE LONDON NAVAL TREATY (1930)

Since the end of World War I, the issue of naval construction had created tension among the world's great powers. The British navy was the largest, but many Americans insisted that the United States should possess a navy that was just as large. Meanwhile, Japan was making a bid to become the premier naval power of the Pacific. The result was a flurry of construction that threatened to turn into a full-scale arms race.

In 1921 delegations from Britain, the United States, Japan, France, and Italy met in Washington, D.C. to set limits on the size of world's navies. It was agreed that each country could build up to a certain tonnage in so-called "capital ships" (battleships and aircraft carriers). Britain and the United States were to have the largest navies, and could build up to the same tonnage. The Japanese, presumably because they had only one ocean to worry about, settled for a navy three-fifths the size of the Americans or the British, while the French and Italians agreed to maintain even smaller fleets.

However, the Washington Treaty said nothing about construction of vessels other than capital ships, and a new competition began to develop in the building of cruisers. The great powers attended a new conference in Geneva, Switzerland, in 1927, in which the U.S. Navy called for "parity" with Britain's Royal Navy. The conference broke up when the British and Americans could not agree on what constituted a "cruiser." The U.S. Navy relied on larger vessels with eight-inch guns, while the British insisted that cruisers had to be smaller, and could carry guns with a caliber of no more than six inches. The collapse of the conference left many Americans believing that the British were unwilling to see the United States build a navy as large as their own.

By the time Hoover took office, the United States and Britain were on the verge of the arms race that diplomats on both sides had hoped to avoid since 1921. Congress in 1928 had passed a bill authorizing the construction of fifteen large cruisers and an aircraft carrier, and the British were prepared to respond with a building program of their own. Hoover, though not actually a pacifist, had distinctly antiwar views; moreover, he felt that money spent on naval construction could be put to better uses elsewhere. He therefore was eager to seek a new arms control agreement.

In October 1929, Ramsay MacDonald became the first sitting British prime minister to visit the United States. After a lengthy meeting with Herbert Hoover at a presidential retreat at Rapidan, Virginia, the two leaders announced that a new conference would be held to revisit the issue of naval limitations. MacDonald assured Americans that he was more than willing to see an American navy as strong as Britain's. "What is all this bother about parity?" he asked. "Parity? Take it, without reserve, heaped up and flowing over."[1]

Delegations from the United States, Great Britain, Japan, France, and Italy met in London in January 1930. Although the French and Italians withdrew from the proceedings, this did not prevent the other three powers from signing a new arms control agreement. All three promised to build no new capital ships until 1936, when a new conference would be called. The British and Americans pledged to limit their total tonnage in cruisers to roughly 1.15 million tons, while the Japanese promised to limit theirs to 714,000.

In May Hoover called the Senate into special session to consider the treaty. It met with spirited opposition, egged on by certain officers of the U.S. Navy as well as several important shipbuilding companies. Opponents of the treaty argued that it would leave the navy inferior to that of Great Britain, and predicted that the Japanese would emerge as a threat in the Pacific. However, public sentiment in favor of the treaty was overwhelming, and in the end the Senate ratified the treaty by a vote of fifty-eight to nine.

The legacy of the London Naval Treaty was mixed. On the one hand, it no doubt ended the threat of an arms race and improved relations between the United States and Great Britain. Both powers, in fact, would continue to cooperate on naval affairs right up through World War II. On the other hand, the treaty's critics were correct to point out the potential threat of Japan. Although the Japanese were prohibited from building a navy as large as those of the United States and Britain, they were free to concentrate all their forces in the Pacific. As a result, after the attack on Pearl Harbor the Japanese navy would enjoy superiority in the Pacific War throughout 1942.

This section features President Hoover's formal request that the Senate ratify the treaty. It also includes the comments of Senator Frederick Hale (R-Maine), the chairman of the Senate Naval Affairs Committee and a powerful "Big Navy" advocate.

NOTE

1. John E. Moser, *Twisting the Lion's Tail: American Anglophobia between the World Wars* (New York: University Press, 1999), 71–72.

HOOVER ASKS THE SENATE TO RATIFY THE LONDON NAVAL TREATY

In requesting the Senate to convene in session for the special purpose of dealing with the treaty for the limitation and reduction of naval armament signed at London April 22, 1930, it is desirable that I should present my views upon it. This is especially necessary because of misinformation and misrepresentation which has been widespread by those who in reality are opposed to all limitation and reduction in naval arms. We must naturally expect opposition from those groups who believe in unrestricted military strength as an objective of the American Nation. Indeed, we find the same type of minds in Great Britain and Japan in parallel opposition to this treaty. Nevertheless, I am convinced that the overwhelming majority of the American people are opposed to the conception of these groups. Our people believe that military strength should be held in conformity with the sole purpose of national defense, they earnestly desire real progress in limitation and reduction of naval arms of the world, and their aspiration is for abolition of competition in the building of arms as a step toward world peace. Such a result can be obtained in no other way than by international agreement.

The present treaty is one which holds these safeguards and advances these ideals. Its ratification is in the interest of the United States. It is fair to the other participating nations. It promotes the cause of good relations.

The only alternative to this treaty is the competitive building of navies with all its flow of suspicion, hate, ill will, and ultimate disaster. History supports those who hold to agreements as the path to peace. . . .

It is folly to think that because we are the richest Nation in the world we can outbuild all other countries. Other nations will make any sacrifice to maintain their instruments of defense against us, and we shall eventually reap in their hostility and ill will the full measure of the additional burden which we may thus impose upon them. The very entry of the United States into such courses as this would invite the consolidation of the rest of the world against us and bring our peace and independence into jeopardy. . . .

The economic burdens and the diversion of taxes from welfare purposes which would be imposed upon ourselves and other nations by failure of this treaty are worth consideration. Under its provisions the replacement of battleships required under the Washington arms treaty of 1921 is postponed for six years. . . . Likewise we make economies in construction and operation by the reduction in our submarine and destroyer fleets. . . . What the possible saving over an otherwise inevitable era of competitive building would be, no one can estimate. . . .

The question before us now is not whether we shall have a treaty with either three more 8-inch cruisers or four less 6-inch cruisers, or whether we shall have a larger reduction in tonnage. It is whether we shall have this treaty or no treaty. It is a question as to whether we shall have no limitation or reduction and shall enter upon a disastrous period of competitive armament.

This treaty does mark an important step in disarmament and world peace. It is important for many reasons that it be dealt with at once. The subject has been under discussion since the Geneva conference three years ago. The lines of this treaty have been known and under discussion since last summer. The actual document has been before the American people and before the Senate for nearly three months. It has been favorably reported by the Senate Foreign Relations Committee. Every solitary fact which affects judgment upon the treaty is known, and the document itself comprises the sole obligations of the United States. If we fail now, the world will be again plunged backward from its progress toward peace.

Congressional Record. 71st Cong., special sess., vol. 73 (July 7, 1930): 4–5.

SENATOR FREDERICK HALE (R-MAINE) URGES
REJECTION OF THE LONDON NAVAL TREATY

... [U]nder the Constitution of the United States it is the duty of Congress to provide and maintain a Navy, and it is the duty of Congress to see that an adequate Navy is maintained. We maintain a navy to support our foreign policies, to protect our commerce, and to guard our possessions at home and abroad. The Navy is the first line of defense of the country. To the minds of many people the word "defense" in this connection suggests a force which will prevent any hostile force from landing on our own coasts or those of our insular possessions. As a matter of fact, a navy that could accomplish no more than this would prove a very inadequate navy and would fail entirely in the ultimate purpose for which we provide a navy, and that is to bring a war to a successful conclusion. . . .

Whatever one may feel about the dangers of competition in world armament, and about the effectiveness of treaty measures that will prevent wars, no one with a spark of patriotism or regard for his country in his make-up will want to see this country, should we by any means be forced into a war, faced with a situation where our Navy is not adequate. When war actually comes every ship of the Navy will be a probable asset to win, and failure to provide in time of peace adequate preparation for possible war will bring down on our heads the just scorn of our people.

Naval strength is and has always been relative. The naval needs of a country are based on the naval strength of possible antagonists. If other countries keep their naval establishments within reasonable limits, there is no reason why the United States cannot do the same; and we have always been willing to do so. We have encouraged attempts to limit naval armament and to bring about treaties for the prevention of war, but if we are to exist as a nation, we must see to it in any limitation of armament that may be brought about that our interests are as well looked after as the interests of other countries, and that we do not, for the purpose of reaching an agreement, sacrifice our right to live. Until treaties outlawing war have proved to be effective, and until the rest of the world has given unquestioned evidence that it intends to abide by such treaties, we have no right to jeopardize our own national interests by relying on such treaties to the extent of weakening relatively our national defense. We have no right to gamble that there will be no future wars. That I fear is precisely what we are doing when we subscribe to the London treaty now before us. . . .

For centuries England has realized the benefits that flow from trade and has maintained a great navy for its protection. She has built up sympathy for herself under the plea that control of the seas is vital to her life as she does not produce sufficient food to be self-supporting. It is true that she must keep certain trade routes open that supply certain commodities necessary for her welfare, but so long as she controls the English Channel, the North Sea, and the Mediterranean, she has all of Europe and the East to draw upon for her food supplies. The real reason for England's desire to control the sea is to retain the prosperity that comes from uninterrupted trade.

Uninterrupted trade is for us no less vital than for Great Britain. Our stake upon the sea is practically the same as hers. Prosperity is as vital for our workingmen and farmers as it is for her people. With her far-flung Empire, her widely scattered bases, and her great merchant marine, she has a tremendous initial advantage, and by every means possible is seeking to maintain and to increase that advantage. . . .

While its proponents claim that the treaty provides for parity with Great Britain, as a matter of fact it provides for no such parity during the life of the treaty. . . .

Under the treaty we attempt to purchase the good will of the world through the sacrifice of the right to safeguard our interests. We will get not good will but the contempt that a supine nation invariably gets and deserves to get. If this treaty is ratified by this Senate, in my judgment, we have definitely and conclusively proved to the world that in international relations we are not capable of looking after our own interests, and do not measure up to the great position of responsibility and legitimate power that we have honorably won for ourselves in the world by ways other than those of war.

Congressional Record. 71st Cong., special sess., vol. 73 (July 11, 1930): 91–102.

THE HAWLEY-SMOOT TARIFF (1930)

A "tariff" is a special tax levied on certain goods that are imported from other countries. At one time tariffs were the primary source of income for the federal government, but they served another purpose as well. By making foreign goods—particularly manufactured products—more expensive, Americans would be more inclined to purchase goods that were produced in the United States. The use of tariffs to protect American manufacturing is as old as the Republic itself, as Secretary of the Treasury Alexander Hamilton had repeatedly advocated tariffs in the 1790s. And since northeastern manufacturers formed the backbone of the Republican Party, tariffs had also been a standard plank in that party's platforms since the formation of the Grand Old Party (GOP) in the 1850s.

The Republican victory in 1920 virtually guaranteed that there would be an increase in tariffs, and, sure enough, the Fordney-McCumber Tariff Act of 1922 set rates high enough that foreign textiles, steel, chemicals, and many other products were practically locked out of the country. Nevertheless, the onset of the Great Depression led to new demands for higher tariff protection as businessmen and farmers alike feared that falling prices overseas would lead to a renewed influx of foreign goods.

Hoover was not a believer in high tariffs; indeed, he thought that the Fordney-McCumber rates had been set too high. He did, however, think that tariffs could serve as a useful tool for propping up farm products, so he and his congressional allies reopened the question of tariff revision with the intent to limit any rate changes to agricultural products. This was a forlorn hope, though, since the mere act of opening the question of trade policy led to a barrage of demands for protection. Under the leadership of Senator Joseph Grundy (R-Pennsylvania), Republicans drafted a tariff bill that offered some help to farmers, but even more to manufacturers. The final bill, named for its main sponsors, Senator Reed Smoot (R-Utah) and Congressman Willis Hawley (R-Oregon), increased the tariff on many items by between 50 and 100 percent over the already high Fordney-McCumber rates. The average rate increased from 33 percent to 40 percent.

Hawley-Smoot had plenty of critics from the start. Farmers, recognizing that tariff reform had been hijacked by manufacturing interests, protested bitterly. While the bill offered some protection for their products, this would be more than offset by the higher prices they would be forced to pay on manufactured items. As one journalist wrote, "there is nothing the Grundyites will not do for the farmer except to give him what he wants. All they wish to do is to tax him out of house and home—perhaps on the theory that the only way to solve the farm problem is to exterminate the farmer."[1] Businessmen involved in international trade predicted that foreign countries would retaliate by raising their own tariffs, and that American exports would be damaged in the end. Thomas Lamont, a partner in J. P. Morgan and Company, begged Hoover to veto the bill, as did the American Economics Association, a prestigious academic organization representing over a thousand leading economists.

Up to this point the president had remained uninvolved in the process, asking only that any bill include provisions to establish an independent Tariff Commission that would set rates "scientifically" in the future. When that provision failed to appear—it was opposed by Republicans and Democrats alike—he seriously considered vetoing the legislation. Since the bill passed the Senate by only a two-vote margin, a veto would undoubtedly be sustained. Nevertheless the president gave in to pressure from Republicans in Congress, and signed the bill into law in June 1930. The prominent journalist Walter Lippmann complained that Hoover "gave up the leadership of his party" in accepting "a wretched and mischievous product of stupidity and greed."[2]

In this case, the critics turned out to be largely correct. Far from encouraging economic recovery at home, the new rates caused the depression to spread overseas. Within three years of the bill's passage, no less than thirty-three foreign countries had raised their own rates. The value of international trade plummeted by more than $1.5 billion by 1931, and banks around the world began to collapse. The American export market all but disintegrated, and the tariff did nothing to prop up the prices of goods on the domestic market. Moreover, Hoover's failure to veto the bill was widely interpreted as a sign of political weakness, so that problems with an assertive Congress would continue to plague him for the remainder of his presidency.

The documents in this section include President Hoover's statement upon signing the Hawley-Smoot Tariff, as well as a speech on the floor of the House by Representative Jacob Milligan (D-Missouri) attacking the bill.

NOTES

1. Michael E. Parrish, *Anxious Decades: America in Prosperity and Depression, 1920–1941* (New York: W. W. Norton, 1992), 248.

2. David M. Kennedy, *Freedom from Fear: The American People in Depression and War, 1929–1945* (New York: Oxford University Press), 50.

HOOVER SIGNS THE HAWLEY-SMOOT TARIFF (1930)

I shall approve the tariff bill. . . .

In my message of April 16, 1929, to the special session of the Congress I accordingly recommended an increase in agricultural protection; a limited revision of other schedules to take care of the economic changes necessitating increases or decreases since the enactment of the 1922 law, and I further recommended a reorganization both of the Tariff Commission and of the method of executing the flexible provisions. . . .

The increases in tariff are largely directed to the interest of the farmer. Of the increases, it is stated by the Tariff Commission that 93.73 per cent are upon products of agricultural origin measured in value, as distinguished from 6.25 per cent upon commodities of strictly nonagricultural origin. . . .

This tariff law is like all other tariff legislation, whether framed primarily upon a protective or a revenue basis. It contains many compromises between sectional interests and between different industries. No tariff bill has ever been enacted or ever will be enacted under the present system, that will be perfect. A large portion of the items are always adjusted with good judgment, but it is bound to contain some inequalities and inequitable compromises. There are items upon which duties will prove too high and others upon which duties will prove to be too low. . . .

On the administrative side I have insisted, however, that there should be created a new basis for the flexible tariff and it has been incorporated in this law. Thereby the means are established for objective and judicial review of these rates upon principles laid down by the Congress, free from pressures inherent in legislative action. Thus the outstanding step of this tariff legislation has been the reorganization of the largely inoperative flexible provision of 1922 into a form which should render it possible to secure prompt and scientific adjustment of serious inequities and inequalities which may prove to have been incorporated in the bill. . . .

The complaints from some foreign countries that these duties have been placed unduly high can be remedied, if justified, by proper application to the Tariff Commission.

It is urged that the uncertainties in the business world which have been added to by the long-extended debate of the measure should be ended. They can be ended only by completion of this bill. Meritorious demands for further protection to agriculture and labor which have developed since the tariff of 1922 would not end if this bill fails of enactment. Agitation for legislative tariff revision would necessarily continue before the country. Nothing would contribute to retard business recovery more than this continued agitation.

As I have said, I do not assume the rate structure in this or any other tariff bill is perfect, but I am convinced that the disposal of the whole question is urgent. I believe that the flexible provisions can within reasonable time remedy inequalities; that this provision is a progressive advance and gives great hope of taking the tariff away from politics, lobbying, and logrolling; that the bill gives protection to agriculture for the market of its products and to several industries in need of such protection for the wage of their labor; that with returning normal conditions our foreign trade will continue to expand.

Congressional Record. 71st Cong., 2d sess., vol. 72, pt. 10 (June 16, 1930): 10859–60.

REPRESENTATIVE JACOB MILLIGAN (D-MISSOURI) DENOUNCES THE HAWLEY-SMOOT TARIFF

. . . [I]t is my opinion that it is most inopportune that the tariff bill should have become a law. We have not only a surplus of farm commodities but also a surplus in all industrial lines, hence must have foreign markets. We can not afford to destroy our foreign trade in order to allow the American manufacturer to plunder the pockets of the consumer. . . .

The tariff bill was under consideration for 17 months. During these 17 months the President had opportunity to inform Congress as to what he meant by "limited tariff revision for the benefit of agriculture." During these 17 months the President remained mute. . . . So the only logical conclusion that can be reached is that the bill was entirely indorsed by the President during its making. So I would not take credit from the President and the "Chief Manipulator" of this legislation in the Senate. I think the bill should be known as the Hoover-Grundy tariff bill. The President assumed full responsibility when he signed the bill, as it could not have become law without his signature.

On the day the tariff bill became a law all grain prices fell to a new low level for the season. Wheat fell to the lowest price in a year, oats to the lowest price in 8 years, rye to the lowest price reached in 30 years. Cotton fell to the lowest price in more than three years.

The steel industry reported a further decline in operations to 69 per cent of capacity.

On the day the bill passed, the Department of Commerce announced that American exports dropped in May to the lowest point in the last six years.

Stocks dropped in value $2,000,000,000 the day the President announced he would sign the bill.

This tariff law carries a general average increase of 20.4 per cent over the Fordney-McCumber law of 1922, which means an additional burden each year to the consumers of this country. The farmers are told they will benefit by this law. The facts are that every dollar of benefit given the farmer will cost him $10 because of the increase in the rates on other than the agricultural rates. . . .

There is an increase carried in this law upon practically every thing a person uses in everyday life from the swaddling cloth of the newborn babe to the tombstone he erects above his dead. This tariff law means an average increased cost of from fifty to one hundred dollars to every average householder in the United States each year. How the now overburdened masses can carry this additional burden I do not know.

We hear from certain quarters that prosperity is raging rampant in every corner of the land; that we are enjoying this unprecedented prosperity because Mr. Hoover is President. I am willing to give President Hoover full credit for the so-called Hoover prosperity we are now enjoying.

I understand that two new planets have been discovered and that some one suggested one be named "Hoover Prosperity" because it is invisible; the other "Farm Relief" because it is so far away.

Congressional Record. 71st Cong., 2d sess., vol. 72, pt. 11 (July 3, 1930): 12675–76.

THE WICKERSHAM COMMISSION (1931)

Ever since the ratification of the Eighteenth Amendment in 1920, and the subsequent passage of the Volstead Act, America was officially "dry." That is, it became illegal to manufacture, sell, or transport beer, wine, and liquor. "Prohibition" was the law of the land.

Prohibition was always controversial. Its supporters—the "drys"— were predominantly churchgoing Protestants, strongest in the small towns and rural areas of the South and the Midwest. Women were often among its most vocal champions. On the other hand, Prohibition's opponents—the "wets"—tended to be Catholics. Many were immigrants from Ireland, Germany, and Southern Europe, and they were strongest in the cities of the Northeast, from Chicago to Boston.

By the end of the 1920s many Americans who had earlier supported Prohibition were beginning to have second thoughts. The law had proved extremely difficult, if not impossible, to enforce. After all, the country had twelve thousand miles of coastline and borders, so that it was almost ridiculously easy for "bootleggers" (those who engaged in the smuggling of liquor) to get their product into the country. Americans also found it easy to brew beer or distill alcohol in their own homes or farms. Illegal nightclubs that served liquor—often referred to as "speakeasies"—flourished in the country's largest cities. According to some reports, there were as many as 32,000 speakeasies in New York City alone. Almost everywhere, it seemed that it was becoming fashionable to break or evade the law. Meanwhile, the movement to repeal the Eighteenth Amendment was gathering steam.

In his acceptance speech at the 1928 Republican National Convention, Hoover called Prohibition "a great social experiment, noble in motive and far-reaching in purpose." On the campaign trail he promised that, if elected, he would appoint a commission to study the breakdown in law and order. However, it is clear that privately he was skeptical. He was enough of a realist to see that Prohibition was not working. Moreover, he did not personally see alcohol as an evil; as secretary of commerce he had been known to visit foreign embassies for the express purpose of enjoying a cocktail or two.

As president, Hoover increased the staff and resources of the various federal agencies responsible for enforcement of the Prohibition laws. He also kept his campaign promise by nominating a commission under the leadership of a former attorney general, George W. Wickersham. The commission was bipartisan, and included a number of distinguished judges and other legal authorities. Nonetheless, many eyebrows were raised when Wickersham himself suggested that enforcement of Prohibition might be best left to the states—thereby insinuating that the federal government was helpless to prevent the sale of alcohol. Drys set up a howl of protest, and accused Hoover of having appointed a wet as chair of the committee. The president, however, remained silent.

The Wickersham Commission issued its final report in January 1931. It came as a bitter disappointment to Hoover, because it did little except to suggest a range of options where Prohibition was concerned. While the commission agreed that the laws had not been effectively enforced, there was no consensus on what should be done. Four of the eleven members recommended maintaining the Eighteenth Amendment as is; the others either called for repeal, or at the very least some revision of laws to allow certain types of mildly intoxicating beverages.

The president dutifully forwarded the report to Congress, but he added his own summary which put a more positive spin on the commission's findings. He claimed that the group "does not favor the repeal of the Eighteenth Amendment as a method of cure." Moreover, he claimed that there had been "continued improvement" in the federal enforcement of the Prohibition laws.[1] It is likely that he made these half-truths because he feared how the report might be interpreted. The Wickersham Commission had been appointed by the president, after all; if it appeared that it was supporting repeal of Prohibition, it might suggest that Hoover himself favored it, and further undermine the enforcement of the law. The Eighteenth Amendment had been approved by a two-thirds vote in Congress and ratified by three-fourths of the states. Whether or not Hoover liked it, he felt that it was his responsibility to uphold the law of the land.

Despite the president's efforts, the report of the Wickersham Commission gave still more ammunition to the advocates of repeal. Nevertheless, Prohibition remained a controversial issue, and at the 1932 Republican National Convention the delegates were deeply divided over it. Ultimately the party platform endorsed repeal of the Eighteenth Amendment, but with the provision that individual states would have the right to ban liquor within their borders. Hoover's opponent in 1932, Franklin D. Roosevelt, supported an outright end to Prohibition. But by now most voters were more concerned about the economy than the liquor traffic, and Hoover's failure to cope with the depression doomed him to defeat. Within months of the election, Congress passed the Twenty-First Amendment, formally repealing the Eighteenth, and making alcohol legal once more.

In this section, we find the message which Hoover sent to Congress and the report of the Wickersham Commission. The counterpoint is a speech from Representative William R. Hull (R-Illinois) calling for the repeal of the Eighteenth Amendment.

NOTE

1. "Message to the Congress Transmitting Report of the National Commission on Law Observance and Enforcement," January 20, 1931, *Public Papers of the Presidents of the United States: Herbert Hoover, 1931* (Washington, D.C.: U.S. Government Printing Office, 1976), pp. 29–30.

HOOVER SUBMITS TO CONGRESS THE REPORT OF THE WICKERSHAM COMMISSION

The first deficiency appropriation act of March 4, 1929, carried an appropriation for a thorough investigation into the enforcement of the prohibition laws, together with the enforcement of other laws. . . .

The commission . . . comprises an able group of distinguished citizens of character and independence of thought, representative of different sections of the country. For 18 months they have exhaustively and painstakingly gathered and examined the facts as to enforcement, the benefits, and the abuses under the prohibition laws, both before and since the passage of the eighteenth amendment. I am transmitting their report immediately. Reports upon the enforcement of other criminal laws will follow.

The commission considers that the conditions of enforcement of the prohibition laws in the country as a whole are unsatisfactory but it reports that the Federal participation in enforcement has shown continued improvement since and as a consequence of the act of Congress of 1927 placing prohibition officers under civil service, and the act of 1930 transferring prohibition enforcement from the Treasury to the Department of Justice, and it outlines further possible improvement. It calls attention to the urgency of obedience to law by our citizens and to the imperative necessity for greater assumption and performance by State and local governments of their share of responsibilities . . . if enforcement is to be successful. It recommends that further and more effective efforts be made to enforce the laws. It makes recommendations as to Federal administrative methods and certain secondary legislation for further increase of personnel, new classification of offenses, relief of the courts, and amendments to the national prohibition act clarifying the law and eliminating irritations which arise under it. Some of these recommendations have been enacted by the Congress or are already in course of legislation. I commend those suggestions to the attention of the Congress at an appropriate time.

The commission, by a large majority, does not favor the repeal of the eighteenth amendment as a method of cure for the inherent abuses of the liquor traffic. I am in accord with this view. I am in unity with the spirit of the report in seeking constructive steps to advance the national ideal of eradication of the social and economic and political evils of this traffic, to preserve the gains which have been made, and to eliminate the abuses which exist, at the same time facing with an open mind the difficulties which have arisen under this experiment. I do, however, see serious objection to, and therefore must not be understood as recommending, the commission's proposed revision of the eighteenth amendment which is suggested by them for possible consideration at some future time if the continued effort at enforcement should not prove successful. My own duty and that of all executive officials is clear—to enforce the law with all the means at our disposal without equivocation or reservation.

The report is the result of a thorough and comprehensive study of the situation by a representative and authoritative group. It clearly recognizes the gains which have been made and is resolute that those gains shall be preserved. There are necessarily differences in views among its members. It is a temperate and judicial presentation. It should stimulate the clarification of public mind and the advancement of public thought.

"Message to the Congress Transmitting Report of the National Commission on Law Observance and Enforcement," January 20, 1931, *Public Papers of the Presidents of the United States: Herbert Hoover, 1931* (Washington, D.C.: U.S. Government Printing Office, 1976), pp. 29–30.

REPRESENTATIVE WILLIAM E. HULL (R-ILLINOIS) CALLS FOR REPEAL OF THE EIGHTEENTH AMENDMENT

[. . .] The voters in the fall election of 1930 spoke in no uncertain terms against the eighteenth amendment and the Volstead law. In other words, prohibition, as it now exists in the United States, has been tried at the bar of public opinion and proven to be, in the minds of every thinking person, unenforceable. The time has come when the honor of the United States is at stake, and this law must be changed. . . .

The prohibition law went into effect in the United States January 16, 1920. Previous to that time the manufacture of whiskies, spirits, gin, alcohol, and rum was conducted under the supervision of the United States Government. Beer and wine were manufactured in the same manner. So there was then a governmental control over all intoxicating liquors.

Since the prohibition law went into effect all of these agencies, which were law-abiding, have been dispensed with, and the process of distillation and brewing has been carried on surreptitiously by criminals and the worst element of citizenship that we have in these United States. It has been an easy matter for them to make a product that would intoxicate, to hide it away, to sell it without the Government's permission, and this has done much to corrupt and destroy the moral fiber of our citizens. . . .

In 1919 there were manufactured 157,276,422 pounds of corn sugar, as against 896,986,000 pounds in 1929. There have been practically no new uses for corn sugar except a small amount in the rayon industry. Therefore, it is estimated that over 600,000,000 pounds of corn sugar were available for distillation, and this would produce at least 61,000,000 gallons of drinkable whisky. In addition to this, there can be no doubt but what large quantities of drinkable whisky have been made from corn, rye, beet sugar, molasses, potatoes, grain mash, and illegally diverted alcohol. So, gentlemen, you have here a production of whisky before prohibition on an average of 62,535,946 gallons a year, and here we have shown by indisputable figures an annual output of an equal amount of drinkable whisky made from one commodity under the Volstead law.

The Department of Agriculture shows by official figures that the wine-grape acreage of California increased from 97,000 acres in 1919 to 174,374 acres in 1926. These grapes were used exclusively to make wine and are not used for other purposes. . . .

It seems impossible to find any accurate figures in regard to the amount of illicit beer sold in the United States, but the output must reach enormous figures, for it is common knowledge that the profit derived from the sale of beer is the basis of the bootleggers' prosperity. We do know that the State of Michigan collects great sums in taxes from the manufacture of malt and wort, which can be immediately transformed into beer, and the National Government is helpless to halt the business. . . .

In 1914 the total amount of all imported spirits amounted to 4,000,000 gallons, and that was the largest amount ever imported into this country in any one year. However, estimates show there are now at least 20,000,000 gallons smuggled into the country as against 4,000,000. Consequently prohibition has increased the use of imported liquors by five times the amount used during the years previous to the prohibition law. . . .

I believe that the figures that I have given are a fair comparison between the conditions that existed in the country before prohibition and conditions that now exist after prohibition has been in force for a 10-year period, and based on this showing there can be no other conclusion than that the eighteenth amendment has failed to accomplish the purpose for which it was enacted.

The Government of the United States is composed of a free people who have always been willing to follow and obey the reasonable dictates of the Government, but being a free people they have ever been quick to rebel against any invasion of their personal rights, and that may be the reason why a large number of our citizens throughout the country have violated the eighteenth amendment openly and without any feeling of shame or disgrace. . . .

. . . [F]or the first time in the history of this country, if not in the history of the world, crime has become a paying institution. The unenforceable prohibition law is responsible for a most vicious development in American community life, and if it is allowed to continue we will be under the combined domination of the bandit, the burglar, the bootlegger, the narcotic vender, and the racketeer.

Congressional Record. 71st Cong., 3rd sess., vol. 74, pt. 3 (January 22, 1931): 2885–86.

THE VETERANS' BONUS BILL (1931)

Congress has a long history of passing legislation benefiting veterans, going back to the granting of public land to those who fought in the War of Independence. After the Civil War, a powerful lobbying organization called the Grand Army of the Republic fought to have all sorts of privileges extended to those who had fought for the Union. Congress, recognizing the power of the veteran vote, seldom refused the Grand Army's requests.

A similar spirit motivated leaders of both parties in Congress during the 1920s. A bill passed in 1924, over President Calvin Coolidge's veto, offering to each veteran of World War I a bonus—called an "adjusted compensation certificate"—based on years of service. These certificates could be redeemed for full value twenty years after the bill was to take effect; that is, in 1945.

By 1931, however, many veterans had begun to feel the effects of the Great Depression, and their organizations started demanding that at least some of the bonuses should be paid sooner. Democratic congressional leaders soon responded with legislation that proposed to offer low-interest loans of up to 50 percent of the value of the adjusted compensation certificates. Supporters argued that during a time of economic distress it was unreasonable to ask veterans to wait another fourteen years to receive what Congress had already said that they deserved. The bill quickly passed by large majorities in both houses.

President Hoover, while not unsympathetic to the plight of veterans, believed that the bonus bill was an unwarranted expenditure. His various spending programs already threatened to unbalance the federal budget, and he estimated that the bonus bill would cost an additional $1.7 billion. Moreover, he claimed, veterans as a group were under no greater economic hardship than anyone else in the country. The vast majority of them were perfectly able to care for themselves; there was simply no need for the legislation. He sent his veto message to Congress on February 26.

The veto was a futile effort, as it was overturned in the House after only forty-three minutes of debate; the Senate did likewise on the following day. But the bonus made little practical difference to suffering veterans, who came back the following year to demand that the entire bonus be paid immediately. Nearly 20,000 veterans, calling themselves the "Bonus Expeditionary Force" (but more commonly known as the "Bonus Army") marched on Washington and assembled near the Capitol building in June 1932. However, this bonus bill never made it to the president's desk; although it passed the House, barely a third of the Senate voted for it.

At this point the Bonus Army moved back across the Anacostia River to a shantytown of tents and tar paper shacks. Hoover signed a $100,000 federal authorization to pay for the marchers' transportation home, and eventually the administration ordered them evicted. However, the local police proved unequal to the task, and called for support from the federal authorities. The president, while rejecting the advice of some in his administration that he declare martial law, did authorize his secretary of war to have the marchers removed. On June 28, units of the U.S. Army under the command of General Douglas MacArthur drove them out of their shanties using tanks and tear gas.

Hoover had not intended that such measures be taken; nevertheless, his popularity hit a new low when reports of the "Battle of Anacostia Flats" reached the American public. The president made the situation worse by claiming that the marchers were "revolutionaries" and "criminals" bent on overthrowing the government. At one point, he told an audience, "Thank God, you have a government in Washington that knows how to deal with a mob."[1] The timing of the incident—just as the 1932 presidential campaign was getting underway—was particularly bad for Hoover, and he would be attacked for his handling of the Bonus March throughout the campaign.

This section features Hoover's veto message on the Bonus Bill, as well as a response in opposition by Senator Arthur Vandenberg (R-Michigan).

NOTE

1. Robert S. McElvaine, *The Great Depression: America, 1929–1941* (New York: Times Books, 1993), 94.

HOOVER VETOES THE VETERANS' BONUS BILL

When the bonus act [of 1925] was passed it was upon the explicit understanding of the Congress that the matter was closed and the Government would not be called upon to make subsequent enlargements. It is now proposed to enlarge the loan rate to 50 per cent of the "face value," at a low rate of interest, thus imposing a potential cash outlay upon the government of about $1,700,000,000, if all veterans apply for loans. . . . According to the Administrator of Veterans' Affairs the probable number who will avail themselves of the privilege under this bill will require approximately $1,000,000,000. There not being a penny in the Treasury to meet such a demand, the Government must borrow this sum through the sale of the reserve fund securities together with further issues or we must need impose further taxation.

The sole appeal made for the reopening of the bonus act is to claim that funds from the National Treasury should be provided to veterans in distress as the result of the drought and business depression. There are veterans unemployed and in need to-day in common with many others of our people. These, like the others, are being provided the basic necessities of life by the devoted committees in those parts of the country affected by the depression or drought. The governments and many employers are giving preference to veterans in employment. Their welfare is and should be a matter of concern to our people. Inquiry indicates that such care is being given throughout the country, and it also indicates that the number of veterans in need of such relief is a minor percentage of the whole. . . .

The principle that the Nation should give generous care to those veterans who are ill, disabled, in need, or in distress, even though these disabilities do not arise from the war, has been fully accepted by the Nation. Pensions or allowances have been provided for the dependents of those who lost their lives in the war; allowances have been provided to those who suffered disabilities in the war; additional allowances were passed at the last session of Congress to all the veterans whose earning power at any time may be permanently impaired by injury or illness; free hospitalization is available not only to those suffering from the results of war but to large numbers of temporarily ill. Together with war-risk insurance and the adjusted compensation, these services now total an annual expenditure of approximately $600,000,000 and under existing laws will increase to $800,000,000 per annum in a very few years for World War veterans alone. A total of five thousand millions of dollars has been expended upon such services since the war. . . .

The need of our people to-day is a decrease in the burden of taxes and unemployment, yet they (who include the veterans) are being steadily forced toward higher tax levels and lessened employment by acts such as this. We must not forget the millions of hard-working families in our country who are striving to pay the debts which they have incurred in acquiring homes and farms in endeavor to build protection for their future. They, in the last analysis, must bear the burden of increasing Government aid and taxes. It is not the rich who suffer. When we take employment and taxes from our people it is the poor who suffer. . . .

The matter under consideration is of grave importance in itself; but of much graver importance is the whole tendency to open the Federal Treasury to a thousand purposes, many admirable in their intentions but in which the proponents fail or do not care to see that with such beginnings many of them insidiously consume more and more of the savings and the labor of our people. In aggregate they threaten burdens beyond the ability of our country normally to bear; and, of far higher importance, each of them breaks the barriers of self-reliance and self-support in our people.

Congressional Record. 71st Cong., 3rd sess., vol. 74, pt. 6 (February 26, 1931): 6098–70.

SENATOR ARTHUR VANDENBERG (R-MICHIGAN) DEFENDS THE VETERANS' BONUS BILL

I cannot agree with the presidential analysis. I shall vote with confidence and conscience to complete the pending legislation. It is my duty to proceed upon the facts as I see them; it is the duty of every Member of the Senate to proceed similarly, no less than it has been the President's duty to exercise the like scruple. . . .

No new addition to the public debt, to be liquidated by otherwise avoidable taxes, is involved in this bill. It merely recognizes an existing debt, and transfers it from one form to another. It is still the same debt. If anything, it might well be argued that this proposed process will ease off the 1945 burden of financing the whole three and a half billion dollars of this particular debt at one time. If anything, it might well be argued that we are forehandedly anticipating and avoiding an ultimate fiscal embarrassment in 1945. . . .

Now, for the President's other general objection—namely, that we extend the option of a loan privilege to veterans not in need, many of whom resent this legislation. . . .

I hope that veterans who do not need these loans will not make them. The American Legion announces its intention to stress this sound philosophy. There is no question but that a veteran is better off if he can leave his certificate intact and if he is happily in a position where that may be done, but there are tens of thousands to whom this loan privilege will be a blessed boon. I make this statement, and invite the Senate's attention to it: I believe it is far more tenable to ask for approval of this legislation lest needy veterans be denied all such relief than it is to ask the defeat of this legislation lest some veterans who are not needy shall share its privileges. . . .

I have no sympathy with the charge, sometimes heard, that the Government has done nothing for the veteran. On the contrary, the Government has been prodigal. We have expended some $5,000,000,000 in his behalf in the last decade, and perhaps 20 cents out of every current tax dollar, without respect to this legislation, goes directly in his behalf. He has not been forgotten or ignored by a grateful Republic.

But neither have I any sympathy with the argument also sometimes heard that we must hold back further legitimate consideration for him lest we open the door to endless raids. I shall vote for no raids. I am prepared to meet that issue if and when it arises. . . .

With greatest respect for the earnestness and the conscience and the pure motive which inspire the President to oppose this view, I must stand my own ground and persist in my support of the pending measure.

Congressional Record. 71st Cong., 3rd sess., vol. 74, pt. 6 (February 27, 1931): 6215–18.

THE MUSCLE SHOALS JOINT RESOLUTION (1931)

During World War I the federal government constructed a series of hydroelectric plants on the Tennessee River at Muscle Shoals, Alabama, for the purpose of extracting nitrates for the manufacture of explosives. During the 1920s there were repeated debates over what was to be done with these facilities now that they were no longer needed for national defense. The Harding and Coolidge administrations favored turning them over to private businesses, but this course was rebuffed again and again by a coalition of southern Democrats and Republicans from the Midwest and West.

George Norris, an elderly Republican senator from Nebraska, had his own ideas as to what should be done with the plants. Norris was one of the so-called "progressive" Republicans, who came mainly from rural parts of the country and believed—even more so that Hoover—in a strong, activist federal government. Driven by a passion for rural electrification, as well as a burning hatred of large power companies, Norris proposed that the plants continue to be operated by the federal government, both as a source of cheap electricity for the rural South and for production of nitrates for fertilizer. He and his allies in Congress proposed a bill creating a government-owned corporation that would run them, and it managed to pass Congress in 1928. However, it ran into the determined opposition of President Coolidge, who vetoed the bill on the grounds that it would place the government in competition with private enterprise.

Norris's pet proposal would meet with no more success under Hoover. Tension between the two men went back to 1928, when the Nebraska senator refused to endorse Hoover's presidential candidacy, even after he had received the nomination of the Republican Party.

As president, Hoover consistently favored conservation and reclamation projects. He backed construction by the federal government of the Hoover Dam on the Colorado River, one of the most ambitious public works projects in U.S. history. Nevertheless, he steadfastly refused to accept Norris's Muscle Shoals project. Hoover Dam, he explained, was mainly built for the purposes of irrigation and flood control; that it also produced hydroelectric power was merely a "by-product." Muscle Shoals, on the other hand, would exist for the primary purpose of providing power; for the government to operate it, he claimed, would amount to socialism.

Hoover had an opportunity to act on his feelings in 1931, when the House and Senate passed a joint resolution that was virtually identical to the one Coolidge had vetoed three years earlier. On March 3 he sent his veto message to Congress. Like Coolidge, he objected to having the federal government go into business in competition with its citizens; he also claimed that it was an unconstitutional expansion of federal power. He proposed instead that the state governments of Alabama and Tennessee operate them, which struck Norris and his allies as ridiculous. The cost of running the plants was far beyond the means of two poor, southern states. Moreover, they wondered why it was acceptable for a state government to compete with its own citizens, but not the federal government. The president, Norris claimed, was being controlled by the hated "Power Trust." Nevertheless, when Democrats and progressive Republicans attempted to override the veto, they failed by six votes. The Nebraska senator's plan was shelved for the time being.

The Muscle Shoals idea did not die. It would resurface early in Franklin Roosevelt's presidency and would form the basis for the Tennessee Valley Authority, which still provides electricity to much of the South today. Moreover, Roosevelt's support for the Muscle Shoals project helped to forge an alliance between Democrats and progressive Republicans that would continue throughout Roosevelt's first term.

This section features President Hoover's message to Congress upon vetoing the Muscle Shoals joint resolution. It also includes an editorial from the pages of the liberal journal *The Nation*, attacking the president for his veto.

HOOVER VETOES THE MUSCLE SHOALS JOINT RESOLUTION

This bill proposes the transformation of the war plant at Muscle Shoals, together with important expansions, into a permanently operated Government institution for the production and distribution of power and the manufacture of fertilizers. . . .

I am firmly opposed to the Government entering into any business the major purpose of which is competition with our citizens. There are national emergencies which require that the Government should temporarily enter the field of business, but they must be emergency actions and in matters where the cost of the project is secondary to much higher considerations. There are many localities where the Federal Government is justified in the construction of great dams and reservoirs, where navigation, flood control, reclamation, or stream regulation are of dominant importance, and where they are beyond the capacity or purpose of private or local government capital to construct. In these cases power is often a by-product and should be disposed of by contract or lease. But for the Federal Government deliberately to go out to build up and expand such an occasion to the major purpose of a power and manufacturing business is to break down the initiative and enterprise of the American people; it is destruction of equality of opportunity amongst our people; it is the negation of the ideals upon which our civilization has been based.

This bill raises one of the most important issues confronting our people. That is squarely the issue of Federal Government ownership and operation of power and manufacturing business not as a minor by-product but as a major purpose. Involved in this question is the agitation against the conduct of the power industry. The power problem is not going to be solved by the Federal Government going into the power business, nor is it to be solved by the project in this bill. The remedy for abuses in the conduct of that industry lies in regulation and not by the Federal Government entering upon the business itself. . . . I hesitate to contemplate the future of our institutions, of our government, and of our country if the preoccupation of its officials is to be no longer the promotion of justice and equal opportunity but is to be devoted to barter in the markets. That is not liberalism, it is degeneration. . . .

I sympathize greatly with the desire of the people of Tennessee and Alabama to see this great asset turned to practical use. It can be so turned and to their benefit. I am loath to leave a subject of this character without a suggestion for solution. Congress has been thwarted for 10 years in finding solution by rivalry of private interests and by the determination of certain groups to commit the Federal Government to Government ownership and operation of power.

The real development of the resources and the industries of the Tennessee Valley can only be accomplished by the people in that valley themselves. Muscle Shoals can only be administered by the people upon the ground, responsible to their own communities, directing them solely for the benefit of their communities and not for purposes of pursuit of social theories or national politics. Any other course deprives them of liberty. . . .

Congressional Record. 71st Cong., 3rd sess., vol. 74, pt. 7 (March 3, 1931): 7046–48.

THE EDITORS OF THE *THE NATION* DENOUNCE THE MUSCLE SHOALS VETO

Disappointed though we are at the loss of the Muscle Shoals bill, we are glad to see the President in his veto message raise a fundamental issue concerning public operation. On that issue, we believe, he is absolutely wrong. We are none the less grateful to him for making the issue clear and inviting public judgment. . . .

The real issue, the President says, is "federal government ownership and operation of power and manufacturing business not as a minor by-product but as a major purpose." With regard to power, we believe this statement to be strictly accurate. . . . We are glad to have the issue squarely presented. For the government to enter on such an undertaking, we learn, "is to break down the initiative and enterprise of the American people; it is the destruction of equality of opportunity among our people; it is the negation of the ideals upon which our civilization has been based." Here we disagree flatly. We do not concede that American civilization is and must be essentially a hard-fisted, hard-headed, hard-hearted grabbing for gain. That appears to be the president's conception, for he is "firmly opposed to the government entering into any business the main purpose of which is competition with our citizens." But the primary purpose of government operation of Muscle Shoals would be, not to compete with citizens, but to furnish them with cheap power and fertilizers. Despite Mr. Hoover, we insist that that is a perfectly legitimate and desirable end of government activity, and an end more important than maintaining the existing profits of private power companies.

Power, the President insists, must be furnished by private enterprise alone. But it can be provided economically only by linking power units into great unified systems; whereupon that competition of citizens so dear to the President becomes a vain and imaginary thing. This fact he recognizes himself; for instead of appealing to competition he declares that the remedy for abuses in the power industry lies in regulation by State and federal authority. Again we believe he is wrong. Experience indicates with increasing clearness that regulation does not and will not cure the abuses of the power business, because the companies, with their great wealth and immensely valuable privileges, constantly manage, in the unashamed pursuit of profits, to circumvent or control the regulating authorities. . . . We entertain no illusion as to the ease of getting efficient and economical public administration of power systems, but we can no longer cherish the romantic idea of satisfactory control of private companies through regulatory commissions. Behind the Muscle Shoals fight lie two conceptions of American government—the President's view that it is simply a referee to see that the rules of a contest among its citizens are observed, and the contrasted belief that it is, and increasingly is to be, an agency of public service. Over that issue we shall continue to wage war on the President.

"The Muscle Shoals Veto," *The Nation* 132 (March 18, 1931): 289.

THE WAR DEBT MORATORIUM (1931)

In the wake of World War I, a complicated and unstable system of international finance developed. During the war, many European countries—but particularly Great Britain and France—borrowed considerable amounts of money from the United States in order to finance the war effort. After the war, they sought to cover these debts by forcing the defeated countries—primarily Germany—to pay reparations to the victors. To complicate matters, in the 1920s American bankers extended huge loans to Germany. Capital, therefore, was flowing from the United States to Germany, from Germany to Britain and France, and then back to the United States.

By 1931 this system threatened to be upset by the worsening economic crisis, which had spread to Europe thanks in large part to the Hawley-Smoot Tariff of the previous year. Early that summer, the German government announced that it was on the verge of bankruptcy, and would be suspending its reparations payments until further notice. This immediately raised fears that the entire system of international finance might collapse.

Wall Street banker Thomas P. Lamont called on President Hoover to take action. The chain of collapse could be broken, he argued, if the United States would cancel or renegotiate the roughly $10 billion in loans that had been made to Britain and France. Hoover recognized that this might relieve the situation, but he knew that this would be extremely dangerous politically. At a time when Americans were struggling to get by, and the government was running a budget deficit, there was little sympathy for the plight of foreign countries. Moreover, many in Congress suspected that bankers like Lamont wanted to see the debt cancelled so that Britain and France were more likely to pay the millions of dollars in private loans that they had taken from Wall Street.

Nevertheless, Hoover was anxious to do something, no matter how small, to alleviate the situation. On June 20 he declared that the United States would delay further collection on the war debts for one year, and called upon the rest of the world to do likewise. His announcement immediately drew fire from his political opponents. While he had held out against legislation that would extend federal funds to ordinary Americans in need, he was willing to help foreign countries and Wall Street bankers. Many claimed that this was only the first step toward complete forgiveness of the debts.

Congress had been out of session when Hoover made his controversial announcement. The moratorium was high on the agenda when Congress reconvened in December, even though by that time it had been in effect for six months. It is likely that most of those who attacked the idea recognized that it was necessary, and that the debts would not be paid that year even if the moratorium were not in effect. Nevertheless, it was difficult for many congressmen and senators to pass up an opportunity to attack a president who was already highly unpopular among the American people. Senator George Norris (R-Nebraska), for example, claimed that the Hoover administration was under British control, and that the moratorium would be the first step on the road to cancellation of the foreign debts. Even though Congress ultimately passed the moratorium bill by a comfortable margin, it did not do so until Hoover had been thoroughly raked over the coals.

The "Hoover moratorium," as it came to be called, was no more than a temporary measure, and it did nothing to stop the slide of the international economy. In January 1932 Britain and France offered to forgive German reparations on the condition that the United States forgive their war debts, but this of course was politically impossible for Hoover. In the meantime, conditions in Europe continued to decline. Unemployment in Great Britain soon reached 25 percent, and, in Germany, Adolf Hitler's National Socialists became the largest single party in the parliament. At home, meanwhile, the moratorium had little effect except to cement the popular, though unfair, image of the president as someone more concerned about the welfare of foreigners and Wall Street than with that of the American people.

Included in this section is a press statement by Hoover on the need for the moratorium on war debt payments. It also contains excerpts from a speech on the floor of the Senate by Lynn Frazier (R-North Dakota), a progressive who was outspoken in his opposition to the moratorium.

HOOVER CALLS FOR A MORATORIUM ON WAR DEBTS AND REPARATIONS (1931)

The American Government proposes the postponement during one year of all payments on intergovernmental debts, reparations, and relief debts, both principal and interest, of course not including obligations of governments held by private parties. Subject to confirmation by Congress, the American Government will postpone all payments upon the debts of foreign governments to the American Government payable during the fiscal year beginning July 1 next, conditional on a like postponement for one year of all payments on intergovernmental debts owing the important creditor powers. . . .

The purpose of this action is to give the forthcoming year to the economic recovery of the world and to help free the recuperative forces already in motion in the United States from retarding influences from abroad.

The world wide depression has affected the countries of Europe more severely than our own. Some of these countries are feeling to a serious extent the drain of this depression on national economy. The fabric of intergovernmental debts, supportable in normal times, weights heavily in the midst of this depression.

From a variety of causes arising out of the depression, such as the fall in the price of foreign commodities and the lack of confidence in economic and political stability abroad, there is an abnormal movement of gold into the United States which is lowering the credit stability of many foreign countries. These and the other difficulties abroad diminish buying power for our exports and in a measure are the cause of our continued unemployment and continued lower prices to our farmers.

Wise and timely action should contribute to relieve the pressure of these adverse forces in foreign countries and should assist in the reestablishment of confidence, thus forwarding political peace and economic stability in the world.

Authority of the President to deal with this problem is limited, as this action must be supported by the Congress. It has been assured the cordial support of leading members of both parties in the Senate and the

House. The essence of this proposition is to give time and to permit debtor governments to recover their national prosperity. I am suggesting to the American people that they be wise creditors in their own interest and be good neighbors. . . .

I do not approve in any remote sense in the cancellation of the debts to us. World confidence would not be enhanced by such action. None of our debtor nations have ever suggested it. But as the basis of the settlement of these debts was the capacity under normal conditions of the debtor to pay, we should be consistent with our own policies and principles if we take into account the abnormal situation now existing in the world. I am sure the American people have no desire to attempt to extract any sum beyond the capacity of any debtor to pay, and it is our view that broad vision requires that our Government should recognize the situation as it exists. . . .

Press statement by Hoover, June 20, 1931, Presidential Press Relations File, Box 1183, Folder 393, Herbert Hoover Presidential Library, West Branch, Iowa.

SENATOR LYNN FRAZIER (R-NORTH DAKOTA) ATTACKS THE "HOOVER MORATORIUM"

I was out in the northwestern part of North Dakota at the time I received the telegram from President Hoover, which was dated June 24. The telegram reached me on the 26th of June, and I replied on the same date. I desire to read the telegram I sent:

"I have been out for two weeks in the drought-stricken counties of this State. Conditions are most deplorable, and assistance must be had. Conditions of farmers everywhere are mighty bad. I believe that a moratorium for all farmers is absolutely necessary; and if that can be provided for I will gladly vote for a moratorium for intergovernmental debts." [. . . .]

. . . [T]here is no question about the hard conditions of the foreign countries; but we have hard conditions here in our own country. If there is anyone who is in a harder situation or harder up than the farmers of these drought-stricken counties out in the middle Northwest, I do not know who he is; and God pity him if he is an any worse condition than those drought-stricken farmers are. Many of those farmers have been foreclosed on during the past few months by the Federal farm land bank of that district.

I have in my office a county paper—the official paper of the county—giving advertisements of nine foreclosures by the Federal farm land bank in that one county at one time. Some of those seemed so unjust that an appeal was taken to the local district judges, asking that these loans be held up and foreclosure be made through the courts; and in six instances out of the nine the injunction was granted by the local judges.

... I believe that our own people should be taken care of in preference to the people of foreign nations. The Government should look after the interests of its own people. Under the present existing conditions, with some eight or ten million men and women out of employment, many of them and their families depending upon charity, and in some instances going hungry; with thousands of farmers who have been foreclosed on and put out of business, yes, hundreds of thousands of them; with the farmers throughout the Nation having been forced this year to sell their products below the cost of production, thus making it impossible for them to meet their expenses or to pay installments on loans, it seems to me it is the duty of Congress to take thought and pass legislation for the benefit of our own people before considering the welfare of foreign countries.

For that reason, unless, as I stated in my telegram . . . , provision can be first made for taking care of our own people, I shall vote against this joint resolution.

Congressional Record. 72nd Cong., 1st sess., vol. 75, pt. 1 (December 22, 1931): 1103.

THE RECONSTRUCTION FINANCE CORPORATION (1932)

Until late in 1931, Hoover believed that private efforts could bring a halt to the depression. By the end of that year, however, recovery seemed as far off as ever. Several of the president's closest advisors began to warn him that direct federal intervention was necessary in order to prevent complete economic chaos. They suggested the creation of an agency modeled on the War Finance Corporation, which had been set up to channel government funds toward the construction of military plants during World War I. In spite of Hoover's squeamishness at the thought of government bailouts of private enterprises, the concept appealed to him; after all, he reasoned, the depression seemed at least as dire an emergency as the war had been.

The result was the creation of the Reconstruction Finance Corporation (RFC), the most radical and innovative of Hoover's initiatives for reviving the economy. The agency would be empowered to make emergency loans to banks, building-and-loan societies, trust companies, credit unions, insurance companies, railroads, and agricultural stabilization corporations. As long as such bodies remained solvent, the reasoning went, the economy as a whole could weather the crisis.

Hoover first asked Congress to pass the necessary legislation in his State of the Union message on December 7, 1931, and the legislature obliged on January 22, 1932. The RFC was granted $500 million in capital, and was authorized to borrow up to $1.5 billion more. In July, Congress voted to increase its funding by nearly 100 percent, to $3.8 billion. *Business Week* magazine praised it as "the most powerful offensive force that governmental and business imagination has . . . been able to command."[1] Even some of Hoover's critics admitted that it was a bold and promising step.

Nevertheless the RFC had its opponents, and they would grow louder and more numerous in the months to come. Most of the criticism was similar to that which had been directed against the previous year's war debt moratorium. Opponents claimed that while workers, farmers, and small businessmen were struggling, Hoover was making strenuous efforts to save not ordinary Americans, but big banks and businesses. And although Hoover denied this, later analysis would reveal that 7 percent of the institutions that borrowed from the RFC in the first two years of its existence received over half its money. Most of these institutions were the largest banks in the country.

The Reconstruction Finance Corporation was probably the boldest domestic initiative of Hoover's presidency, and it certainly represented a turning point in his approach to the depression. The president had always stood firm against direct or indirect government relief, but now he was willing to spend hundreds of millions of dollars to keep large banks and corporations in business. Now that this step had been taken, it would be far more difficult to refute the claims of other groups—workers, farmers, and small businesses—who asked when their relief would come. To be sure, by late 1932 there were plenty of Americans who wondered why the administration's chief concern seemed to be helping the "plutocrats."

For all of its boldness, it is difficult to assess the RFC's effectiveness. It probably did for a time prevent certain major financial institutions from going under, but it did little or nothing to ease the economic crisis. By 1932 the problem was lack of confidence on the part of investors and consumers, and a massive infusion of credit could do little or nothing to address this. Moreover, when, in January 1933, banks began to close at an alarming rate, the RFC proved powerless to stop the crisis. But in spite of its shortcomings, the Reconstruction Finance Corporation would in many ways serve as a model for Franklin Roosevelt's New Deal, and would remain an important government agency until the late 1950s.

The first document in this section is Hoover's message to Congress asking for the establishment of the Reconstruction Finance Corporation. The second is a rejoinder by Representative Fiorello LaGuardia (R-New York), who charges that the RFC is nothing more than a "millionaire's dole."[2]

NOTES

1. Quoted in David M. Kennedy, *Freedom from Fear: The American People in Depression and War, 1929–1945* (New York: Oxford University Press, 1999), 84.

2. *Congressional Record.* 72nd Cong., 1st Sess., vol. 75, pt. 2 (January 11, 1932): 1742–44.

HOOVER PROPOSES THE RECONSTRUCTION FINANCE CORPORATION (1932)

At the convening of the Congress on December 7 I laid proposals before it designed to check the further degeneration in prices and values, to fortify us against continued shocks from world instability, and to unshackle the forces of recovery. The need is manifestly even more evident than at the date of my message a month ago. I should be derelict in my duty if I did not at this time emphasize the paramount importance to the Nation of constructive action upon these questions at the earliest possible moment. These recommendations have been largely developed in consultation with leading men of both parties, of agriculture, of labor, of banking, and of industry. They have no partisan character. We can and must replace the unjustifiable fear in the country by confidence.

The principal subjects requiring immediate attention are: [. . .]

. . . The creation of a reconstruction finance corporation to furnish during the period of the depression credits otherwise unobtainable under existing circumstances in order to give confidence to agriculture, industry, and labor against further paralyzing influences. By such prompt assurance we can reopen many credit channels and reestablish the normal working of our commercial organization and thus contribute greatly to reestablish the resumption of employment and stability in prices and values. . . .

Combating a depression is indeed like a great war in that it is not a battle upon a single front but upon many fronts. These measures are all a necessary addition to the efficient and courageous efforts of our citizens throughout the Nation. Our people through voluntary measures and through State and local action are providing for distress. Through the organized action of employers they are securing distribution of employment and thus mitigating the hardships of the depression. Through the mobilization of national credit associations they are aiding the country greatly. Our duty is so to supplement these steps as to make their efforts more fruitful.

The United States has the resources and resiliance [*sic*] to make a large measure of recovery independent of the rest of the world. Our internal economy is our primary concern and we must fortify our economic structure in order to meet any situation that may arise and by so doing lay the foundations for recovery. . . .

Action in these matters by the Congress will go far to reestablish confidence, to restore the functioning of our economic system, and to rebuilding of prices and values and to quickening employment. Our justified hope and confidence for the future rests upon unity of our people and of the Government in prompt and courageous action.

Congressional Record. 72nd Cong., 1st sess., vol. 75, pt. 2 (January 11, 1932): 1263.

REPRESENTATIVE FIORELLO LAGUARDIA (R-NEW YORK) BLASTS THE RECONSTRUCTION FINANCE CORPORATION

. . . [W]hen the House of Representatives votes the passage of this bill, . . . it will go down as one of the darkest days in the history of parliamentary government. . . . This plan is indeed more than putting the cart before the horse. It is giving aid to the unsuccessful bankers before giving aid to the innocent depositors. Let us first secure the depositors by the passage of a proper guarantee fund to depositors, and that will take care of the liquidity in currency for a great many banks. Restore confidence to depositors and $2,000,000,000 will be restored to the banks. Then compel banks to do only legitimate banking instead of wild speculation. . . .

This is a millionaire's dole and you can not get away from it. It is a subsidy for broken bankers—a subvention for bankrupt railroads—a reward for speculative and unscrupulous bond pluggers. . . .

. . . We are in this position: Of a man in his country home, having finished his day's work. His wife and his children are upstairs in bed and he is reading. Two men come to the door and say, "Hand over your money," and point to the window. There stands a third hold-up man with a bomb in his hand. The head of the house would be able to go out and lick all three of the stick-up men, but the man with the bomb in his hand would destroy his wife and his children if he attempted to put up a fight, so he submits. And that is what is happening today. You talk about the railroads. . . . The railroads tell Congress, with a leer and a sneer, "Give us this money, because if you do not we will default on our bonds and we will impair every insurance company and every savings bank of the country." . . . The railroads have resisted Government control and supervision during the time of their financial manipulation and crooked financing. They resisted and complained of regulation when they were on a profit-earning basis. Now that they are broke they come to the Government on bended knees for a dole. . . .

This bill takes care of what? Of the banks. It provides to take over their securities, which have depreciated in value, and, of course, the Government is going to be stuck with them. . . .

Now, gentlemen, I want to ask anyone if it would not be a fair proposition . . . to take out of this $2,000,000,000, $150,000,000 as a first loan to a fund to be created and increased to a sufficient size for the guaranty of deposits and establish a system of deposit guaranty in our national and Federal reserve banks and put that into the bill? [. . .] Let the people of the country know that the American Congress can not be fooled; that we realize the coercion and the force that is put back of this bill by the bankers; but that we will first look after the interest of depositors, and if any banker violates his trust after a guaranty fund is provided, then that banker should have not the aid of the Reconstruction Finance Corporation but be in the custody of a Federal penitentiary.

Congressional Record. 72nd Cong., 1st sess., vol. 75, pt. 2 (January 11, 1932): 1742–44.

THE EMERGENCY RELIEF BILL (1932)

By the middle of 1932, unemployment was the most serious problem facing the nation. It is estimated that at this point more than ten million people were out of work, nearly 20 percent of the total labor force. In certain industries, such as steel and automobiles, the unemployment rate was closer to 50 percent; in Detroit alone, 223,000 autoworkers were jobless by the end of 1931.

Such levels of unemployment, for so long a period, were unprecedented in U.S. history. Traditionally, people without jobs could turn to their state or local governments or to private charities for relief, but the sheer magnitude of the crisis stretched their resources to the limit. In Chicago, for example, relief expenditures averaged $100,000 per day; lost wages from unemployment, however, were estimated at $2 million per day. Some journalists and politicians were beginning to predict revolution if something were not done quickly.

The creation of the Reconstruction Finance Corporation marked a turning point in Hoover's response to the Great Depression. By offering loans to banks, railroads, and other corporations, the federal government was for the first time involved in direct relief efforts. But relief for whom? Critics of the RFC noted that most of the loans made by that agency went to the country's largest banks and companies. What about the millions who had been laid off by some of those same corporations?

By mid-1932 the demands for federal unemployment relief were growing harder and harder to resist. That summer an Emergency Relief Bill, sponsored by Representative John Nance Garner (D-Texas) and Senator Robert Wagner (D-New York) passed both houses of Congress. The bill authorized an expansion of RFC activities, allowing that agency to extend loans to state and local governments, as well as to private charities, so that they might continue their relief efforts. It further provided funds to state and local governments to engage in public works projects.

Hoover vetoed the bill on July 11, 1932, claiming that "[n]ever before has so dangerous a suggestion been seriously made in our country." He argued that it would make the RFC "the greatest banking and money-lending institution of all history," and would thus jeopardize the existence of the same private banks that it had been designed to preserve. While he advocated federal funding for public works projects, he insisted that those covered under the Garner-Wagner bill were "nonproductive" make-work projects that would employ few people and would ultimately be a drain on the taxpayers. Finally, he feared that the states might see it as an opportunity to dump all their financial liabilities on the federal government.[1]

Congress was unable to muster enough votes to overturn the veto. However, just ten days later the president agreed to a compromise bill called the Relief and Reconstruction Act. This bill authorized the RFC to finance up to $1.5 billion in what he called "self-liquidating" public works; that is, projects such as toll roads, which promised to pay for themselves. It also permitted the RFC to loan up to $300 million to state and local governments for continued relief efforts.

Given the vehemence with which he rejected the Emergency Relief Bill, it is somewhat surprising that he signed a bill so similar only ten days later. Indeed, one senator characterized it as a "remarkable somersault."[2] No doubt politics had a great deal to do with it, as the presidential elections were only a few months away. However, the Relief and Reconstruction Act came far too late to save Hoover's presidency, and he would go down to defeat in November.

This section features a speech by Senator Robert Wagner (D-New York) backing the Emergency Relief Bill, and President Hoover's veto message to Congress.

NOTES

1. *Congressional Record.* 72nd Cong., 1st sess., vol. 75, pt. 14 (July 11, 1932): 15040–41.

2. David M. Kennedy, *Freedom from Fear: The American People in Depression and War, 1929–1945* (New York: Oxford University Press, 1999), 91.

SENATOR ROBERT WAGNER (D-NEW YORK) ADVOCATES UNEMPLOYMENT RELIEF

What is our problem? I know of no shorter way to describe it than to call it the vicious spiral of depression. When men lost their jobs they stopped buying. As buying was curtailed prices fell, profits disappeared, and factories reduced production. Reduced production meant that more men were laid off, deprived of their wages, and in turn more families curtailed their buying. So the vicious cycle continued. As it spread a great apprehension began to sweep through the country. A man who was at work was uncertain how long his job would continue and he, too, reduced his purchases. That quickened the decline. Then home owners out of work found that they could not meet interest and amortization on their mortgages; business houses unable to sell their merchandise could not pay their debts; and foreclosure and bankruptcy joined the forces of destruction. . . .

This is not the first time that I speak of this problem. Long before the Nation was aware of any sign of approaching depression I publicly advocated adequate preparedness to meet this very situation which has brought untold agony to our people. Since then I have repeatedly urged action along the lines now proposed in the bill I shall describe. I am convinced that now, at last, all elements of responsible public opinion in this country have come to recognize the irresistible necessity of taking such action.

What do we propose to do? First, we propose to help relieve the desperate and irrepressible needs of the destitute so that no one in the United States shall have cause to go cold or hungry. Second, we propose to launch and finance a gigantic program of construction, both public and private. And, third, we propose to help finance agricultural, industrial, and commercial undertakings, where credit for proper enterprises can not be obtained through normal banking channels. Our ultimate object is to initiate a program which will create a demand for commodities and labor. We hope thereby to help check the decline of prices. When prices stop falling private business will resume its normal activity without government insurance. . . .

Whatever theories we may personally entertain as to where responsibility lies for the relief of distress, it can no longer be denied that many communities throughout this country and many States are no longer able to carry unaided the crushing burden which the unprecedented demands for relief has placed upon them. These are days of emergency and it is, therefore, the sacred duty of the Federal Government to help meet that emergency and to mitigate the human misery which has been the unmerited lot of many of our citizens. . . .

We shall resume employment to check and counteract the spiral of depression. For employment breeds more employment. There is no greater force for recovery than a job for the man who is eager to work.

The American people have never yet admitted defeat or succumbed to despair. We have the resources, the means, and the energy not only to check the depression but to lift our people to a higher level of prosperity than we have ever known. Our immediate task is to deal with the present emergency. The relief and construction bill is in my judgment a well-designed lever to give American industry a lift and a start until its own great native strength can be brought into vigorous action again. I repeat the hope that before the week is over the country may hear the encouraging news that the relief and construction bill has become a law and that this program of rehabilitation is under way.

Congressional Record. 72nd Cong., 1st sess., vol. 75, pt. 13 (July 6, 1932): 14640–41.

HOOVER VETOES THE EMERGENCY RELIEF BILL

I have expressed myself at various times on the extreme undesirability of increasing expenditure on nonproductive public works beyond the $500,000,000 of construction already in the Budget. It is an ultimate burden upon the taxpayer. It unbalances the Budget after all our efforts to attain that object. It does not accomplish the purpose in creating employment for which it is designed, as is shown by the reports of the technical heads of the bureaus concerned that the total annual direct employment under this program would be less than 100,000 out of the 8,000,000 unemployed. . . .

[This bill represents a] major extension of the authority of the Reconstruction Finance Corporation. The creation of the Reconstruction Finance Corporation itself was warranted only as a temporary measure to safely pass a grave national emergency which would otherwise have plunged us into destructive panic in consequence of the financial collapse in Europe. Its purpose was to preserve the credit structure of the Nation and thereby protect every individual in his employment, his farm, his bank deposits, his insurance policy, and his other savings, all of which are directly or indirectly in the safe-keeping of the great fiduciary institutions. Its authority was limited practically to loans to institutions which are under Federal or State control or regulation and affected with public interest. These functions were and are in the interest of the whole people. . . .

This expansion of authority of the Reconstruction Corporation would mean loans against security for any conceivable purpose on any conceivable security to anybody who wants money. It would place the Government in private business in such fashion as to violate the very principle of public relations upon which we have builded [sic] our Nation, and render insecure its very foundations. Such action would make the Reconstruction Corporation the greatest banking and money-lending institution of all history. It would constitute a gigantic centralization of banking and finance to which the American people have been properly opposed for the past 100 years. . . .

One of the most serious objections is that under the provisions of this bill those amongst 16,000 municipalities and the different States that have failed courageously to meet their responsibilities and to balance their own budgets would dump their financial liabilities and problems upon the Federal Government. All proper and insuperable difficulties they may confront in providing relief for distress are fully and carefully met under other provisions in the bill. . . .

This proposal violates every sound principle of public finance and of government. Never before has so dangerous a suggestion been seriously made to our country. Never before has so much power for evil been placed at the unlimited discretion of seven individuals [i.e., the board of directors of the RFC]. . . .

With the utmost seriousness I urge the Congress to enact a relief measure, but I can not approve the measure before me, fraught as it is with possibilities of misfeasance and special privileges, so impracticable of administration, so dangerous to public credit, and so damaging to our whole conception of governmental relations to the people as to bring far more distress than it will cure.

Congressional Record. 72nd Cong., 1st sess., vol. 75, pt. 14 (July 11, 1932): 15040–41.

RECOMMENDED READINGS

Burner, David. *Herbert Hoover: A Public Life.* New York: Alfred A. Knopf, 1979.

Daniels, Roger. *The Bonus March: An Episode of the Great Depression.* Westport, Conn.: Greenwood Press, 1971.

Fausold, Martin L., and George T. Mazuzan, eds. *The Hoover Presidency: A Reappraisal.* Albany: State University of New York Press, 1974.

Ferrell, Robert H. *American Diplomacy in the Great Depression: Hoover-Stimson Diplomacy, 1929–1933.* New Haven, Conn.: Yale University Press, 1957.

Hubbard, Preston J. *Origins of TVA: The Muscle Shoals Controversy, 1920–1932.* Nashville: Vanderbilt University Press, 1961.

Lisio, Donald J. *The President and Protest: Hoover, Conspiracy, and the Bonus Riot.* Columbia: University of Missouri Press, 1974.

O'Conner, Raymond. *Perilous Equilibrium: The United States and the London Disarmament Conference of 1930.* Lawrence: University Press of Kansas, 1962.

Olson, James S. *Herbert Hoover and the Reconstruction Finance Corporation, 1931–1933.* Ames: Iowa State University Press, 1977.

Romasco, Albert U. *The Poverty of Abundance: Hoover, the Nation, the Depression.* New York: Oxford University Press, 1965.

Smith, Richard Norton. *An Uncommon Man: The Triumph of Herbert Hoover.* New York: Simon & Schuster, 1984.

Wilson, Joan Hoff. *Herbert Hoover: Forgotten Progressive.* New York: Harper-
Collins, 1975.

Internet Sources

The Herbert Hoover Page—http://www.bayserve.net/falkland/hoover/.

Herbert Hoover Presidential Library and Museum—http://www.hoover.nara.gov.

Herbert Hoover on the World Wide Web—http://www.cs.umb.edu/~rwhealan/jfk/
hoover_links.html.

2

FRANKLIN DELANO ROOSEVELT

(1933–1945)

In the opinion of many historians and political scientists, Franklin D. Roosevelt was one of the greatest presidents in U.S. history, and probably the single most noteworthy since Abraham Lincoln. Part of the reason for this is the sheer amount of time he spent in the White House—he was the only president to serve more than two terms. In fact, he was elected president no less than four times, although he would die only a few months into his fourth term. But even more important than his tenure of office were the actual changes that took place during his presidency. The years 1933–1945 saw a tremendous growth in the size and scope of the American government, the product both of Roosevelt's so-called "New Deal" to bring the nation out of the depression and of the effort of the United States to help the Allies defeat Nazi Germany and Japan in World War II.

In some ways, Franklin Roosevelt seemed destined for high office. He was born an only child to a wealthy family that lived on an estate along the Hudson River in upstate New York. His fifth cousin had been Theodore Roosevelt, an important president in his own right. After an elite education that included Harvard University and Columbia Law School, he entered politics. He was elected to the New York state assembly in 1910, and several years later President Woodrow Wilson appointed him assistant secretary of the navy. In 1920 he received the nomination of the Democratic Party for vice president, but his candidacy fell victim to the Republican landslide that put Warren G. Harding in the White House.

Less than one year after the 1920 presidential election, Roosevelt faced a more severe crisis—polio. Today there is a vaccination to prevent polio, so it is quite rare in the United States, but in the 1920s, it was prevalent.

For the rest of his life, he was virtually paralyzed below the waist, and he was unable to walk without assistance. But while many people—including his mother—urged him to retire permanently from public life, Roosevelt refused. He returned to the limelight in 1924, when he gave an important speech at the Democratic National Convention. Four years later he was elected governor of New York—an office which, as he well knew, had often been a springboard for the presidency.

For most of the country the Great Depression was a tragedy of colossal proportions, but for Franklin Roosevelt it was a grand opportunity. Herbert Hoover had entered office a much-admired public figure, but as the 1932 elections approached it became more and more likely that the next president was going to be a Democrat. And, as a popular governor of an important state, Roosevelt was in a position to make sure that he was that Democrat. When he received the party's nomination, he gave a speech in which he promised a "new deal" for the American people. While he was never clear on what that meant, the phrase caught on and would be applied to his entire agenda once he became president.

Roosevelt was a vigorous campaigner who seemed constantly to exude an aura of cheery optimism. This in itself was enough to put him in stark contrast to Herbert Hoover, who came across as perpetually gloomy despite his attempts to reassure Americans that recovery was "just around the corner." Roosevelt's attitude was summed up in his campaign song—"Happy Days Are Here Again"—and although he avoided specifics about how he would end the depression, his temperament had a positive impact on the voters. On election day, he won by a landslide.

The Roosevelt administration began in 1933 with what came to be known as the first "Hundred Days," a period of intense activity designed to solve many problems at once. Roosevelt announced a "bank holiday," in which all the nation's banks would close, each one to be reopened after federal investigators determined whether or not it was solvent. Within a couple of weeks most of the banks had reopened, and the long string of bank failures that characterized the depression at last came to an end.

More legislation soon followed. In an effort to restore confidence in the stock market, new restrictions were placed on the buying and selling of stocks and other securities. To relieve unemployment, Roosevelt created the Civilian Conservation Corps, which provided work for young men on projects such as reforestation, soil conservation, flood control, and road construction. The president also won the support of many in the Midwest and South by endorsing the creation of the Tennessee Valley Authority (set up to bring inexpensive electric power to much of the South), a body similar to the one called for in the Muscle Shoals legislation vetoed by Hoover two years earlier.

Roosevelt believed that the way to promote recovery was to raise incomes, both for industrial workers and farmers. To promote the former, Roosevelt signed the National Industrial Recovery Act, by which the National Recovery Administration (NRA) was created. The NRA established a series of boards—one for the automobile industry, one for the steel industry, etc.—made up of representatives from the most important companies in each industry. Each board was to establish a code of conduct for all companies within the industry, setting production levels, maximum hours of work, minimum wages and prices. Although adherence to the codes was supposedly voluntary, the NRA's director, General Hugh S. Johnson, threatened those who failed to comply with "a sock right on the nose."[1]

To raise prices for agricultural produce, Roosevelt pressed for and signed the Agricultural Adjustment Act (AAA), which encouraged farmers to produce less by paying them to take land out of cultivation by destroying existing crops of wheat and cotton, and by slaughtering thousands of farm animals.

Such seemingly drastic measures could not help but spark opposition. Many business leaders and bankers claimed that Roosevelt's policies were actually delaying recovery by creating a climate of insecurity. Farmers, meanwhile, objected that the NRA was making manufactured goods too expensive, and that the AAA was not doing enough to raise the prices of agricultural products. Nevertheless, it appeared as though the reforms were beginning to have their desired effects—the stock market began to move upward again, and businesses were reporting increased profits. Some were even beginning to speak of a "Roosevelt boom." Many on the Left believed that the president should use his authority to push for more dramatic action; they urged that capitalism could not be reformed, but had to be scrapped.

Faced with opposition from both the Left and the Right, Roosevelt decided in 1935 to co-opt some of his more radical critics by launching a new round of reforms. The result was the so-called "Second Hundred Days," a period which saw the passage of numerous new laws, most notably the National Labor Relations Act and the Social Security Act. The former guaranteed that industrial workers could form unions, and forced employers to bargain with them instead of with individual workers. The latter was a government-sponsored pension plan, in which employers and employees were required to pay into a fund that would be used to support the elderly after they retired. The Second Hundred Days also produced huge new public works programs, and a "Wealth Tax" that placed new levies on corporations and wealthy individuals.

If conservatives were annoyed by the New Deal legislation of 1933, the measures of 1935 enraged them. They predicted that business would never recover if companies were forced to recognize labor unions, pay for their workers' retirement, and pay higher taxes. Such legislation, they claimed, would deter businessmen from hiring new employees. Roosevelt responded by calling his critics "economic royalists," and claimed that "greedy businessmen" had brought on the depression. Many radicals applauded, as did the millions of industrial workers who rushed to join unions in the mid-1930s.

Roosevelt's conservative critics were correct in saying that the New Deal would not bring about lasting recovery. Except for very brief periods, the unemployment rate continued to hover at around 20 percent. The critics were wrong, however, in thinking that this would matter to the voters. The president's charisma, underlined by his frequent "fireside chats" to the American people via radio, made him a beloved figure, and his policies promised tangible benefits—unemployment insurance, old-age pensions, public works jobs, etc.—even if recovery itself proved elusive. In 1936 Roosevelt stood for reelection against the Republican candidate, Kansas governor Alfred M. Landon. Landon did not stand a chance against the popular president, who mobilized a powerful coalition of union workers and small farmers. Millions of African Americans, who had traditionally voted for Republicans, moved into the Democratic camp as well, having benefited from Roosevelt's public works programs. The president won with more than 62 percent of the popular vote; Landon failed to win even in his home state. Moreover, the Democrats won an overwhelming majority in both houses of Congress. The New Deal, it seemed, was here to stay.

Yet Roosevelt soon ran into trouble in his second term, beginning with his attempt to reorganize the Supreme Court. The Court had ruled in 1935 and 1936 that several New Deal measures, most notably the National Industrial Recovery Act and the Agricultural Adjustment Act, were unconstitutional. Fearing that the same fate might await his other programs, the president in early 1937 proposed that six new justices be added to the Court. It was his first big political mistake. The measure came across as a naked attempt to "pack" the Court with Roosevelt supporters, and this time the conservatives were not the only ones to object. In Congress, Democrats and Republicans alike denounced the move and accused the president of trying to establish a dictatorship. Ultimately the bill was defeated, but the battle had even broader implications. Many Democrats, particularly from the South and West, concluded that the New Deal had gone far enough, and began to work with Republicans to block further presidential initiatives.

Nor was the "court-packing" incident the only problem for Roosevelt. By 1937 the economy had shown some improvement, as the number of unemployed dipped below eight million for the first time since 1930. However, by the end of the year even this modest recovery was snuffed out, and the unemployment rate soared back to 19 percent. By 1938, in fact, there were more Americans unemployed than there had ever been during Herbert Hoover's presidency. It was a grim reminder that the New Deal was failing to live up to its promises.

In 1938 Roosevelt took the bold step of intervening in the Democratic primaries. His targets were conservative Democrats who had joined Republicans in opposing New Deal measures. In races across the country, he stumped for liberal candidates and denounced conservative incumbents as traitors to the cause of reform. There were even cases in which those employed on public works projects were threatened with dismissal if they failed to support those favored by Roosevelt. Yet, in spite of such tactics, the plan backfired. Critics accused Roosevelt of attempting to "purge" the party, and once again began to accuse him of wanting to create a dictatorship. In the end, nearly all of the conservatives won against their primary challengers; Roosevelt's intervention had only earned him their enmity. When the president proposed a bill to reorganize the executive branch of the government he was handed a decisive defeat. It was only with difficulty that he managed to persuade Congress to pass the Fair Labor Standards Act, which set minimum wages and maximum hours of work. It would prove to be the final act of the New Deal.

It was perhaps just as well, for by the end of the 1930s the public's attention was increasingly focused on events beyond America's shores. In the middle of the decade Congress had taken steps to ensure that the country would never again be drawn into a foreign war. From 1935 to 1937 it passed a series of Neutrality Acts that prohibited loans and arms sales to countries at war. Moreover, in 1938 Congress considered a proposed constitutional amendment that would require a national referendum on any declaration of war. Only after strenuous lobbying by the president was the amendment defeated, and by the narrowest of margins.

But while Americans sought to insulate themselves from war, war in Europe was becoming increasingly likely. Germany, which came under the control of Adolf Hitler's Nazi Party in 1933, had managed to build a powerful army and air force. In 1938 German forces occupied Austria, which was then absorbed into Germany. Later that year, Hitler demanded that Czechoslovakia cede some if its territory, and when that country's leaders realized that Great Britain and France would not come to their aid, they reluctantly agreed to do so. Early in 1939, however, the German army invaded the rest of Czechoslovakia, and Hitler declared most of it to be German territory.

In September 1939, after signing a treaty of nonaggression with Joseph Stalin's Soviet Union, Hitler launched an invasion of Poland. This time Britain and France pledged to fight, and declared war on Germany, marking the beginning of World War II. Roosevelt declared that the United States would remain neutral, although he spoke for most Americans when he expressed his hope that Britain and France would win. He also called upon Congress to revise the neutrality laws so that Britain and France could purchase arms from the United States. After a spirited debate, both houses agreed to do so, and as a result of purchases of American arms and other products abroad the economy finally rebounded from the depression. Within two years, U.S. industrial production exceeded what it had been in October 1929, and would continue to grow.

Despite the willingness of America to sell arms to Britain and France, it appeared for a time that Germany would actually triumph. After several months of relative inactivity, German forces invaded and conquered Denmark, Norway, the Netherlands, Luxembourg, Belgium, and France within the span of three months in the spring of 1940. Moreover, Italy also decided to enter the war as an ally of Germany, so that Britain stood alone against a hostile alliance that controlled nearly all of Europe.

In mid- to late 1940, therefore, the president sought a variety of means to assist the British and to prepare to fight if it became necessary. He first authorized the transfer of fifty old destroyers to the British navy, mainly to be used to defend supply convoys from German submarines. To expand the size of the army, Roosevelt also pressed Congress to enact the country's first peacetime draft. The public seemed to give its approval when, in November 1940, the president stood once again for reelection. This time the Republican candidate was Wendell Willkie, a corporate lawyer from Indiana who had never held elected office. Willkie conducted a spirited campaign, but in the end Roosevelt triumphed again, this time with nearly 55 percent of the popular vote.

The president interpreted his victory as a popular mandate for further aid to Great Britain, so in January 1941 he announced his proposal for "lend-lease," a plan by which millions of dollars' worth of tanks, aircraft, and other military hardware could be transferred to the British. He told the American people that Germany posed a direct threat to national security, and that Britain was the country's first line of defense. The lend-lease proposal triggered one of the most memorable debates in the history of U.S. foreign relations, but in the end Roosevelt got what he wanted. Moreover, when in June Hitler's armed forces invaded the Soviet Union, Congress voted to extend lend-lease aid to that country as well.

While all of this was going on, new crises were developing in Asia. Japan had launched an invasion of China in 1937, and by 1940 the offensive had bogged down in that country's vast expanses. In an effort to cut off China's supply routes, Japanese troops occupied French Indochina. The Japanese government also signed an alliance—the Axis Pact—with Germany and Italy, hoping that this would deter the United States from interfering in Asian affairs. However, it had precisely the opposite effect. Although Japan had never been popular in the United States, the alliance with Hitler made Americans even more anti-Japanese. Roosevelt responded with a series of economic sanctions, culminating in an embargo on oil to Japan.

But just as the Japanese had miscalculated the likely effect of their policies on American opinion, Roosevelt failed to see how his sanctions might affect Japanese strategy. Japan was almost completely dependent on the United States for its oil supplies, and without such imports, the campaign in China could not continue. The Japanese army and navy, therefore, concluded that the war would have to be expanded. Neighboring oil-producing territories would have to be invaded and conquered, and to make sure that the United States could not interfere, there would be an attack on the U.S. Pacific Fleet, based at Pearl Harbor in Hawaii.

Japanese aircraft struck Pearl Harbor on the morning of Sunday, December 7, 1941. The attack came as a complete surprise, and the air raid managed to sink six battleships, as well as several smaller vessels. Americans were outraged, and when Roosevelt asked for a declaration of war on Japan, Congress swiftly complied. Three days later Germany and Italy declared war on the United States, making the war a conflict of truly global proportions.

In 1942, after a series of defeats in the Pacific, the U.S. Navy dealt a devastating blow to the Japanese at the battle of Midway. Several months later American marines captured a Japanese base on the island of Guadalcanal, and for the next two-and-a-half years advanced slowly across the Pacific. Some islands were captured outright, others ignored, their Japanese garrisons left to starve from lack of supplies. This tactic, called "leap-frogging" or "island-hopping," brought American forces within range of the Japanese home islands.

In Europe, Germany and its allies were being pounded in the East by the Soviet Union, and by the end of 1942 Axis forces were pressured into a slow retreat. British and American troops landed in North Africa in November 1942, and then crossed the Mediterranean Sea to invade Italy in May 1943. But the crowning glory of the U.S. armed forces came on June 6, 1944, when the British and Americans landed on the Normandy coast of France in the largest amphibious invasion in the history of warfare. Germany was now being squeezed from three different directions.

Domestically, the war concentrated far more power in Washington than the New Deal ever had, with a variety of new agencies set up to coordinate industrial and agricultural production, to mobilize manpower and resources, and to maintain public morale. The war cost more than any conflict in history, and taxes steadily increased in an effort to finance it. (Even with the increased taxation, the national debt grew fivefold to nearly $260 million.) Many items, including rubber, oil, sugar, and coffee, were subject to rationing. On the other hand, the war effort provided a tremendous stimulus to the economy, and the problem of unemployment was virtually eliminated. War had finally accomplished what the New Deal had failed to do.

Politics, for the most part, took a back seat during the war, particularly since Roosevelt had backed away from further New Deal reforms. There were, however, some contentious issues, most notably the War Labor Disputes Act of 1943. Backed by Republicans and conservative Democrats, the bill authorized the president to seize plants in which labor disturbances threatened to impede war production, and made striking workers subject to the draft. Roosevelt vetoed the bill, but Congress promptly overturned the veto.

In November 1944 Roosevelt stood for reelection yet again, this time against the popular Republican governor of New York, Thomas E. Dewey. This race was the closest yet, but most Americans were unwilling to have a change of leadership in the midst of a war—the president once again emerged victorious, with more than 53 percent of the popular vote. However, it would be his last election. Throughout the campaign he had succeeded in keeping news of his failing health from reaching the voters, but it was clear that by early 1945 he was a sick man. At the end of March he went for a vacation to his retreat at Warm Springs, Georgia. Two weeks later, on April 12, he died of a cerebral hemorrhage. He would not live to see the final defeat of the Axis powers; from that point on, conduct of the war would lie in the hands of Roosevelt's successor, Vice President Harry S. Truman.

NOTE

1. Arthur M. Schlesinger, *The Coming of the New Deal* (Boston: Houghton Mifflin, 1957), 153.

THE AGRICULTURAL ADJUSTMENT ACT (1933)

Farmers had enjoyed little of the prosperity of the 1920s, and their situation grew even worse with the coming of the Great Depression. Despite the efforts of the Federal Farm Board, farm prices dropped sharply after the Wall Street crash of October 1929, and remained well below even the already-low levels of the late 1920s. Farmers were also more heavily in debt than any other sector of the population, and when prices fell many were unable to make their payments. Foreclosure and eviction notices nailed to farmhouse doors became an all-too-common feature of rural America.

Franklin Roosevelt's choice for secretary of agriculture was Henry

Wallace, a progressive Republican whose father had served in the same position under Warren Harding. Wallace gathered an impressive group of economists and lawyers to consider the farm problem, and the end result was the Agricultural Adjustment Act. The act aimed at achieving "parity" for farmers by forcing the prices of farm goods to what they had been in the years before World War I. It created an Agricultural Adjustment Administration (AAA), which was authorized to set production quotas for various commodities and make cash payments to farmers in exchange for their agreement to produce less. For example, corn growers could receive thirty cents a bushel for corn not raised; hog producers could receive $5 a head for pigs not raised. The program was to be paid for by special taxes levied on those who processed agricultural commodities, such as flour millers and meat packers. The size of the taxes would be determined by difference between the market price for a particular commodity and the "parity" price. For example, if wheat were selling at fifty cents a bushel, and the target price was eighty-eight cents, then the tax on flour millers could not exceed thirty-eight cents per bushel. Therefore the taxes would be phased out gradually as agricultural prices increased.

Roosevelt presented the plan to Congress just two weeks after his inauguration. Opponents charged that it would exacerbate the economic distress of workers who would be forced to pay more for food and clothing; moreover, they argued that it was an unconstitutional infringement on the freedom of farmers to control their crops. However, these arguments were quickly brushed aside, as midwestern Republicans joined with Democrats in support of the bill. The president signed it into law in May and by the following spring more than three million farmers had signed on to the AAA's production quotas.

However, the AAA's efforts ran into serious problems from the beginning. Many farmers distrusted the agency's officials, mainly young lawyers from the East who often knew little about the practical aspects of farming. Even more ominously, a bumper crop of hogs and cotton from the previous year threatened any immediate hope of raising prices. Wallace's solution was to order ten million acres of cotton that was ready for picking to be plowed under, and the slaughter of six million baby pigs and more than 200,000 sows. The decision evoked a storm of protest; at a time when millions of unemployed could not afford decent food or clothing, the destruction of so much cotton and livestock seemed nothing less than an atrocity.

As the bill's opponents predicted, the Supreme Court declared the Agricultural Adjustment Act unconstitutional in 1936, although a bill passed Congress that same year that continued the plan's basic functions under a different structure. All told, the AAA channeled about $4.5 million into the pockets of American farmers between 1934 and 1940. However, farm income never exceeded 80 percent of the plan's goals, and most farm families continued to struggle on incomes that were significantly less than the national average. Many farmers claimed that by basing subsidies on the size of farms rather than on need, the AAA acted in the interest of the largest landowners, and actually worked against those with smaller holdings. Nevertheless, the program remained generally popular, with large majorities of farmers choosing to participate.

The first document in this section is an excerpt from Secretary of Agriculture Wallace's message to Congress recommending passage of the Agricultural Adjustment Act. The counterpoint comes from a speech by Senator David A. Reed (R-Pennsylvania), an outspoken opponent of the bill.

HENRY WALLACE PUSHES THE AGRICULTURAL ADJUSTMENT ACT

Its basic purpose . . . is to increase the purchasing power of farmers. It is, by that token, farm relief, but it is also by the same token, national relief, for it is true that millions of urban unemployed will have a better chance of going back to work when farm purchasing power rises enough to buy the products of city factories.

The method to be used in increasing the farmer's purchasing power is by restoring the balance between production and consumption as rapidly as possible. Let us help the farmer, the bill says in effect, plan his production to fit the effective demands of today's and tomorrow's— rather than yesterday's—market.

The goal of the bill, in terms of price, is pre-war parity between the things the farmer sells and the things the farmer buys. Let me explain that. In the pre-war years, 1909–1914, wheat brought around 88 or 90 cents a bushel on the farm, cotton better than 12 cents a pound, and hogs better than 7 cents a pound. But at the same time, the prices of the things the farmer had to buy—his fertilizer, farm machinery, and the like— were on a comparable level. In general, these items bought by the farmer were a little lower than they are right now. But the prices the farmer got for his wheat and cotton and hogs were, in those pre-war days, more than twice as high as they are now. It is that gap that we want to bridge. And this bill provides the bridge. . . .

This bill . . . follows a new and untrod path. The successful operation of it depends on the whole-hearted cooperation of farmers, processors, and consumers. Has the time come when all elements of our society are willing to pull together to restore economic balance and attain social justice?

It may be true that the things which this bill strives to attain here and now may be brought about 10 or 15 years hence by the slow working of economic law. This action, we hope, will speed the inevitable readjustments with much less suffering than under the harsh hand of uncontrolled competition.

Some farmers join with urbanites in repudiating with horror the idea of reducing production at this time. They point out, very properly, that the world is full of hungry people and that the great quantities of surplus foodstuffs should be used to feed them. No supporter of this new farm bill will disagree with this as an ideal program.

As our economic system works, however, it seems that the greater the surplus of wheat on Nebraska farms the longer the change it seems to be necessary to maintain a balance between different groups of producers if we are to avoid suffering. Our surpluses of food crops seem to have had as disastrous an effect upon national well-being as crop shortage used to have on the isolated communities of a simpler age.

This bill attempts a major social experiment. It looks toward a balanced social state. It is trying to subdue the habitual anarchy of a major American industry and to establish organized control in the interest not only of the farmer but of everybody else.

Congressional Record. 77th Cong., 1st sess., vol. 77, pt. 1 (March 20, 1933): 642–43.

SENATOR DAVID A. REED (R-PENNSYLVANIA) OPPOSES THE AGRICULTURAL ADJUSTMENT ACT

I sincerely believe that it offers the most serious threat to the welfare of the workingmen of America that has been presented to them in those decades in which I have had any knowledge of the American Government; and I believe that in the guise of offering relief to the farmers of the country, in reality this bill would impose upon them a slavery which they would find to be utterly intolerable. . . .

To begin with, the bill is based upon a false premise—a premise that the farmers of the United States are in a worse case than are the industrial workers in the more concentrated communities.

I know full well that the price of farm products has sunk to a smaller percentage of its predepression level than has the price of most manufactured products, but that is only a part of the picture. If we will consider it from the standpoint of the income of the citizen, we will realize that the farmer is getting approximately 50 percent of his predepression prices for his entire crop, and that nature is working for him just as it was before the depression; and his output is a full output, on which he gets a 50-percent price. Then consider, on the other hand, the situation of the worker in industry, and we realize that he has suffered a very substantial diminution of his prices; and, besides that, an additional diminution of his output. The combination of those factors—diminished prices and diminished output—means that the income of the average urban worker today is a lower percentage of his predepression income than is the farmer's present-day income. . . .

. . . [I]n times of prosperity the Department of Labor has determined that the average workingman spends about 32 percent of his income for the food of himself and his family. Inevitably, as income shrinks that proportion increases, so that men who are working but half-time—as so many of us are these days—find themselves spending all their income for shelter and food. . . . Consequently, if by this law we double the cost of foodstuffs to the poorest elements of our population, we are doubling the cost not of that 32 percent but probably of 60 or 70 percent of the spending of the average workman of America. . . .

. . . [H]ow do Senators suppose the population of our cities, undernourished as they are in these dreadful times, are going to submit to a tax of over 100 percent on their cereals, on their meats, on their textiles, because all of them are going to be taxed under one section or another of this bill. How long are they going to submit to that? How long can we successfully explain to them that they are being subjected to a burden so cruel, not for the general purposes of their Government, but so that a particular group of farmers, most of them in the upper Mississippi Valley and in Texas, are to be given these vast sums as a bounty on their production? . . .

. . . The immediate effect of the bill is going to be to increase the cost of all products manufactured from basic agricultural products. With an agricultural price double that of the world market, how in the world can the manufactured products of American agriculture hope to compete in the markets of the world with those from other countries? How can an American packing plant, paying 100 percent more for its raw material, compete with a British packing plant, to which the bill provides we shall sell at the world level and not at the pegged price? It means the immediate extinction of American exports in products manufactured from the basic products of agriculture. . . .

Congressional Record. 73rd Cong., 1st sess., vol. 77, pt. 2 (April 13, 1933): 1638–45.

THE CIVILIAN CONSERVATION CORPS (1933)

The most dangerous feature of the Great Depression, the one that directly affected the lives of most Americans, was unemployment. When Franklin Roosevelt became president, nearly one in four adult males in the country were without work. Of particular concern were the large numbers of young men—recent high school graduates—with little prospect of employment. As men between the ages of seventeen and twenty-four made up (as they continue to do today) the segment of society most likely to commit violent crimes, finding some way to relieve their situation was of immediate importance.

The idea for the Civilian Conservation Corps (CCC), unlike many New Deal programs, originated with Roosevelt himself. His plan was to create public works jobs specifically for men between the ages of seventeen and twenty-four, with an emphasis on projects such as reforestation, soil conservation, flood control, and road construction. Unlike most such projects, these would be carried out under the auspices of the U.S. Army, and the employees would live in camps under military-style discipline. For $30 per month they would plant trees, fight forest fires, repair reservoirs, and refurbish national parks and historic sites. Of their wages, they would be allowed to keep only $5 each month; the rest they would be required to send home to their families. Presumably this would enable them to purchase more consumer goods, and thus to reinvigorate the economy.

In addition to his concern about unemployment, the CCC reflected two other of the president's longstanding priorities—a commitment to the preservation of natural resources, and an interest in exposing urban youths to a rural environment. The regimentation and "army camp" aspects of the program also demonstrates Roosevelt's lifelong interest in military affairs.

On March 21, 1933, Roosevelt sent a message to Congress recommending the passage of legislation to create the Civilian Conservation Corps, which he promised could give employment to 250,000 men by early summer. Critics charged that the proposed projects were unnecessary, and that the plan was too expensive. However, as was the case with most of the legislation proposed by the president during the Hundred Days, the opposition amounted to only a small minority, and the bill passed within days.

Ultimately, the Civilian Conservation Corps would prove to be one of the most popular programs of the New Deal, and at one time or another it employed more than three million young men. Congress voted to extend and expand the program in 1935, and it was only dissolved in 1943, when the immense numbers of young men in the armed services made it unnecessary.

One other point is worth mentioning. Among those who benefited from the CCC were thousands of African Americans, although in many states black workers were segregated from their white counterparts. The program's popularity among the black community goes a long way in explaining why Roosevelt became the first Democrat to win over large numbers of African American voters.

This section features excerpts from Roosevelt's address to Congress calling for the passage of legislation that would create the Civilian Conservation Corps. It also includes a rebuttal by Representative John Taber (R-New York), a conservative who argued that the program was too costly given the meager results that were expected to come from it.

ROOSEVELT PROPOSES THE CIVILIAN CONSERVATION CORPS

It is essential to our recovery program that measures immediately be enacted aimed at unemployment relief. A direct attack in this problem suggests three types of legislation.

The first is the enrollment of workers now by the Federal Government for such public employment as can be quickly started and will not interfere with the demand for or the proper standards of normal employment.

The second is grants to States for relief work.

The third extends to a broad public-works labor-creating program.

With reference to the latter, I am now studying the many projects suggested and the financial questions involved. I shall make recommendations to the Congress presently.

In regard to grants to States for relief work, I advise you that the remainder of the appropriation of last year will last until May. Therefore, and because a continuance of Federal aid is still a definite necessity for many States, a further appropriation must be made before the end of this special session.

I find a clear need for some simple Federal machinery to coordinate and check these grants of aid. I am, therefore, asking that you establish the office of Federal relief administrator, whose duty it will be to scan requests for grants and to check the efficiency and wisdom of their use.

The first of these measures which I have enumerated, however, can and should be immediately enacted. I propose to create a civilian conservation corps to be used in simple work, not interfering with normal employment, and confining itself to forestry, the prevention of soil erosion, flood control, and similar projects. I call your attention to the fact that this type of work is of definite, practical value, not only through the prevention of great present financial loss but also as a means of creating future national wealth. This is brought home by the news we are receiving today of vast damage caused by floods on the Ohio and other rivers.

Control and direction of such work can be carried on by existing machinery of the Departments of Labor, Agriculture, War, and Interior.

I estimate that 250,000 men can be given temporary employment by early summer if you give me authority to proceed in the next two weeks.

I ask no new funds at this time. The use of unobligated funds, now appropriated for public works, will be sufficient for several months. This enterprise is an established part of our national policy. It will conserve our precious natural resources. It will pay dividends to the present and future generations. It will make improvements in National and State domains which have been largely forgotten in the past few years of industrial development.

More important, however, than the material gains will be the moral and spiritual value of such work. The overwhelming majority of unemployed Americans, who are now walking the streets and receiving private or public relief, would infinitely prefer to work. We can take a vast army of these unemployed out into healthful surroundings. We can eliminate to some extent at least the threat that enforced idleness brings to spiritual and moral stability. It is not a panacea for all the unemployment, but it is an essential step in this emergency. I ask its adoption.

Congressional Record. 73rd Cong., 1st sess., vol. 77, pt. 1 (March 21, 1933): 650.

REPRESENTATIVE JOHN TABER (R-NEW YORK) DENOUNCES THE CIVILIAN CONSERVATION CORPS

. . . I am in favor of every measure which will relieve unemployment, but this measure will not relieve unemployment. It provides for further extending the Government indebtedness, because if we did not spend the money on this we would not spend it at all, and the money that we have to borrow from the people of the country must come through the selling of bonds, and that money must come out of the banks. The money that we spend on this will be frozen up in a nonliquidating project. The result of the whole thing is a further contraction of credit on the part of the banks and a further liquidation in the prices of labor and commodities. As a result, it means less employment than we had before.

This bill will cost a lot of money for every man that it puts to work. We hear it said, though it is hard to put your finger on the exact situation, that it is going to cost $500,000,000 and the bill is going to put 250,000 men to work. That is $2,000 per man. Then they are going to pay these men $1 a day. The rest of the money is going somewhere—into organization, into material—and it is going to cost about six times as much as it would to feed a whole family to put one man to work.

The way to work out of this situation is to stop spending money . . . and give industry and mining and farming and business generally a chance to work out of this picture. We have not given them a single chance without a lot of deflationary tactics since 1929. Let us begin now, because when we do recover we are going to recover because we put things on a sound basis. Let us stop doing the things that prolong the depression and begin to do such things as we did when we started in on this session of Congress—that is, balance the Budget and put this country in the black and out of the red; put it where it can and has a decent chance to recover. The farther we go into this sort of thing, the farther we go with this sort of spreading out, the worse the country will get. Why should we not stop this sort of thing and begin to give business and industry a chance to recover?

In order to understand how this bill would work, one must have an understanding of economic principles. In ordinary times a certain amount of capital can be tied up by the Government, when its Budget is balanced, in unnecessary and nonproductive public works without serious damage, but when the Budget is unbalanced and that money must come not from the regular income of the Government but the sale of securities, and every time you sell a million dollars' worth of bonds the result is that you take that much capital out of the channels of trade and industry and away from the credit channels of the banks which are available, and thereby you slow up and make more difficult dealings in commodities, agriculture, and otherwise, and the operation of farms, factories, mines, and railroads.

You do more damage to the unemployment situation by such operations than you do good. This bill is another deflationary operation. It will further increase unemployment beyond the numbers who will be put to work by this bill, and it will further reduce commodity prices and the prices of securities and make credit conditions more distressing. . . .

We have not tried once to stick to sound measures which under normal circumstances have always resulted in a price rise. Is it not time that we tried the old-fashioned way of balancing the Budget and stop experimenting with legislation on a vast scale which prevents the things which we most desire? If we had tried the sound way and it had failed, I would be willing to experiment. Not having tried the sound way and it not having failed, I believe it is entitled to the first choice.

Congressional Record. 73rd Cong., 1st sess., vol. 77, pt. 1 (March 29, 1933): 967–68.

THE NATIONAL INDUSTRIAL RECOVERY ACT (1933)

President Roosevelt and his advisors believed that the way out of the depression was to reverse the vicious cycle by which decreasing demand led falling prices, leading further to decreased wages, which further depressed demand. If prices and wages could be forced upward, they reasoned, the country's economic problems would be solved. However, getting companies to increase wages and prices was tricky; there was always the risk that some would seek to offer their products at lower prices—what the Roosevelt administration called "cutthroat competition."

The National Industrial Recovery Act (NIRA) was an attempt to eliminate "unfair trading practices" through a partnership among government, business, and labor. Designed largely by Senator Robert F. Wagner (D-New York) and Secretary of Labor Frances Perkins (who was, incidentally, the first woman to hold a cabinet position), it called for the creation of codes of "fair competition" to eliminate price cutting and overproduction. Each industry would form a committee made up of representatives of corporations, labor unions, and the federal government, and these committees would be charged with drafting the code for that industry. While these codes varied from industry to industry, all codes were to include a minimum hourly wage, a maximum number of hours worked per week, and a ban on child labor. A special feature of the NIRA was Section 7(a), which guaranteed the right of workers to organize and bargain collectively. Although adherence to the codes was technically voluntary, the law also included provisions authorizing the president to impose codes where industries failed to draft them voluntarily.

The NIRA faced little opposition in Congress; even many conservatives appreciated that private businessmen instead of government bureaucrats would draw up the codes. In June 1933, it passed both houses, and the president signed it into law. Within two years, however, it had proved a bitter disappointment even to its original supporters.

To administer the law, the NIRA created the National Recovery Administration (NRA), which was placed under the direction of General Hugh S. Johnson, a hard-drinking, chain-smoking Texan who had directed the draft during World War I. He crisscrossed the country by plane, making speeches and organizing rallies to promote adherence to the codes. Those who agreed to do so won the right to display the NRA's symbol, the blue eagle, bearing the motto, "We Do Our Part." As for those who refused to go along, Johnson threatened them with "a sock right on the nose."[1] By the end of September, more than five hundred codes had been written and approved by Johnson and the White House.

The initial enthusiasm over the NRA and its flamboyant director did not last long. In practice, large businesses played the most significant roles in the drafting of the codes, setting prices and production quotas at levels that many smaller businesses could not meet. To critics, it appeared that the NRA codes had done nothing more than help big corporations drive their competitors out of business. Moreover, union leaders charged that the wages and hours provisions of the NIRA were being neither observed by employers nor enforced by the government.

Membership in unions soared, and nearly 2,000 strikes—many of them violent—erupted across the country in 1934.

Eventually, the bombastic Johnson was eased out of his position, but by 1935 it appeared that the program was beyond saving. The Supreme Court delivered the final blow when on May 27 it declared the NIRA unconstitutional. In the case of *Schechter Poultry Corp. v. United States*, the court ruled that the bill delegated too much power to the executive branch. For many of the act's initial supporters, it was a mercy killing.

It would be a mistake to suggest that the NIRA had no positive achievements. It dealt a death blow to the use of child labor, which had still been prevalent in many southern cotton mills, and Section 7(a) would lay the groundwork for the modern labor movement. However, in its fundamental goal—the raising of prices and wages—it had failed miserably, making it one of the most disappointing contributions of the New Deal.

In the first document of this section, Roosevelt, in a "fireside chat" to the American people, defends the measures proposed under the National Industrial Recovery Act. The second document is a speech by former president Herbert Hoover, who claims that the NIRA places a stranglehold on small business.

NOTE

1. Paul M. Johnson, *A History of the American People* (New York: HarperCollins, 1997), 756.

ROOSEVELT PROMOTES THE NATIONAL INDUSTRIAL RECOVERY ACT

Last autumn . . . I expressed my faith that we can make possible by democratic self-discipline in industry general increases in wages and shortening of hours sufficient to enable industry to pay its workers enough to let those workers buy and use the things that their labor produces. This can be done only if we permit and encourage cooperative action in industry, because it is obvious that without united action a few selfish men in each competitive group will pay starvation wages and insist on long hours of work. Others in that group must either follow suit or close up shop. We have seen the result of action of that kind in the continuing descent into the economic hell of the past four years.

There is a clear way to reverse that process: If all employers in each competitive group agree to pay their workers the same wages—reasonable wages—and require the same hours—reasonable hours—then higher wages and shorter hours will hurt no employer. Moreover, such action is better for the employer than unemployment and low wages, because it makes more buyers for his product. That is the simple idea which is the very heart of the Industrial Recovery Act.

On the basis of this simple principle of everybody doing things together, we are starting out on this nationwide attack on unemployment. It will succeed if our people understand it—in the big industries, in the little shops, in the great cities, and in the small villages. There is nothing complicated about it and there is nothing particularly new in the principle. It goes back to the basic idea of society and of the nation that people acting in a group can accomplish things which no individual acting alone could even hope to bring about.

Here is an example. In the Cotton Textile Code and in other agreements already signed, child labor has been abolished. That makes me personally happier than any other thing with which I have been connected since I came to Washington. In the textile industry—an industry which came to me spontaneously and with a splendid cooperation as soon as the Recovery Act was signed—child labor was an old evil. But no employer acting alone was able to wipe it out. If one employer tried it, or if one state tried it, the costs of operation rose so high that it was impossible to compete with the employers or states which had failed to act. The moment the Recovery Act was passed, this monstrous thing which neither opinion nor law could reach through years of effort went out in a flash. . . .

We have sent out to all employers an agreement which is the result of weeks of consultation. This agreement checks against the voluntary codes of nearly all the large industries which have already been submitted. This blanket agreement carries the unanimous approval of the three boards which I have appointed to advise in this, boards representing the great leaders in labor, in industry, and in social service. This agreement has already brought a flood of approval from every state, and from so wide a cross-section of the common calling of industry that I know it is fair for all. It is a plan—deliberate, reasonable, and just—intended to put into effect at once the most important of the broad principles which are being established, industry by industry, through codes. . . .

There are, of course, men, a few men, who might thwart this great common purpose by seeking selfish advantage. There are adequate penalties in the law, but I am now asking the cooperation that comes from opinion and from conscience. These are the only instruments we shall use in this great summer offensive against unemployment. But we shall use them to the limit to protect the willing from the laggard and to make the plan succeed.

In war, in the gloom of night attack, soldiers wear a bright badge on their shoulders to be sure that comrades do not fire on comrades. On that principle, those who cooperate in this program must know each other at a glance. That is why we have provided a badge of honor for this purpose, a simple design with a legend, "We do our part," and I ask that all who join with me shall display that badge prominently. It is essential to our purpose.

Already all the great, basic industries have come forward willingly with proposed codes, and in these codes they accept the principles leading to mass reemployment. But, important as is this heartening demonstration, the richest field for results is among the small employers, those whose contribution will be to give new work for from one to ten people. These smaller employers are indeed a vital part of the backbone of the country, and the success of our plan lies largely in their hands. . . .

While we are making this great common effort there should be no discord and dispute. This is no time to cavil or to question the standard set by this universal agreement. It is time for patience and understanding and cooperation. The workers of this country have rights under this law which cannot be taken from them, and nobody will be permitted to whittle them away but, on the other hand, no aggression is now necessary to attain those rights. The whole country will be united to get them for you. The principle that applies to the employers applies to the workers as well, and I ask you workers to cooperate in the same spirit.

The Third "Fireside Chat"—"The Simple Purposes and the Solid Foundations of Our Recovery Program," July 24, 1933, see *The Public Papers and Addresses of Franklin D. Roosevelt, Volume Two* (New York: Random House, 1938), pp. 295–303.

FORMER PRESIDENT HERBERT HOOVER BLASTS THE NRA

This whole idea of ruling business through code authorities with delegated powers of law is un-American in principle and a proved failure in practice. The codes are retarding recovery. They are a cloak for conspiracy against the public interest. They are and will continue to be a weapon of bureaucracy, a device for intimidation of decent citizens. . . .

The multitude of code administrators, agents or committees has spread into every hamlet, and, whether authorized or not, they have engaged in the coercion and intimidation of presumably free citizens. People have been sent to jail, but far more have been threatened with jail. Direct and indirect boycotts have been organized by the bureaucracy itself. Many are being used today. Claiming to cure immoral business practices, the codes have increased them a thousand fold through "chiseling." They have not protected legitimate business from unfair competition but they have deprived the public of the benefits of fair competition.

The whole NRA scheme has saddled the American people with the worst era of monopolies we have ever experienced. However monopoly is defined, its objective is to fix prices or to limit production or to stifle competition. Any one of those evils produces the other two, and it is no remedy to take part of them out. These have been the very aim of certain business elements ever since Queen Elizabeth. Most of the 700 NRA codes effect those very purposes. . . .

My investigations over the country show that the codes have increased costs of production and distribution, and therefore prices. Thus they have driven toward decreased consumption and increased unemployment. They have increased the cost of living, and placed a heavier burden on the American farmer.

NRA has been crushing the life out of small business, and they are crushing the life out of the very heart of the local community body. There are 1,500,000 small businesses in this country, and our purpose should be to protect them.

The codes are preventing new enterprises. In this they deprive America's youth of the opportunity and the liberty to start and build their independence, and thus stop the men and women of tomorrow from building soundly toward a true social security. . . .

The whole concept of NRA is rooted in a regimented "economy of scarcity"—an idea that increased costs, restricted production and hampered enterprise will enrich a Nation. That notion may enrich a few individuals and help a few businesses, but it will impoverish the nation and undermine the principles of real social justice upon which this Nation was founded.

If the NRA has increased employment, it is not apparent. If we subtract the persons temporarily employed by the coded industries as the direct result of the enormous Government expenditures, we find that the numbers being employed are not materially greater than when it was enacted. NRA's pretended promises to labor were intentionally vague and have never been clarified. They have only promoted conflict without establishing real rights.

That original ballyhoo used to hypnotize and coerce the people into acquiescence is now gone. Most of the originally grandiose schemes now are conceded to be a violation of the spirit and the letter of the American Constitution.

Some business interests already have established advantages out of the codes, and therefore seek the perpetuation of the NRA. Even these interests should recognize that in the end they, themselves will become either the pawns of a bureaucracy that they do not want or the instruments of a bureaucracy the American people do not want.

Statement by Hoover to the Associated Press on the NRA, May 15, 1935, "Bible," 2195, Herbert Hoover Presidential Library, West Branch, Iowa.

THE SOCIAL SECURITY ACT (1935)

For decades liberals had been seeking government assistance for those who, through no fault of their own, remained unemployed, as well as for those who could not work due to age, sickness, or physical disability. During the 1920s, some corporations offered private pension plans, as did many fraternal orders, but few of these had managed to survive the economic crisis of the early 1930s. By 1935 Wisconsin was the only state to operate a functioning system of unemployment insurance, and fewer than 500,000 of the nation's 6.6 million elderly received any sort of government assistance.

Adding to the pressure for a federal pension system was Dr. Francis Townsend, a California physician who founded Old Age Revolving Pensions, Limited, in 1933. Townsend advocated a plan by which all persons over the age of sixty would receive $200 per month from the federal government on the condition that they retire from their jobs and promise to spend the entire amount during that month. The retirements, he argued, would free up many jobs for younger unemployed workers, while the spending requirement would help boost consumer demand, and thus encourage recovery. When critics pointed out that the cost of such a program would exceed the entire federal budget, Townsend remained unmoved; "I'm not in the least interested in the cost of the plan," he told a congressional committee.[1]

Nevertheless, the Townsend Plan attracted many supporters, particularly (and unsurprisingly) among the elderly. When a bill based on the plan appeared before Congress in January 1935, Old Age Revolving Pensions, Limited managed to collect twenty million signatures calling for its immediate passage. That bill did not even make it to a vote, but many in both political parties believed that it was only a matter of time before some form of "social insurance" would be enacted.

Designing such a plan involved many difficult questions. Who would be covered? Who should pay for it? Who should direct the program? To address these, President Roosevelt appointed a special committee, to be chaired by Labor Secretary Frances Perkins. With enthusiastic input from Agriculture Secretary Henry Wallace and Treasury Secretary Henry Morgenthau, as well as from the president himself, a bill was introduced to the House and Senate in January 1935.

The Social Security Act's main provision was for unemployment insurance and old-age pensions to be paid through a 6 percent payroll tax divided between employers and employees. The revenues generated from these payroll taxes would be more than sufficient to provide for the current elderly; the surplus would go into a special fund that would maintain the program in perpetuity. Other aspects of the plan directed that federal money would also be passed along to the states to support assistance programs for the blind, the disabled, and families with dependent children. But while the benefits to the elderly would be managed at the federal level by a Social Security Administration, unemployment insurance and other assistance programs would remain under the control of the states.

The act fell far short of what liberals in the administration had in mind, and certainly was a far cry from what was envisioned under the Townsend Plan. Liberals had hoped that the program would be funded from revenues generated by the income tax, so that it might redistribute wealth from rich to poor. Moreover, they had hoped for federal control over the entire program, not just the old-age portion. However, Roosevelt recognized that such provisions were unlikely to fly in Congress. As he later explained, funding Social Security through payroll taxes gave recipients "a legal, moral, and political right to collect their pensions and their unemployment benefits. With those [payroll] taxes in there, no damn politician can ever scrap my social security program."[2]

The bill that went before Congress appeared sufficiently moderate that it aroused little real opposition, except from a few die-hard conservatives who predicted that it would destroy incentives to work and save. Some claimed that the proposed payroll tax was excessive; not only would it retard recovery, but they feared that the resulting surplus might be used to fund other attempts at New Deal "social engineering." In spite of such criticism, though, the bill passed both houses by wide margins, and Roosevelt signed it into law on August 14.

Social Security has been one of the most enduring legacies of the New Deal. It was and remains one of Roosevelt's most popular accomplishments, but in many ways it has also proved the most troublesome. The first problems appeared in 1937, when the program's payroll taxes first began to be withheld from paychecks. The resulting decrease in the purchasing power of American workers played a major role in bringing on the so-called "Roosevelt Recession" of that year. Over the long term, however, more serious problems would arise. In 1938, Congress voted to reduce the payroll tax to 2 percent, making it a strictly "pay-as-you-go" plan that transferred wealth from the young to the elderly. This posed no problem at a time when the working population vastly exceeded the number of retired people. But in recent years, thanks to demographic patterns and longer life expectancies, the proportions have reversed, so that fewer are paying into the system and many more are drawing from it. Without major changes, some have suggested that the Social Security system could actually go bankrupt in the early twenty-first century.

The documents in this section include Roosevelt's message to Congress endorsing the Social Security Act, plus an address by Representative James Wadsworth (R-Pennsylvania) in which he labels the bill "undemocratic and dangerous."[3]

NOTES

1. William E. Leuchtenburg, *Franklin D. Roosevelt and the New Deal, 1932–1940* (New York: Harper & Row, 1963), 105.

2. David M. Kennedy, *Freedom from Fear: The American People in Depression and War, 1932–1940* (New York: Oxford University Press, 1999), 267.

3. *Congressional Record.* 74th Cong., 1st sess., Vol. 79, pt. 6 (April 19, 1935): 6060–61.

ROOSEVELT PROPOSES SOCIAL SECURITY LEGISLATION

In addressing you on June 8, 1934, I summarized the main objectives of our American program. Among these was, and is, the security of the men, women, and children of the Nation against certain hazards and vicissitudes of life. This purpose is an essential part of our task. In my annual message to you I promised to submit a definite program of action. This I do in the form of a report to me by a Committee on Economic Security, appointed by me for the purpose of surveying the field and of recommending the basis of legislation. . . .

It is my best judgment that this legislation should be brought forward with a minimum of delay. Federal action is necessary to and conditioned upon the actions of States. Forty-four legislatures are meeting or will meet soon. In order that the necessary State action may be taken promptly, it is important that the Federal Government proceed speedily.

The detailed report of the committee sets forth a series of proposals that will appeal to the sound sense of the American people. It has not attempted the impossible nor has it failed to exercise sound caution and consideration of all the factors concerned: the national credit, the rights and responsibilities of States, the capacity of industry to assume financial responsibilities and the fundamental necessity of proceeding in a manner that will merit the enthusiastic support of citizens of all sorts. . . .

Three principles should be observed in legislation on this subject. In the first place, the system adopted, except for the money necessary to initiate it, should be self-sustaining in the sense that funds for the payment of insurance benefits should not come from the proceeds of general taxation. Second, excepting in old-age insurance, actual management should be left to the States subject to standards established by the Federal

Government. Third, sound financial management of the funds and the reserves and protection of the credit structure of the Nation should be assured by retaining Federal control over all funds through trustees in the Treasury of the United States.

At this time, I recommend the following types of legislation looking to economic security:

First. Unemployment compensation.

Second. Old-age benefits, including compulsory and voluntary annuities.

Third. Federal aid to dependent children through grants to States for the support of existing mother's pension systems and for services for the protection and care of homeless, neglected, dependent, and crippled children. . . .

With respect to unemployment compensation I have concluded that the most practical proposal is the levy of a uniform Federal pay-roll tax, 90 percent of which should be allowed as an offset to employers contributing under a compulsory State unemployment compensation act. The purpose of this is to afford a requirement of a reasonably uniform character for all States cooperating with the Federal Government and to promote and encourage the passage of unemployment compensation laws in the States. The 10 percent not thus offset should be used to cover the costs of Federal and State administration of this broad system. Thus, States will largely administer unemployment compensation, assisted and guided by the Federal Government. . . .

In the important field of security for our old people, it seems necessary to adopt three principles—first, noncontributory old-age pensions for those who are now too old to build up their own insurance; it is, of course, clear that for perhaps 30 years to come funds will have to be provided by the States and the Federal Government to meet these pensions. Second, compulsory contributory annuities, which in time will establish a self-supporting system for those now young and for future generations. Third, voluntary contributory annuities by which individual initiative can increase the annual amounts received in old age. It is proposed that the Federal Government assume one-half of the cost of the old-age-pension plan, which ought ultimately to be supplanted by self-supporting annuity plans. . . .

The establishment of sound means toward a greater future economic security of the American people is dictated by a prudent consideration of the hazards involved in our national life. No one can guarantee this country against the dangers of future depressions, but we can reduce these dangers. We can eliminate many of the factors that cause economic depressions and we can provide the means of mitigating their results. This plan for economic security is at once a measure of prevention and a method of alleviation.

We pay now for the dreadful consequence of economic insecurity—and dearly. This plan presents a more equitable and infinitely less expensive means of meeting these costs. We cannot afford to neglect the plain duty before us. I strongly recommend action to attain the objectives sought in this report.

Congressional Record. 74th Cong., 1st sess., vol. 79, pt. 1 (January 17, 1935): 545–46.

REPRESENTATIVE JAMES W. WADSWORTH (R-NEW YORK) OPPOSES SOCIAL SECURITY

. . . I realize perfectly well that this bill is going to pass the House of Representatives . . . without any substantial change, and nothing that I can say will prevent it or even tend to prevent it, in view of the determination of the majority.

It is not my purpose to discuss it in detail . . . but I am going to endeavor to glance a little toward the far future and analyze some one or two things which seem to me to be susceptible of analysis, and certainly worth serious thought on the part of Members of the House regardless of their political affiliations.

First, as to the financing of the major portion of this program. As I understand it . . . these funds are to be established in the Treasury Department, through the collection of pay-roll taxes. . . . The bill provides in general that those moneys shall be invested solely in the bonds of the Government of the United States or bonds guaranteed as to the principal and interest by the Government. As I read the report and have listened to the discussion on the floor, it is apparent that the proponents of this bill expect that this fund will grow from time to time, year after year, until about 1970, if I am not mistaken, the fund will approximate $32,000,000,000, every penny of which must be invested in government bonds.

It is apparent that unless the national debt of the United States goes far, far beyond $32,000,000,000 in the time over which this calculation is extended, by the time this fund has been built up to any considerable degree it will become a fund large enough to absorb at least a major portion of the national debt, and finally absorb it all. . . .

Now, that may seem an effective and adequate way to finance the Government's financial activities in all the years to come. I am trying to look to the future. Heretofore the Government has financed its undertakings primarily and fundamentally as a result of the confidence of the individual citizen in the soundness of the Government's undertaking, but from this point on we are apparently going to abandon that philosophy of public confidence and resort to a very different practice. The Government is to impose a pay-roll tax through one of its agencies, collect the money into the Treasury Department, then the Treasury Department with its left hand on the proceeds of these taxes is to turn around and buy bonds of the United States government issued by the right hand of the Treasury Department. Thus the Government of the United States, after this thing gets going, is no longer to be financed directly by its citizens, confident in the soundness of the Government, but it is to be financed instead by arrangements made within the bureaucracy—an undemocratic and dangerous undertaking. . . .

Now, this may not seem important at this moment. I may be old-fashioned. . . . It seems to me that we are moving away from democracy in this new and manipulative method of financing the obligations of the United States. I do not question the integrity and the honor of the men who are going to manage this fund or the men who will be Secretaries of the Treasury down through the years to come, but there is something offensive to me in the spectacle of one branch of the Treasury Department having collected a fund by taxing the working people of America, and then using that money for the floating of its own bonds. It seems to me to present the possibility of a vicious circle, and is certainly removing the financial support of the Government of the United States far from the people themselves and confining it to an inner ring, bureaucratic in character. I am trying to look ahead and visualize what that may mean in the preservation of democracy. . . .

One other thing looking toward the future. . . . I know the appeal this bill has to every human being, that it appeals to the humane instincts of men and women everywhere. We will not deny, however, that it constitutes an immense, immense departure from the traditional functions of the Federal Government for it to be projected into the field of pensioning the individual citizens of the several States. It launches the Federal Government into an immense undertaking which in the aggregate will reach dimensions none of us can really visualize and which in the last analysis, you will admit, affects millions and millions of individuals. Remember, once we pay pensions and supervise annuities, we cannot withdraw from the undertaking no matter how demoralizing and subversive it may become. Pensions and annuities are never abandoned; nor are they ever reduced. The recipients ever clamor for more. To gain their ends they organize politically. They may not constitute a majority of the electorate, but their power will be immense. On more than one occasion we have witnessed the political achievements of organized minorities. This bill opens the door and invites the entrance into the political field of a power so vast, so powerful as to threaten the integrity of our institutions and so pull the pillars of the temple down upon the heads of our descendants.

We are taking a step here today which may well be fateful. I ask you to consider it, to reexamine the fundamental philosophy of this bill, to estimate the future and ask yourselves the questions, "In what sort of country shall our grandchildren live? Shall it be a free country or one in which the citizen is a subject taught to depend upon government?"

Congressional Record. 74th Cong., 1st sess., vol. 79, pt. 6 (April 19, 1935): 6060–61.

THE NATIONAL LABOR RELATIONS ACT (1935)

Section 7(a) of the National Industrial Recovery Act stipulated that every NRA code guarantee "the right of employees to organize and bargain collectively through representatives of their own choosing." It also prohibited employers from interfering with attempts to establish unions. The result of this legislation was a tremendous boom in union membership. In a single month, 100,000 men joined the United Mine Workers, while another 50,000 joined unions for rubber tire workers. As the labor leader John L. Lewis told workers, "The president wants you to unionize."[1]

But organized labor soon became disillusioned with Section 7(a). Many employers, they claimed, simply ignored its provisions, or set up "company unions" which were subservient to management. At the same time, the rising expectations of workers led to a series of strikes, many of them violent, during 1934. Particularly serious disputes took place in the trucking, coal mining, textile, and shipping industries. One walkout by longshoremen in San Francisco led to a general strike in which thousands of workers throughout the city left their jobs.

The National Labor Relations Act was the brainchild of Senator Robert F. Wagner, and for that reason it is often referred to as simply the Wagner Act. The bill established an independent, three-person National Labor Relations Board with the power to mediate labor disputes and enforce its decisions in the courts. It also laid out procedures by which workers could choose which union (if any) would represent them, and required that employers bargain "in good faith" with any union so chosen.

The bill instantly generated fierce opposition from the business community, who claimed that it would destroy the free enterprise system. In Congress, northeastern Republicans claimed that it was unconstitutional, would jeopardize recovery by deterring businessmen from hiring new workers, and would lead to more, not less, labor unrest. They were joined by some southern Democrats who feared that the need to negotiate with unionized labor would keep industry from developing in their mostly rural home states.

Representatives from both sides brought their case before President Roosevelt. Wagner countered that the failure of the federal government to enforce the rights of labor under Section 7(a) threatened recovery by promoting industrial conflict. He noted that many of the country's leading corporations had seen a marked increase in profits since 1933, but that industrial wages on average had fallen. As long as profits rose and wages fell, Wagner argued, the depression would continue.

Roosevelt sympathized with Wagner's position, but was unwilling to alienate southern Democrats, many of whom held leadership positions in Congress. As a result, he remained silent on the issue; indeed, as late as two days before the bill came to a vote in the Senate, he told reporters that he had not "given it any thought one way or the other."[2] After the bill passed, however, he embraced it enthusiastically, particularly after the Supreme Court declared the NIRA unconstitutional.

As expected, the passage of the National Labor Relations Act led to an unprecedented growth in labor unions. However, as the bill's critics predicted, the next two years saw a whole series of strikes that dwarfed those of 1934 in both numbers involved and violence. Nevertheless, the National Labor Relations Act proved to be one of the most important pieces of legislation of the New Deal. The mediation of the National Labor Relations Board forced even the country's most powerful corporations—such as General Motors and U.S. Steel—to recognize unions. Organized labor, it appeared, was here to stay.

Although Roosevelt had remained on the sidelines during much of the fight for the Wagner Act, he was more than happy to take credit for its results. While it did nothing to assist economic recovery, the bill gave Roosevelt a reputation as the most pro-labor president in U.S. history, and this helped to cement an alliance between labor unions and the Democratic Party that still exists today.

This section features excerpts from a speech by Senator Robert Wagner (D-New York) explaining the National Labor Relations Act and the desirability of its passage. It also includes a counterpoint in the form of a speech by Representative Robert Rich (R-Pennsylvania), who argues that it will result in an unprecedented wave of labor unrest.

NOTES

1. Michael E. Parrish, *Anxious Decades: America in Prosperity and Depression, 1920–1941* (New York: W. W. Norton, 1992), 313.
2. Ibid., 356.

SENATOR ROBERT WAGNER (D-NEW YORK) EXPLAINS THE NATIONAL LABOR RELATIONS BILL

The breakdown of section 7(a) brings results equally disastrous to industry and to labor. Last summer it led to a procession of bloody and costly strikes, which in some cases swelled almost to the magnitude of national emergencies. It is not material at this time to inquire where the balance of right and wrong rested in respect to these various controversies. If it is true that employees find it difficult to remain acquiescent when they lose the main privilege promised them by the Recovery Act, it is equally true that employers are tremendously handicapped when it is impossible to determine exactly what their rights are. Everybody needs a law that is precise and certain. . . .

The national labor relations bill which I now propose is novel neither in philosophy nor in content. It creates no new substantive rights. It merely provides that employees, if they desire to do so, shall be free to organize for their mutual protection or benefit. . . .

There is not a scintilla of truth in the wide-spread propaganda to the effect that this bill would tend to create a so-called "labor dictatorship." It does not encourage national unionism. It does not favor any particular union. It does not display any preference toward craft or industrial organizations. Most important of all, it does not force or even counsel any employee to join any union if he prefers to deal directly or individually with his employers. It seeks merely to make the worker a free man in the economic as well as the political field. Certainly the preservation of long-recognized fundamental rights is the only basis for frank and friendly relations in industry.

The erroneous impression that the bill expresses a bias for some particular form of union organization probably arises because it outlaws the company-dominated union. Let me emphasize that nothing in the measure discourages employees from uniting on an independent- or company-union basis, if by these terms we mean simply an organization confined to the limits of one plant or employer. Nothing in the bill prevents employers from maintaining free and direct relations with their workers or from participating in group insurance, mutual welfare, pension systems, and other such activities. The only prohibition is against the sham or dummy union which is dominated by the employer, which is supported by the employer, which cannot change its rules or regulations without his consent, and which cannot live except by the grace of the employer's whims. To say that that kind of a union must be preserved in order to give employees freedom of selection is a contradiction in terms. There can be no freedom in an atmosphere of bondage. No organization can be free to represent the workers when it is the mere creature of the employer. . . .

A great deal of interest centers around the question of majority rule. The national labor relations bill provides that representatives selected by the majority of employees in an appropriate unit shall represent all the employees within that unit for the purposes of collective bargaining. This does not imply that an employee who is not a member of the majority group can be forced to enter the union which the majority favors. It means simply that the majority may decide who are to be the spokesmen for all in making agreements concerning wages, hours, and other conditions in employment. Once such agreements are made the bill provides that their terms must be applied without favor or discrimination to all employees. . . .

The enactment of this measure will clarify the industrial atmosphere and reduce the likelihood of another conflagration of strife such as we witnessed last summer. It will stabilize and improve business by laying the foundations for the amity and fair dealing upon which permanent progress must rest. It will give notice to all that the solemn pledge made by Congress when it enacted section 7(a) cannot be ignored with impunity, and that a cardinal principle of the new deal for all and not some of our people is going to be supported and preserved by the Government.

Congressional Record. 74th Cong., 1st Sess., vol. 79, pt. 8 (February 21, 1935): 2371–72.

REPRESENTATIVE ROBERT RICH (R-PENNSYLVANIA) DENOUNCES THE NATIONAL LABOR RELATIONS ACT

I cannot conform to all of the things suggested in this bill because of the fact that I believe as the bill is drawn today it will cause us to see more strikes in the next 2 or 3 years than we have ever seen in the history of this country, and Members of Congress know that in the past 2 years we have had more strikes than we have ever had in the history of the country. . . .

If an employee must be left free to join a union, so should he be left free not to join a union. There are rights of the employees and there are rights of the employers, and all of those rights must be considered if we are going to pass legislation that will eliminate strikes and make conditions in the country better for the employer and for the employee; because . . . labor and capital are inseparable. They must work together. The majority of business men are honest and are striving to do the thing that is best for labor and for their business, and if the politicians make such laws that [permit] radicals and intimidators . . . to close industry, foment strikes, then greater harm than good will be done, men will be put out of jobs instead of employed, industry will be closed rather than operated. . . .

I have always thought that the most elementary right of an American is that of selecting and pursuing the employment of his choice. In that right he is to be free from molestation or intimidation by anyone. This

House is asked to write in the law the proposition that he shall be free only from employers and that the equally notorious coercion of labor organizations shall be ignored. How long do you think that this kind of arbitrary classification will stand in a court? You also propose to give to this labor board, with only the guidance of your vague definitions, the power to determine what constitutes these unfair labor practices. You give that board a jurisdiction and an authority greater than is possessed by any of our courts. Without rules of evidence it is to make findings of facts and they are to bind the court which reviews them. . . .

But are the gentlemen gaining new rights for labor? On the contrary, I think they are inflicting new wrongs upon the worker, for, if this bill is enacted, his right of self-organization and association will not be enlarged—it will be contracted. First of all, the labor board, not himself, will determine the unit of employment which is to select representatives. Unless he is part of the majority in that unit he will not be represented by an agent of his own selection. As an individual, whether he is in a big or a little unit of employment, he cannot make his own contract and sell his own labor if a majority of his fellow employees want to sell it collectively. This is not enlarging the right of self-organization or association. This bill gives fellow employees the right to coerce and intimidate their fellows in the exercise of every one of these rights. It destroys individual bargaining, takes away the right to determine their own unit of employment, and, unless you are part of a majority, the worker will have to let someone whom he did not select sell his labor for him. I predict with confidence that, if this measure is enacted, it will have a short life but an unhappy one, for it will breed strife and bitterness, as it is neither practical nor effective to protect the rights it pretends to safeguard. On the contrary, it is defective, biased class legislation and deserves from this House the condemnation it will receive from the courts. . . .

The Wagner Act will work in the interest of only a small minority of workers represented by professional labor leaders, will promote industrial strife, will bring about an epidemic of labor disputes, will drive employers and employees apart, and will substantially impede recovery.

It will in practice tend to make a closed shop of every plant and to make every employee carry a union card if he is to earn a living.

It penalizes employers for so-called "unfair practices" but will leave the agents and organizers of labor unions or the labor unions themselves completely free to use violence, intimidation, and other coercive methods which they may seek to employ. . . .

Congressional Record. 74th Cong., 1st sess., vol. 79, pt. 9 (June 19, 1935): 9688–91.

THE WEALTH TAX (1935)

Although the New Deal had been in effect for over two years by mid-1935, economic recovery still seemed distant, and unemployment remained dangerously high. A variety of public figures began pressing Roosevelt to take more radical steps. Chief among these was Senator Huey P. Long (D-Louisiana). As governor of Louisiana, Long had built a political empire by taxing the wealthy and corporations and by bringing new social services to the poor. Now in the Senate, he argued that the true cause of the depression was that wealth had been badly distributed in American society—the rich had far too much, and the poor far too little.

In February 1934 Long announced that he was creating a nationwide pressure group called the Share Our Wealth Society. This group would advocate a plan by which every American family would be given $5,000 plus a guaranteed minimum income of $2,500 per year. The plan would be paid for through high taxes on the rich, including a law limiting personal fortunes to $5 million and annual income to $1.8 million. The federal government would seize anything over and above these figures.

The scheme was highly impractical, as even the draconian taxes prescribed by Long would produce nowhere near the revenues that would be necessary to fund it. Nevertheless people flocked to Long's banner, so that by early 1935 the Share Our Wealth Society boasted more than eight million members in 27,000 local clubs around the country. There was talk that Long himself would make a run for the presidency in 1936, and while it was unlikely that he could win, supporters of the administration feared that he might take enough votes away from the president to allow a Republican to be elected.

It was largely to cope with the threat of Long's Share the Wealth movement that Roosevelt proposed the Revenue Act of 1935. It called for a graduated tax on corporate income, a federal inheritance tax, an increase in the maximum income tax rate from 59 to 79 percent, and a constitutional amendment to permit the federal government to tax interest derived from state and municipal bonds. Since all of these provisions would fall hardest on the wealthiest Americans, the president referred to it as a "wealth tax." Many others, however, began to call it the "soak-the-rich" plan. When Roosevelt sent the proposal to Congress, Huey Long claimed rightly to have provided the inspiration for the bill.

The bill turned out to be one of the most controversial measures of the New Deal. The newspaper publisher William Randolph Hearst declared it "Communism," while the wealthy denounced Roosevelt as "a traitor to his class."[1] For ten weeks the plan was the subject of heated debate in Congress as conservative southern Democrats began to whittle down its provisions. The corporate income tax remained part of the final bill, as did the 79 percent tax level (although it would apply only to incomes over $5 million, and in 1935 only one man in the entire country—John D. Rockefeller—had an income of that size). The inheritance tax and the proposed constitutional amendment were both removed. When Roosevelt failed to protest against these revisions, Long accused him of being "a liar and a fake."[2]

The watered-down "Wealth Tax" that passed Congress was one of the worst products of the New Deal. It ended up producing no more than $250 million in new revenues, and while it did nothing to alter the distribution of national income, it was enough to convince businessmen and other wealthy Americans that the administration was out to get them. In the uncertain climate of the 1930s, this made them far less likely to invest in new enterprises and hire new employees.

Nevertheless, the bill was good politics, for it allowed Roosevelt to portray himself as a champion of the common man and an enemy of those whom he would later call "economic royalists." In fact, Treasury Secretary Henry Morgenthau admitted as much when he called the plan "more or less a campaign document."[3] Public reaction was overwhelmingly positive, with more than 80 percent of those who wrote to the president on the issue praising the plan. As for the wealthy, the president seemed to enjoy the fury that they directed at him, and the rhetoric of class warfare would play an important role in his 1936 reelection campaign.

The documents in this section include Roosevelt's address to Congress recommending passage of the Wealth Tax, as well as a speech by Senator William W. Barbour (R-New Jersey), who warns that the bill is likely to retard recovery.

NOTES

1. David M. Kennedy, *Freedom from Fear: The American People in Depression and War, 1929–1945* (New York: Oxford University Press, 1999), 276–77.

2. Michael E. Parrish, *Anxious Decades: America in Prosperity and Depression, 1920–1941* (New York: W. W. Norton, 1992), 346.

3. Kennedy, *Freedom from Fear*, 276.

ROOSEVELT PROPOSES THE WEALTH TAX

[. . .] The movement toward progressive taxation of wealth and of income has accompanied the growing diversification and interrelation of effort which marks our industrial society. Wealth in the modern world does not come merely from individual effort; it results from a combination of individual effort and of the manifold uses to which the community puts that effort. The individual does not create the product of his industry with his own hands; he utilizes the many processes and forces of mass production to meet the demands of a national and international market.

Therefore, in spite of the great importance in our national life of the efforts and ingenuity of unusual individuals, the people in the mass have inevitably helped to make large fortunes possible. Without mass cooperation great accumulations of wealth would be impossible to save by unhealthy speculation.... Whether it be wealth achieved through the cooperation of the entire community or riches gained by speculation— in either case the ownership of such wealth or riches represents a great public interest and a great ability to pay....

My first proposal, in line with this broad policy, has to do with inheritance and gifts. The transmission from generation to generation of vast fortunes by will, inheritance, or gift is not consistent with the ideals and sentiments of the American people.

The desire to provide security for one's self and one's family is natural and wholesome, but it is adequately served by a reasonable inheritance. Great accumulations of wealth cannot be justified on the basis of personal and family security. In the last analysis such accumulations amount to the perpetuation of great and undesirable concentration of control in a relatively few individuals over the employment and welfare of many, many others.

Such inherited economic power is as inconsistent with the ideals of this generation as inherited political power was inconsistent with the ideals of the generation which established our Government....

I recommend, therefore, that in addition to the present estate taxes there should be levied an inheritance, succession, and legacy tax in respect to all very large amounts received by any one legatee or beneficiary; and to prevent, so far as possible, evasions of this tax, I recommend further the imposition of gift taxes suited to this end....

The disturbing effects upon our national life that come from great inheritances of wealth and power can in the future be reduced, not only through the method I have just described, but through a definite increase in the taxes now levied upon the very great individual net incomes....

Social unrest and a deepening sense of unfairness are dangers to our national life which we must minimize by rigorous methods. People know that vast personal incomes come not only through the effort or ability or luck of those who receive them, but also because of the opportunities for advantages which government itself contributes. Therefore, the duty rests upon the Government to restrict such incomes by very high taxes....

In the modern world scientific invention and mass production have brought many things within the reach of the average man which in an earlier age were available to few. With large-scale enterprise has come the great corporation drawing its resources from widely diversified activities and from a numerous group of investors. The community has profited in those cases in which large-scale production has resulted in substantial economies and lower prices.

The advantages and the protections conferred upon corporations by Government increase in value as the size of the corporation increases. Some of these advantages are granted by the State which conferred a charter upon the corporation, others are granted by other States which, as a matter of grace, allow the corporation to do local business within their borders. But perhaps the most important advantages, such as the carrying on of business between two or more States, are derived through the Federal Government—great corporations are protected in a considerable measure from the taxing power and the regulatory power of the States by virtue of the interstate character of their businesses. As the profit to such a corporation increases, so the value of its advantages and protections increases. . . .

It seems only equitable, therefore, to adjust our tax system in accordance with economic capacity advantage and fact. The smaller corporations should not carry burdens beyond their powers; the vast concentrations of capital should be ready to carry burdens commensurate with their powers and their advantages. . . .

Congressional Record. 74th Cong., 1st sess., vol. 79, pt. 9 (June 19, 1933): 9657–59.

SENATOR WILLIAM W. BARBOUR (R-NEW JERSEY) ATTACKS THE WEALTH TAX

The power to tax its citizens is the most sacred trust lodged in the hands of any government. Rightfully used, it is a legitimate source of revenue exacted from those best able to pay. Wrongfully used, it becomes the weapon of a tyrant, more dangerous than any other in the destruction of human liberties, threatening the confiscation of private property, and a constant encouragement to excesses in governmental spending.

It must be the purpose of any civil society to encourage the production of wealth, rather than curtail it, because by its production and distribution the people find their employment, and as total internal production is increased national living standards are also increased. From national production is obtained the revenue which supports the civil society in the form of government.

Any national policy, therefore, which threatens to curb the creation of wealth, which operates as a curb upon private initiative, is contrary to all sound economics, and is a threat both to living standards and to employment. . . .

Never in this history of this country has a more flagrant proposal to violate all these tenets and to misuse the taxing power come from a high official of the Government than the recent taxation message of the President of the United States, deliberately thrown into the tail end of a congressional session, when it could not have due consideration. . . .

Taxation has but one function. It is to raise revenue for the legitimate operating expenses of government. The Constitution so provides, and the Supreme Court in the past has rejected the theory that the taxing power may be used to effectuate devious policies.

Yet no member of this administration has dared to challenge the repeated statement made by eminent newspaper writers that this is not a bill to raise revenues, but is designed solely as a political gesture. To the contrary, it is brazenly admitted that this is not a Budget-balancing measure; that it has no relation to making income meet outgo, but is intended to accomplish some weird social objective. . . .

There is but one issue and one objective before this country today. We must seek recovery, which means reemployment, above all else. We must gratify the eternal craving of every American for a job in private employment, and any policy which does not aim directly at this objective is obnoxious to me at this time. Any policy which threatens to create new obstacles to recovery and to delay reemployment is doubly ill-advised. . . .

What this bill actually attempts is to climb upon that hard-ridden steed, "Share-the-Wealth," and ride him away while the demagogues who have pressed him so sorely in the past are looking in the other direction. Particularly it aims its punitive features at corporations which have grown large.

These corporations and those who profit greatly from them should and must carry their just burden of the Nation's tax load. But in trying to reach this source of revenue we must avoid the pitfalls so obvious in this bill of penalizing the millions of small shareholders whose income is derived from the profits of these corporations, and the other millions of employees whose living might be endangered.

In this country there are more than 10,000,000 stockholders in corporations. Many of them have no other source of revenue. Many of these investments represent the thrifty savings of a lifetime, and mostly they are in large corporations. In 103 industrial companies alone there are nearly 4,000,000 shareholders.

Are we, in a mad quest for reforming our social structure, to imperil these savings and penalize the person of small means who has invested in these corporations? [. . .]

This bill should be laid away until the next session of Congress when the Budget for the following fiscal year will be presented. Then, in the light of carefully appropriated federal moneys, we can determine how much revenue will be needed to operate. Taxes can be levied deliberately as a true revenue measure. Any other program is not good business and it is not good government.

Congressional Record. 74th Cong., 1st sess., vol. 79, pt. 12 (August 7, 1935): 12867.

SUPREME COURT REORGANIZATION (1937)

Franklin Roosevelt's New Deal received its first setbacks not from Congress, not from the voters, but rather from the Supreme Court. In a series of decisions in 1935 and 1936, the Court declared unconstitutional several pieces of New Deal legislation, most notably key sections of the Agricultural Adjustment Act and the National Industrial Recovery Act. Moreover, as 1937 opened, lawsuits challenging the constitutionality of several other New Deal reforms—such as Social Security and the National Labor Relations Act—were working their way through the judicial system. The president feared that if some sort of action were not taken, much of his agenda would be swept away.

For Roosevelt and other liberals, much of the problem stemmed from a bloc of four conservative Supreme Court justices—the so-called "Four Horsemen"—who opposed any federal intrusion into economic affairs, or into what they saw as the proper jurisdiction of the states. Given that there were a total of nine justices on the Court, all the Horsemen needed to do to block any New Deal measure was to convince one more justice that their interpretation of the Constitution was correct.

There were a number of methods by which the president might have dealt with this dilemma. He could have waited for one or more of the conservative justices to retire, thus giving him an opportunity to appoint more liberal men to the bench. However, the Four Horsemen were convinced that Roosevelt was a true threat to free enterprise, and resolved to outlast the president. In the meantime, they might throw out much of what he had accomplished since 1933. Some suggested amending the Constitution to make it more difficult for the Court to declare laws unconstitutional, or to allow Congress to override Court decisions. But to amend the Constitution could take years, so this course was rejected as well.

On February 5, 1937, Roosevelt called congressional leaders and members of his cabinet to a meeting at the White House, and informed them that the Judicial Procedures Reform Act was being put before Congress that same day. Many of the justices on the Supreme Court were elderly, the president explained, and needed more assistance in working through the Court's heavy caseload. The act, therefore, proposed to add a new justice for every member above seventy years of age. Given the makeup of the current court, this would allow Roosevelt to name no less than six new justices.

The president did not expect the furor that would result. After all, the Constitution says nothing about how many justices would be on the Supreme Court, and indeed the number had changed several times during the nineteenth century. Moreover, the 1936 elections, in addition to returning him to the White House with 62 percent of the popular vote, had been an overwhelming Democratic victory in Congress. Democrats had huge majorities in both houses, and up to this point they had never failed to give the president what he wanted. Roosevelt therefore believed that he would have no problem in getting approval for this particular bill.

He was wrong, and Democrats and Republicans alike quickly attacked what they called the "court-packing" plan. Although he had defended the reorganization on the grounds that it would make the Court more efficient, everyone knew what the president's real motives were. Moreover, he had taken the congressional leadership for granted, failing to involve them in the drafting of the bill—the whole affair had the appearance of a royal proclamation, placed before Congress for a rubber stamp of approval. The proposal even drew fire from members of Roosevelt's own administration.

Two events occurred that spring that combined to doom the Judicial Procedures Reform Act. The first was a public letter by the Court's chief justice, Charles Evans Hughes, that demolished point-by-point every one of the president's arguments for the bill. Even more damaging to Roosevelt was that Justice Louis Brandeis, the Court's most liberal member (as well as the oldest) had signed the letter as well. The second was the announcement in late March and early April that the Court had reversed two of its previous anti-New Deal rulings. Many believed that the "court-packing" plan had frightened two of the justices into changing their positions, but this later proved to be untrue—the decisions had been made even before the plan had been announced.

In any case, the Senate Judiciary Committee voted against the bill, and when it came before the entire Senate, it fell by a vote of seventy to twenty. Roosevelt could argue that, since the Supreme Court had now begun to validate the New Deal, the defeat of his proposal was not such a disaster. Moreover, since one of the Four Horsemen announced his retirement in May, Roosevelt would have an opportunity to nominate a more liberal justice and thereby permanently alter the makeup of the Court. However, the fight showed a new willingness on the part of congressional Democrats to oppose the president. It also permanently damaged his relationship with certain liberal midwestern Republicans who had supported him throughout his first term. Finally, the court-packing plan suggested to many in both parties that Roosevelt would use any means to press his New Deal agenda. Never again would he enjoy the happy relations with Congress that he had experienced before 1937.

The first document in this section comes from one of Roosevelt's "fireside chats" to the nation, in which he defends his plan for reorganization of the federal judiciary. The second comes from a radio address by Senator Carter Glass (D-Virginia), a conservative southerner who saw the plan as an attempt to subvert the Constitution.

ROOSEVELT DEFENDS HIS SUPREME COURT REORGANIZATION PLAN

[. . .] We have . . . reached the point as a Nation where we must take action to save the Constitution from the Court and the Court from itself. We must find a way to take an appeal from the Supreme Court to the Constitution itself. We want a Supreme Court which will do justice under the Constitution—not over it. In our Courts we want a government of laws and not of men.

I want—as all Americans want—an independent judiciary as proposed by the framers of the Constitution. That means a Supreme Court that will enforce the Constitution as written—that will refuse to amend the Constitution by the arbitrary exercise of judicial power—amendment by judicial say-so. It does not mean a judiciary so independent that it can deny the existence of facts universally recognized.

How then should we proceed to perform the mandate given us? . . .

When I commenced to review the situation with the problem squarely before me, I came by a process of elimination to the conclusion that, short of amendments, the only method which was clearly constitutional, and would at the same time carry out other much needed reforms, was to infuse new blood into all our Courts. We must have men worthy and equipped to carry out impartial justice. But, at the same time, we must have Judges who will bring to the Courts a present-day sense of the Constitution—Judges who will retain in the Courts the judicial functions of a court, and reject the legislative powers which the courts today have assumed. . . .

What is my proposal? It is simply this: whenever a Judge or Justice of any Federal Court has reached the age of seventy and does not avail himself of the opportunity to retire on a pension, a new member shall be appointed by the President then in office, with the approval, as required by the Constitution, of the Senate of the United States.

The plan has two chief purposes. By bringing into the judicial system a steady and continuing stream of new and younger blood, I hope, first, to make the administration of all Federal justice speedier and, therefore, less costly; secondly, to bring to the decision of social and economic problems younger men who have had personal experience and contact with modern facts and circumstances under which average men have to live and work. This plan will save our national Constitution from hardening of the judicial arteries. . . .

Those opposing this plan have sought to arouse prejudice and fear by crying that I am seeking to "pack" the Supreme Court and that a baneful precedent will be established.

What do they mean by the words "packing the Court"?

Let me answer this question with a bluntness that will end all *honest* misunderstanding of my purposes.

If by that phrase . . . it is charged that I wish to place on the bench spineless puppets who would disregard the law and would decide specific cases as I wished them to be decided, I make this answer: that no President fit for this office would appoint, and no Senate of honorable men fit for their office would confirm, that kind of appointees to the Supreme Court.

But if by that phrase the charge is made that I would appoint and the Senate would confirm Justices worthy to sit beside present members of the Court who understand those modern conditions, that I will appoint Justices who will not undertake to override the judgment of the Congress on legislative policy, that I will appoint Justices who will act as Justices and not as legislators—if the appointment of such Justices can be called "packing the Courts," then I say that I and with me the vast majority of the American people favor doing just that thing—now. . . .

Like all lawyers, like all Americans, I regret the necessity of this controversy. But the welfare of the United States, and indeed of the Constitution itself, is what we all must think about first. Our difficulty with the Court today rises not from the Court as an institution but from human beings within it. But we cannot yield our constitutional destiny to the personal judgment of a few men who, being fearful of the future, would deny us the necessary means of dealing with the present.

This plan of mine is no attack on the Court; it seeks to restore the Court to its rightful and historic place in our system of Constitutional Government and to have it resume its high task of building anew on the Constitution "a system of living law." The Court itself can best undo what the Court has done. . . .

A "Fireside Chat" Discussing the Plan for Reorganization of the Judiciary, March 9, 1937, see *The Public Papers and Addresses of Franklin D. Roosevelt, 1937 Volume* (New York: Macmillan, 1941), pp. 122–33.

SENATOR CARTER GLASS (D-VIRGINIA) ATTACKS THE COURT-PACKING PLAN

What does this Court-packing scheme signify if it does not reflect the fury of its proponents against the Supreme Court of the United States for certain of its recent decisions asserting the rights of the States and individuals and private business under the law and prohibiting the proposed invasion of these by ill-digested congressional legislation, largely devised by inexperienced and incompetent academicians? That is precisely what it is all about. Had the judicial decisions sanctioned these rankly unconstitutional measures, who believes there would have been this unrestrained abuse of the Court and this unprecedented attempt to flank the Constitution by putting on the bench six judicial wet nurses to suckle the substance out of the opinions of jurists whose spirit of independence keeps pace with their profound knowledge of the law? . . .

What other and how many peculiar schemes of government are to be presented for submissive legislative action in confident expectation that they will meet with the favor of the "biased" half dozen who are to adorn the bench is left to our imagination because not exactly specified in the proclaimed program. We are simply given to understand that the President has a "mandate from the people" to so reconstitute the Supreme Court as to have it sanction whatever the White House proposes to an agreeing Congress, particularly if it involves no "check upon unauthorized freedom," to quote Grover Cleveland . . . or "restraint on dangerous liberty."

But we know there has been no such mandate from the people to rape the Supreme Court or to tamper with the Constitution. The Constitution belongs to the people. It was written by great representatives of the people, chosen for the purpose, and was ratified by the people as the Supreme Charter of their Government, to be respected and maintained with the help of God. With the consent and by mandate of the people their Constitution provides how it may be amended to meet the requirements of the ages. It has always been so, and no administration in the history of the Republic has attempted to flank the Constitution as a legislative short-cut so vividly denounced by Woodrow Wilson as "an outrage upon constitutional morality. . . ."

The predominant question is whether the practice of a century under an independent judiciary is to be abruptly terminated by authorizing the President to seize the Court by the process of packing in order to compel agreement with the Executive views. Should this be done without "a mandate from the people"? Should the people be ignored and, without asking their consent in the usual way, submit helplessly to having their

Constitution tortured unto meanings which have been declared in contravention of the fundamental law? . . . The talk about "party loyalty" being involved in the opposition to this extraordinary scheme is a familiar species of coercion. It is sheer poppycock. No political party since the establishment of the Government ever dared to make an issue of packing the Supreme Court. . . .

I am far from intimating that the President of the United States is incapable of selecting suitable men for the Supreme Court. I am simply accepting his own word and that of his spokesmen to the effect that he wants men "biased" in behalf of his legislative and administrative projects, who may be counted on to reverse the Supreme Court decisions already rendered and give such other decisions of policy as may be desired. This is not my view alone; it is the conclusion of millions of alarmed citizens throughout the Nation. . . .

Abraham Lincoln at Gettysburg thought the Civil War was a test of whether a "government of the people, by the people, for the people" should perish from the face of the earth. Just as profoundly are some of us convinced that no threat to representative democracy since the foundation of the Republic has exceeded in its evil portents this attempt to pack the Supreme Court of the United States and thus destroy the purity and independence of this tribunal of last resort.

Radio Address by Honorable Carter Glass [D-Virginia], March 29, 1937, Post-Presidential Files, Box 306, Herbert Hoover Presidential Library, West Branch, Iowa.

EXECUTIVE REORGANIZATION (1937–1938)

In the short term, it did not appear that the failure of Roosevelt's Supreme Court Reorganization plan would do much damage to his presidency. After all, the Supreme Court had upheld all of the legislation from the Second Hundred Days, and few were willing to cry over the fate of the ineffective National Recovery Administration in any case. Moreover, the announced retirement of one of the conservative "Four Horsemen" of the Court meant that the president would have an opportunity to place a more liberal man on the bench.

However, it soon appeared that the "court-packing" fight had done serious damage to the president's credibility in Congress. In the minds of many—Democrats and Republicans alike—Roosevelt had tried to make the Supreme Court subservient to the executive branch of government. Similar thoughts would come to mind in connection with his proposed plan of executive reorganization, which he had submitted to Congress at roughly the same time.

The executive reorganization plan was the product of the President's

Committee on Administrative Management, a group of three nationally known experts in public administration who had been appointed by the president to suggest ways in which the executive branch could become more efficient. They made a host of recommendations, including the addition of six new executive assistants to the president and two new cabinet-level posts. Most importantly, the executive reorganization plan increased the president's control over budgetary, administrative, and personnel matters within the various departments and bureaus. It was a fairly innocuous piece of legislation, and under normal circumstances the bill would probably have faced little opposition. Indeed, even Republicans such as Herbert Hoover had been talking about increasing the efficiency of the executive branch, so that chances of passage when Roosevelt first submitted the bill in January 1937 were quite high. However, the arrival of the "court-packing" plan the following month made congressmen and senators extremely wary of any White House proposal containing the word "reorganization." Almost immediately, critics in both parties began to connect the two, and to argue that they were part of a grand plan by Roosevelt to set himself up as a dictator. As Massachusetts Democrat David I. Walsh put it, the bill amounted to "plunging a dagger into the very heart of democracy."[1]

At a time when democracies were rapidly giving way to dictatorships in Europe, such rhetoric had profound effects. When the bill came before the Senate in March 1938, even some of the president's most stalwart supporters—including Senator Robert Wagner of New York—voted against it. Ultimately, it passed the upper house by a margin of only seven votes, but in the House the president's opponents managed to send it back to committee—effectively killing it—by a vote of 204 to 196. In one of the greatest defections in history, no fewer than 108 House Democrats had opposed the bill. As a political defeat, it was even more devastating than the court-packing debacle. "I didn't expect the vote," Roosevelt confided to a friend. "I can't understand it. There wasn't a chance for anyone to become a dictator under that bill."[2]

The incident did not completely destroy the cause of executive reorganization, although it certainly crippled it. The following year, Congress approved a watered-down version of the plan that authorized the hiring of six new executive assistants, but which included none of the other recommendations of the President's Committee on Administrative Management. In the end, however, the bill served only to remind Roosevelt of the strength of the forces arrayed against him in Congress.

The first document in this section comes from a public letter that Roosevelt addressed to one of his allies in the Senate. In this letter, the president ridicules those who claim that he is attempting to establish a dictatorship. The second document is a series of excerpts from the comments of Senator Josiah Bailey (D-North Carolina), a southern Democrat who suggests that executive reorganization is a violation of the Constitution.

NOTES

1. James MacGregor Burns, *Roosevelt: The Lion and the Fox* (New York: Harcourt, Brace, 1956), 344.
2. William E. Leuchtenburg, *Franklin D. Roosevelt and the New Deal, 1932–1940* (New York: Harper & Row, 1963), 279–80.

ROOSEVELT DENIES EXECUTIVE REORGANIZATION IS "DICTATORIAL"

... [S]everal newspapers [have charged] that the reorganization bill now before the Congress would make me a dictator.

1. As you well know, I am as much opposed to American dictatorship as you are, for three simple reasons:

A. I have no inclination to be a dictator.

B. I have none of the qualifications which would make me a successful dictator.

C. I have too much historical background and too much knowledge of existing dictatorships to make me desire any form of dictatorship for a democracy like the United States of America.

2. The reorganization bill now before the Congress is the culmination of an effort starting over 40 years ago to make the business end—i.e., the executive branch—of the Federal Government more businesslike and more efficient. Seven or eight of my immediate predecessors in the Presidency have recommended similar reorganization measures.

There are two methods of effecting a businesslike reorganization. It can be done by complex and detailed legislation by the Congress going into every one of the hundreds of bureaus in the executive departments and other agencies.

Or it can be done by giving the President as Chief Executive authority to make certain adjustments and reorganizations by Executive order, subject to overriding of these Executive orders by the Congress itself.

I would have been wholly willing to go along with the first method, but attempts at detailed reorganization by the Congress itself have failed many times in the past, and every responsible Member of the Senate or the House is in agreement that detailed reorganization by the Congress is a practical impossibility.

We come, then, to the second alternative—reorganization by Executive order subject to overriding by the Congress.

3. In any reorganization you will realize, I am sure, that if it changes existing administrative set-ups, consolidates jobs, or makes other kinds of savings, either from the point of view of cost or from the point of view of bureaucratic authority, such changes are bitterly fought by those who stand to lose some authority and by those who are so wedded to existing practices that they go to any length to prevent the slightest change that seeks greater efficiency. . . .

4. You know that when over a year ago I recommended a reorganization to the Congress all parties and all factions agreed on the need for such a measure. You know, too, that a year later a carefully manufactured partisan and political opposition to any reorganization has created a political issue—created it deliberately of whole cloth.

5. The opposition has planted bogies under every bed. It was said, for example, that the work of the Army engineers was to be abolished in spite of the fact that the Congress, and the Congress alone, can determine who will do river and harbor dredging and build flood-control levies. It is charged that the splendid work of the Forestry Service is to be hamstrung—hamstrung, I suppose, by the best friend forestry ever had in the United States. It is charged that the extremely efficient Veterans' Bureau or the excellent Railroad Mediation Board is to be damaged beyond repair. I cite these merely as an example of a score of equally silly nightmares conjured up at the instigation either of those who would restore the Government to those who owned it between 1921 and 1933 or those who for one reason or another seek deliberately to wreck the present administration of the Government of the United States. . . .

. . . [T]here are two cogent reasons why the bill should go through as it is now drawn. The first is the constitutional question involved in the passage of a concurrent resolution, which is only an expression of Congressional sentiment. Such a resolution cannot repeal Executive action taken in pursuance of a law. The second is the very remote possibility that some legislative situation might possible arise in the future where the President would feel obligated to veto a joint resolution of the Congress and properly require a two-thirds vote to override his veto. I repeat that I visualize no such possibility between now and 1940, when the authority given is to end. Thus you will see that charges of dictatorship are made out of whole cloth—even if I wanted to be a dictator, which Heaven knows, I do not.

Congressional Record. 75th Cong., 3rd sess., vol. 83, pt. 10 (April 5, 1938): A1337–39.

SENATOR JOSIAH BAILEY (D-NORTH CAROLINA) CLAIMS EXECUTIVE REORGANIZATION WILL BRING DICTATORSHIP

[. . .] We created these departments. We have the legislative authority over them. If they are to be changed, the power to change them is within us. What right have we to give away that power to start with?

The Constitution says in the plainest language that—

All legislative powers herein granted shall be vested in a Congress of the United States.

The word "vested" means that the power goes, and goes forever. When a thing vests, it vests. It is all there. A thing cannot be vested and then taken back. That would be a gift on condition. Whereas this power now is vested in us, we are asked to vest it in another power without knowing how far it goes, or what is to be done. . . .

I dwell on another matter. I take it that every intelligent man on earth knows that democracy is at stake in the world today. The question in America is not whether we can maintain the capitalistic system. The question in America is not whether we can recover. The question in America is whether we can maintain the democratic structure, the democratic spirit, and the democratic method. It is gone across the sea. It is not altogether gone in England, I thank God, but everywhere else it has gone up in a reversion to the barbaric tyrannies which we had hoped were buried in history 2,000 years ago.

. . . [I]f we take this bill for our precedent, what becomes of our legislative function? What becomes of that which is predicated in the legislative process here? Where is the notification to the people? Where is the opportunity for them to resolve our doubts in their judgment? . . .

We are told by the philosophers to resist the beginnings, and that injunction is so old that it has been written in Latin for 3,000 years— "osbta principiis," resist beginnings—and if some of us here are very much concerned to resist now, it is because we feel that, with the beginnings of the attrition of the democratic process here, where a great continent has been dedicated to it, where it will have its last stand, and die, if it must die, we must resist. We must beg our fellow Senators to refuse to yield to the little argument of expediency or the seductive plea of agreeableness, or compromise, or accord. So here is a matter in which the legislative process ought to be preserved as in all other matters which affect the Government and affect the people. . . .

Many persons forget that our Constitution is a constitution which fixed the checks and balances of the Government so that no one part of the Government could exercise power over another. Sometimes I think we do not sufficiently respect the men who wrote our Constitution. They did not sit down at Philadelphia and work it up out of their own minds. The Constitution of the United States is the consummation of the experience of the human race in matters of government. The framers of the Constitution were afraid to put power in the President. They were afraid of a king. They knew what a king meant. They were afraid of a tyrant. They knew what a tyrant meant. They were afraid to put executive powers in the legislature for fear of tyranny. They knew what tyranny meant. They would not put more power in the Supreme Court than was necessary to maintain its independent existence, and I must say they trusted the Congress to do that. But here we are, time after time, a little here, and a little there, destroying the balance of powers in the United States, and we think we are merely passing a bill concerning which some of us get assurances. Hear me on that subject. The man does not live who can get assurances against a disturbance of the balance of power, and the man never will live who can give such assurances. Our forefathers knew that. They checked power because they would not trust it. They distributed power because they were afraid of its concentration. . . .

So . . . while I began discussing the pending measure, I have broadened my discussion into all the implications of the careless disregard of the constitutional obligations under which we legislate here. I am saying that as we love our Constitution, as we would preserve the democratic process in America, in an hour when the night seems to be approaching . . . let us, you and I, resist the beginnings of every move, every motion, every bill, every amendment that tends to impair the force and the effect of the constitutional obligation in a matter resting upon us as Senators, who have the legislative power vested in us, and who have no right to vest it in anyone else whomsoever.

Congressional Record. 75th Cong., 3rd sess., vol. 83, pt. 4 (March 17, 1938): 3563–70.

THE LUDLOW AMENDMENT (1938)

When it came to foreign policy in the 1930s, the most pressing concern for most Americans was how to avoid getting involved in another foreign war. It was commonly believed that U.S. intervention in World War I had accomplished nothing except add to the wealth and power of the British Empire. Moreover, the belief—first expressed by President Hoover, but widely accepted among Americans—that the depression had started overseas encouraged a public attitude in favor of "isolationism." According to this view, the country needed to isolate itself from the problems of Europe and focus on national economic recovery.

During the 1930s Congress passed a series of laws with just that goal in mind. Much of this legislation stemmed from the belief that loans made to belligerent countries had brought about U.S. involvement in World War I. Therefore, in 1934 the Johnson Act banned private loans to countries that had failed to pay their war debts. The Neutrality Acts of 1935, 1936, and 1937 went further by not only prohibiting all loans to countries that were at war, but also all arms sales to such countries. It also made it illegal for Americans to travel on cruise ships owned by countries at war, for fear that the sinking of such ships might encourage pro-war sentiment. And although President Roosevelt expressed certain reservations about some aspects of the Neutrality Acts, he openly endorsed them and willingly signed all of them into law.

To its supporters, the Ludlow Amendment was the logical next step. In 1935 Louis Ludlow, a Democratic congressman from Indiana, proposed an amendment to the Constitution that would require a national referendum before the country could declare war, except in case of actual invasion. But in spite of public opinion polls that showed large majorities in favor of the amendment (as many as 73 percent, according to one survey) and the endorsement of several popular magazines (most notably *Good Housekeeping*, which encouraged housewives and mothers to write their congressmen in support of it), it had made little headway in Congress. In late 1937 it remained stuck in the House Judiciary Committee, since Ludlow had failed to garner enough support to bring it to a vote by the full House.

All that changed on December 12, when Japanese aircraft attacked and sank the gunboat USS *Panay*, then lying at anchor on the Yangtse River in China. A few in the administration called for war, and the president himself considered seizing Japanese property in the United States. However, the reaction of the public was quite different. Rather than demanding retaliation against Japan, the main question was, "What was an American gunboat doing in China?" A poll in *Fortune* magazine showed that a clear majority of Americans favored a complete U.S. withdrawal from Asia.

The main effect of the *Panay* incident, however, was that it rescued the Ludlow Amendment from legislative oblivion. Within two days of the attack, the amendment had received sufficient support to move to a floor vote in the House of Representatives. It received endorsement from a wide array of congressman, from liberal to conservative. As Representative Gerald Boileau (R-Wisconsin) put it, if it was fair to hold plebiscites under the Agricultural Adjustment Act to ask farmers "whether or not they should lead little pigs to slaughter," then "all of the people should be permitted by a referendum vote to determine whether or not the sons and daughters of these same farmers should be led to slaughter upon the battlefields of foreign countries."[1]

Roosevelt quickly registered his opposition to the amendment, and sent a message to Congress objecting that it "would cripple the President in his conduct of our foreign relations."[2] The White House launched a massive lobbying campaign, and ultimately convinced forty-four Democrats to change their minds. When the amendment came to a final vote, it lost by a vote of 209 to 188. It was a narrow victory for the administration, but it showed the extent to which anti-interventionism dominated the American public mind.

The documents in this section include a speech by Representative Louis Ludlow promoting the amendment that bore his name, and an address by Representative Charles Faddis (D-Pennsylvania), a Roosevelt loyalist who argues that the amendment would make national defense impossible.

NOTES

1. William E. Leuchtenburg, *Franklin D. Roosevelt and the New Deal, 1932–1940* (New York: Harper & Row, 1963), 230.
2. Ibid.

REPUBLICAN LOUIS LUDLOW (D-INDIANA) CALLS FOR A NATIONAL REFERENDUM ON WAR

The purpose and essence of the proposal which I bring to your thoughtful attention is that the people of our country may have an opportunity to express themselves before our boys are sent away into foreign lands to die like sheep in a shambles in the settlement of quarrels of alien origin. . . .

I insist that it is the business of our fathers and mothers and our young men whether the flower of our manhood is to be sent into foreign countries to be maimed and slaughtered, and I contend that that question, whenever it arises, should be submitted to a vote of all the citizens. . . . The demand for a vote on foreign war will not be satisfied without action. If we disregard it now, that will not stop it. It will ring in our ears more and more, and it will be heard in the next congressional elections, and it will keep on being heard, because it is the voice of humanity crying in the wilderness. . . .

What is there that is unsound about this proposal that the people shall have a right to vote on declarations of war, except in the case of attack and invasion?

How can anyone who is steeped in the genius and spirit of our free American institutions say that it is unsound? It is as sound as [the] Magna Carta is sound. It is as sound as the Bill of Rights is sound. It is as sound as "government of the people, by the people, and for the people" is sound. It is in entire harmony with the philosophy of the Bill of Rights, and if adopted it would round out and complete that immortal chart of freedom. . . .

The only tenable argument ever made against the plan for a referendum on foreign war is the time required to take a referendum which it is claimed might give an enemy nation the advantage.

That was a valid argument in 1837 but not in 1937.

In the early days of the Republic the time objection was, indeed, an insuperable obstacle. Had it not been for imperfection in the means of communication at that early time I believe that Jefferson and his compatriots would have included a provision for a referendum on war in their cherished Bill of Rights. The railroad, the telegraph, the radio, the airplane were then in the bosom of the unknown future. Even the pony express was as yet undreamed of. Letters mailed on the eastern seaboard were 6 months arriving at the uttermost frontiers, if, indeed, they ever reached there at all. Now it is all different. The fast train roars its way across the continent in 100 hours, the airplane in 24. The President, sitting before the microphone in Washington, talks to the entire Nation.

Thus the only real objection ever made against a war referendum, namely, that it would consume too much time, has been completely nullified by modern perfection in the means of communication. . . .

If anyone has jumped to the conclusion that the constitutional amendment I am advocating is a pacifist position, as the word "pacifist" is generally understood, I want to correct that impression. This proposition has nothing whatever to do with the size of our national defense. It in no way, sense, or degree impairs our national defense, since under the very terms of the resolution there would be no referendum in the case of attack or invasion. . . .

While no one realizes more keenly than I do the danger of our involvement in foreign war, I do not subscribe for one minute to the defeatist theory that if another world war breaks out America cannot escape it. I believe that is a wholly erroneous theory. America will not enter a foreign war if the people have a chance to vote on the proposition. If the counsel of calmness and reason prevails and the people are allowed to settle the question in the privacy of ballot booths we will keep out of war. I think I know something about American sentiment on war as a result of my years of hard struggle to promote my war referendum amendment. I saw that as a nation we do not want to enter foreign wars and we will not do so if the people have a chance to decide the question. . . .

I believe that the real question here is whether we Members of Congress are willing to shut the people from that one great awful decision which, once made, cancels the power of Congress and of the people for years to come. Once the decision to declare war has been made by Congress, it follows that civil liberties are suspended, the press can be controlled, men can be sent to danger and death, billions must be spent, billions must be loaned to foreign nations, foreign exchange must be supported with American money. After that one great decision Congress becomes by it a rubber stamp. The Nation becomes an armed camp. It seems to me, my colleagues, that we should be willing to allow our constituents to participate in this major decision.

Speaking for myself, I am not going to say that my constituents are not intelligent and well-informed enough to vote on a question of sending our boys away to be killed in foreign wars. I know that they are and I believe that the American concept of free government will remain imperfect and incomplete until the people are given a right to vote on a question that affects so intimately their homes, their families, and their well-being.

Congressional Record. 75th Cong., 2d sess., vol. 82, pt. 1 (November 22, 1937): 242–48.

REPRESENTATIVE CHARLES FADDIS (D-PENNSYLVANIA) ATTACKS THE LUDLOW AMENDMENT

[. . .] This [amendment] . . . would take from the Congress the power to declare war—a power which was imposed upon this body by the founders of the Constitution. The power to declare war is a grave, and, indeed, an awful responsibility, one to be exercised only after the most serious, careful, and prayerful consideration. In the exercise of this power may depend the very fate of our Nation.

Let me say . . . that I sympathize with the desire of the distinguished gentleman from Indiana and with the desires of those who view the matter as he does to prevent this Nation from becoming engaged in any wars, either foreign or domestic. Their purpose is most commendable and, I am sure, is actuated by the very highest of motives. However, let me make this observation. A nation, rendered helpless by the very highest of motives, is just as helpless as though rendered so by the very basest of treachery.

The Members of Congress . . . are the direct representatives of the people in foreign as well as in domestic affairs. That is the way a democratic form of government functions. I have the highest respect for this body. I believe it is composed of patriotic men of ability. They endeavor to represent the sentiment of their constituents. From their constituents they obtain their ideas regarding domestic affairs. In regard to foreign affairs, however, they are in a different position. In such matters they must be guided to a large extent by information which their constituents do not in general possess. In connection with the foreign affairs of the Nation, and especially in the conduct of war, it is impossible to disclose all of the facts and conditions involved. The idea in waging war is to win the war, and in time of war, or an emergency due to the imminence of war, it is impossible to make too much information public without giving the enemy information. . . .

Action must be prompt, effective, and positive. Modern mechanization, transportation, and equipment have brought nations more closely together, have neutralized natural defensive barriers, and have made the need for prompt action more imperative. The factor of time is more vital than ever. . . . Today wars are fought and not declared. The former *code duello* among nations, in which communications were exchanged and diplomatic representatives were recalled before a formal declaration of war, has been replaced by the methods of a metropolitan gangster. The first notice of hostilities is a blast of machine-gun fire, a rain of bombs from the skies, and deadly clouds of gas falling most devastatingly upon the innocent and helpless noncombatants. If we must ever fight in another war, or if our sons must ever fight in one, it should be as far from our mothers, wives, and daughters as possible. . . .

Amendments to the Constitution are meant to remedy defects in our own system of government which our experience proves should be remedied. What is there in our past to justify such a demand? Never have our forces been used except in defense of justice, national and international. No intelligent person can read history and accuse our military forces of being habitual and tyrannical pursuers of invasion and conquest. But year by year, decade after decade, our system of national defense has been built around the sound theory that its most valuable asset in keeping the peace is its freedom to use its initiative in impending emergencies. That initiative does not extend to declaring war. But it does permit constant readiness to move to thwart any potential enemy, before that enemy has destroyed lives, homes, and property on American soil. Should we change this tried and proven policy because of the actions of Napoleon or Kaiser Wilhelm or any other foreign war lord? Not any more than we should change our monetary system because of their mistakes in that respect.

Let the people speak through their elected representatives in this as in other matters.

Congressional Record. 75th Cong., 2d sess., vol. 82, pt. 1 (November 23, 1937): 320–21.

THE FAIR LABOR STANDARDS ACT (1938)

At the beginning of 1937, Franklin Roosevelt had every reason for confidence. He had just been reelected by one of the widest margins in

U.S. political history. Just as importantly, Democrats controlled huge majorities in both the House and the Senate. The president looked toward further reforms; as he put it in his second inaugural address, "I see one-third of a nation ill-housed, ill-clad, ill-nourished. . . . The test of our progress is not whether we add more to the abundance of those who have much; it is whether we provide enough for those who have too little."[1]

By the end of 1937, this seemed like just so much brash talk. The president's ill-advised attempt to reorganize the Supreme Court alienated many in Congress who had at one time been his key supporters. Even more frightening was another stock market crash in October, which effectively wiped out the meager economic gains that had occurred during Roosevelt's first term. The failure of the administration's proposed executive reorganization bill in the summer of 1938 showed just how far the president's fortunes had fallen.

It was in this atmosphere of defeat that Congress passed the only significant domestic reform of Roosevelt's second term—the Fair Labor Standards Act of 1938. The bill was a direct consequence of the Supreme Court's declaration that crucial portions of the National Industrial Recovery Act were unconstitutional. When the Court later ruled that legislation to set minimum wages and maximum hours *was* constitutional, administration supporters in Congress set about to draft a new law that would restore the wages and hours clauses of the defunct National Industrial Recovery Act codes.

The Fair Labor Standards Act set a minimum wage of twenty-five cents per hour, with a series of scheduled increases to raise it to forty cents by 1945. It also established a maximum work week of forty-four hours, to be reduced gradually to forty hours by 1940; employers who wanted their employees to work beyond that were forced to pay 50 percent more ("time and a half") for overtime. Finally, the law prohibited the employment of children under sixteen years of age.

Although the bill had first been proposed in early 1937, it was subject to several delays. The "court-packing" fight occupied much of the legislature's time during that year, and conservative Democrats managed to keep the bill from reaching the floor of the House for several months thereafter. Southerners found it particularly offensive; as they pointed out, less than 3 percent of industrial workers outside the South earned below the proposed minimum wage, while in the South nearly 20 percent did. The new law, they argued, was nothing but a means of destroying southern industry. Indeed, many of the bill's biggest supporters were northern businessmen who feared competition from lower-paying southern firms.

Ultimately the bill passed in late May 1938, but not without substantial revision, as one legislator after another sought immunity for the industries in his or her district. As a result, the final version contained so many exemptions and loopholes that one supporter suggested that the Secretary of Labor report within ninety days "whether anyone is subject to this bill."[2]

Despite the loopholes, the Fair Labor Standards Act remains one of the most important features of the New Deal. Such standard features of the modern workplace as overtime and the minimum wage first became federal law at that time. Opponents had charged that the so-called "wages and hours" bill would be the death knell of American free enterprise. It was instead the final gasp of the New Deal. As Roosevelt affixed his signature to it, he was heard to sigh, "That's that."[3] Although he may not have realized it at the time, he had just signed the last piece of New Deal legislation.

This section features Roosevelt's message to Congress asking for federal regulation of wages and hours. It also includes a rebuttal by Representative Wade Kitchens (D-Arkansas), who predicts that the bill will have dire consequences for the economy of the southern states.

NOTES

1. David M. Kennedy, *Freedom from Fear: The American People in Depression and War, 1929–1945* (New York: Oxford University Press, 1999), 287.

2. William E. Leuchtenburg, *Franklin D. Roosevelt and the New Deal, 1932–1940* (New York: Harper & Row, 1963), 263.

3. James MacGregor Burns, *Roosevelt: The Lion and the Fox* (New York: Harcourt, Brace, 1956), 343–44.

ROOSEVELT ASKS CONGRESS FOR REGULATION OF LABOR STANDARDS

The time has arrived for us to take further action to extend the frontiers of social progress. Such further action initiated by the legislative branch of the Government, administered by the executive, and sustained by the judicial, is within the common-sense framework and purpose of our Constitution and receives beyond doubt the approval of our electorate.

The overwhelming majority of our population earns its daily bread either in agriculture or in industry. One-third of our population, the overwhelming majority of which is in agriculture or industry, is ill-nourished, ill-clad, and ill-housed. . . .

Today you and I are pledged to take further steps to reduce the lag in the purchasing power of industrial workers. . . . Our Nation, so richly endowed with natural resources and with a capable and industrious population, should be able to devise ways and means of insuring to all our able-bodied working men and women a fair day's pay for a fair day's work. A self-supporting and self-respecting democracy can plead no justification for the existence of child labor, no economic reason for chiseling workers' wages or stretching workers' hours.

Enlightened business is learning that competition ought not to cause bad social consequences, which inevitably react upon the profits of business itself. All but the hopelessly reactionary will agree that to conserve our primary resource of manpower, government must have some control over maximum hours, minimum wages, the evil of child labor, and the exploitation of unorganized labor. . . .

One of the primary purposes of the formation of our Federal Union was to do away with the trade barriers between the States. To the Congress, and not to the States, was given the power to regulate commerce among the several States. Congress cannot interfere in local affairs; but when goods pass through the channels of commerce from one State to another, they become subject to the power of the Congress, and the Congress may exercise that power to recognize and protect the fundamental interests of free labor.

And so to protect the fundamental interests of free labor and a free people we propose that only goods which have been produced under conditions which meet the minimum standards of free labor shall be admitted to interstate commerce. Goods produced under conditions which do not meet rudimentary standards of decency should be regarded as contraband and ought not to be allowed to pollute the channels of interstate trade.

These rudimentary standards will of necessity at the start fall far short of the ideal. Even in the treatment of national problems there are geographical and industrial diversities which practical statesmanship cannot wholly ignore. Backward labor conditions and relatively progressive labor conditions cannot be completely assimilated and made uniform at one fell swoop without creating economic dislocations. . . .

Allowing for a few exceptional trades and permitting longer hours on the payment of time and a half for overtime, it should be not difficult to define a general maximum working week. Allowing for appropriate qualifications and general classifications by administrative action, it should also be possible to put some floor below which the wage ought not to fall. There should be no difficulty in ruling out the products of the labor of children from any fair market. And there should also be little dispute when it comes to ruling out of the interstate markets products of employers who deny to their workers the right of self-organization and collective bargaining, whether through the fear of labor spies, the bait of company unions, or the use of strikebreakers. The abuses disclosed by the investigations of the Senate must be properly curbed.

With the establishment of these rudimentary standards as a base, we must seek to build up, through appropriate administrative machinery, minimum-wage standards of fairness and reasonableness, industry by industry, having due regard to local and geographical diversities and to the effect of unfair labor conditions upon competition in interstate trade and upon the maintenance of industrial peace. . . .

As we move resolutely to extend the frontiers of social progress, we must be guided by practical reason and not by barren formula. We must ever bear in mind that our objective is to improve and not to impair the standard of living of those who are now undernourished, poorly clad, and ill-housed.

We know that overwork and underpay do not increase the national income when a large portion of our workers remain unemployed. Reasonable and flexible use of the long-established right of government to set and to change working hours can, I hope, decrease unemployment in those groups in which unemployment today principally exists.

Our problem is to work out in practice those labor standards which will permit the maximum but prudent employment of our human resources to bring within the reach of the average man and woman a maximum of goods and of services conducive to the fulfillment of the promise of American life.

Legislation can, I hope, be passed at this session of the Congress further to help those who toil in factory and on farm. We have promised it. We cannot stand still.

Congressional Record. 75th Cong., 1st sess., vol. 81, pt. 5 (May 24, 1937): 4983–84.

REPRESENTATIVE WADE KITCHENS (D-ARKANSAS) CRITIQUES THE FAIR LABOR STANDARDS ACT

. . . [T]he proposed bill has most far-reaching implications of injustice and discrimination to southern labor and industry. In fact, it is directed against southern, western, and mid-western labor and industry. We have very little interstate industry in Arkansas. We are just beginning to obtain some industry for our labor. Our great trouble is lack of industry and jobs. There can be no jobs nor wages without industry. . . .

[. . .] This bill, in my opinion, will create, centralize, and sectionalize industry in the New England States, and further protect and foster monopolies. I hear Members on the floor of the House and in the cloakrooms say that all small businesses, if unable to pay what they call a "living wage," should be destroyed. But, they lose sight of the fact that what is a living wage in one section is not in another. What is a living wage? This bill purports to define it, but I disagree with the definition.

It falls far too short. They prefer that he receive no wage at all unless he receives the same wages as paid by a large million-dollar factory. By their votes and their efforts, they are against all southern, western, and midwestern labor and industry, and favor monopolies and million-dollar corporations. They are against the farmers and the consumers likewise, because any aid to the large industrial corporations, . . . and to their labor, will be at the expense of farmers and other laborers and consumers. . . .

Pay rolls are met with money from bank deposits. They cannot be met without money. These pay rolls are met from demand deposits in our banks. The State of New York has about $750 demand deposits for each man, woman, and child in that State. In our State, and many other Southern, Western, and Midwestern States, we have around $50 in demand deposits per capita. In other words, in New York State there is available for labor 15 times as much money per capita as there is in Arkansas. In the State of New Jersey there is seven times as much money available for labor in demand deposits as in Arkansas. In Connecticut, where the population is 250,000 less than in Arkansas, the demand deposits are two and a half times that of Arkansas.

No Southern State has attained anywhere near as high per capita demand deposits as these New England industrial States. American wages must, of necessity, vary widely from State to State because of this great difference in available money for pay rolls. Wages are governed by the amount of money available and by the conditions existing at the particular plant. These discriminations and inequalities cannot be put upon the same basis, and a uniform wage, if attempted, will be impractical. . . .

I submit, if we are going to fix a minimum wage for some laborers, then fix minimum wage or price for the farmer and his products. Why not help him and his family, because his sweatshop requires as much hard work, perspiration, and longer hours than any other sweatshop in this country? If the farmer be given a fair price, the industrial laborer will prosper. If Congress, under this law, can fix minimum wage, it can fix maximum wage and price on all things in interstate commerce or having to do with interstate commerce. If Congress can fix minimum or maximum wage under this bill, then it can fix minimum or maximum salaries for all business in the United States. I submit that when all this great business is turned over to some bureau or secretary in Washington to manage, to define what is and what is not interstate commerce, then we have destroyed individual rights, collective rights, State rights, constitutional rights, and substituted the dictates of man for law and the Constitution. . . .

It is my opinion that the title of this bill should read: "A bill for an act in the interest of and to help create more monopolies, aid the financiers and controllers of large industry, . . . regiment labor and industry, take away from labor the right to contract individually or collectively, cripple, if not destroy, present southern labor and industry, prevent further industry locating in the South, West, or Midwest, deprive citizens in four-fifths of the country of jobs and opportunities for jobs, further deprive the children of southern, western, and midwestern parents of educational advantages, fair share of industrial taxes and wealth, occupational opportunities, and for other discriminatory purposes."

Congressional Record. 75th Cong., 3rd sess., vol. 83, pt. 6 (May 16, 1938): 6911–13.

THE NEUTRALITY REVISION (1939)

One of the most important and controversial features of the neutrality legislation of the mid-1930s was the ban on arms sales to belligerent countries. During the debates over the issue, President Roosevelt had expressed his preference for a provision that would allow him to apply the embargo selectively. That is, if one country invaded another, the president could choose to withhold weapons and ammunition from the attacker, while continuing to permit arms sales to the victim. The sponsors of the neutrality acts, however, would hear nothing of this; the United States had been drawn into World War I by those who wanted to trade with Britain and France but not Germany. For a president to take sides would represent a fatal step on the road to intervention, and would therefore defeat the purpose of the legislation. Roosevelt reluctantly agreed to go along with this, and the impartial arms embargo became law.

By 1939 the president believed that the international situation had changed sufficiently to ask for revision of the law. For the past three years, Germany, Italy, and Japan had committed acts of aggression against other countries. Roosevelt concluded that the arms embargo, far from being impartial, actually aided aggressors, since presumably a country that was planning to attack its neighbors would already have stockpiled a sufficient supply of arms and ammunition. On the contrary, it was the victim that needed to be able to purchase weapons abroad, and so as long as the United States refused to sell them, it was tacitly supporting the invader. Moreover, it was appearing more and more likely that a war could break out in Europe between Nazi Germany on the one hand, and France and Britain on the other. Under no circumstances did the president want to appear to be helping the Nazis.

Therefore, in his 1939 State of the Union message, Roosevelt asked Congress for revision of the neutrality laws. Two months later he approached Key Pittman (D-Nevada), the chairman of the Senate Foreign Relations Committee, and asked for a discretionary embargo that would allow him to discriminate between aggressor and victim. If he could not get that, he told Pittman, he preferred an outright repeal of the embargo. Pittman suggested a third option—that arms and ammunition be made available to all belligerents, but on a "cash-and-carry" basis. That meant that arms could only be purchased with money up front—no credits— and could not be transported on American vessels.

Roosevelt was willing to go along with this. He realized that in the event of a European war only Britain and France would have easy access to the high seas, so that in reality they would be the only countries able to purchase American arms. Unfortunately for him, however, the other members of the Senate Foreign Relations Committee also recognized this fact. The president, they claimed, wanted to take sides in a European war, and that was all that they needed to know. The committee refused to release the bill to a floor vote in the Senate. When Pittman then agreed to sponsor a bill to end the embargo altogether, the committee voted twelve to eleven to postpone consideration of any revision of the neutrality laws until the next session. But there was no reason for worry, Senator William E. Borah (R-Idaho) added; his sources assured him that there would be no war in Europe.

Six weeks later, Borah was proven wrong. German troops invaded Poland on September 1, 1939, and two days later Britain and France declared war on Germany. Public opinion clearly favored the Allies; in one poll no less than 84 percent of respondents hoped for a British and French victory. Hoping to capitalize on this sentiment, Roosevelt called a special session of Congress to revisit the issue of neutrality revision, again calling for the repeal of the arms embargo.

Opposition came swiftly and vigorously. Senator Borah predicted that ending the embargo would be the first step toward actual intervention. The famous aviator Charles Lindbergh gave a radio address asserting that the United States was impervious from attack, and should thus mind its own business in foreign affairs. Many others charged that neutrality revision was a plot by arms manufacturers who stood to make millions from the tragedy in Europe. Letters, telegrams, and postcards flooded into the offices of senators and congressmen, demanding that the embargo remain in place.

However, after six weeks of impassioned debate the president won out. The result reflected a strange reversal of alliances, as northeastern Republicans and southern Democrats—traditionally the groups most hostile to Roosevelt—supported the president's proposal. On the other hand, many urban Democrats and midwestern Republicans who had consistently backed the New Deal voted against it. And while the Neutrality Act of 1939 ended the arms embargo, Congress insisted on maintaining the "cash-and-carry" provisions. It also included a prohibition on the entry of U.S. merchant vessels into a so-called "danger zone" that included most of the sea-lanes to Western Europe. Nevertheless, the president signed the bill into law on November 4, 1939.

One of the most immediate effects of the end of the arms embargo was an upswing in the country's economic fortunes, as Britain and France rushed to purchase weapons and other supplies in the United States. Anti-interventionists warned that the country was becoming too dependent on trade with the Allies for its recovery, and that this would lead to increased demands for aid to the British and French. As it turned out, they were largely correct, although it would take the fall of France in June 1940 to convince most Americans that this sort of aid was required.

The documents in this section include Roosevelt's message to Congress requesting revision of the neutrality laws, as well as a speech by Senator William E. Borah (R-Idaho) warning that ending the arms embargo would ultimately mean direct U.S. intervention in the European war.

ROOSEVELT REQUESTS REVISION OF THE NEUTRALITY LAWS

I have asked the Congress to reassemble in extraordinary session in order that it may consider and act upon the amendment of certain legislation, which, in my best judgment, so alters the historic foreign policy of the United States that it impairs the peaceful relations of the United States with foreign nations. . . .

For many years the primary purpose of our foreign policy has been that this Nation and this Government should strive to the utmost to aid in avoiding war among other nations. But if and when war unhappily comes, the Government and the Nation must exert every possible effort to avoid being drawn into the war.

The executive branch of the Government did its utmost, within our traditional policy of noninvolvement, to aid in averting the present appalling war. Having thus striven and failed, this Government must lose no time or effort to keep the Nation from being drawn into the war.

In my candid judgment we shall succeed in these efforts. . . .

. . . [T]he Neutrality Act of 1935 . . . [was passed] only 4 years ago . . . despite grave doubts expressed as to its wisdom by many Senators and Representatives and by officials charged with the conduct of our foreign relations, including myself. I regret that the Congress passed that act. I regret equally that I signed that act.

On July 14 of this year I asked the Congress, in the cause of peace and in the interest of real American neutrality and security, to take action to change that act.

I now ask again that such action be taken in respect to that part of the act which is wholly inconsistent with ancient precepts of the law of nations—the embargo provisions. I ask it because they are, in my opinion, most vitally dangerous to American neutrality, American security, and American peace. . . .

The enactment of the embargo provisions did more than merely reverse our traditional policy. It had the effect of putting land powers on the same footing as naval powers, so far as sea-borne commerce was concerned. A land power which threatened war could thus feel assured in advance that any prospective sea-power antagonist would be weakened through denial of its ancient right to buy anything anywhere. . . . Removal of the embargo is merely reverting to the sounder international practice, and pursuing in time of war as in time of peace our ordinary trade policies. . . .

To those who say that this program would involve a step toward war on our part, I reply that it offers far greater safeguards than we now possess or have ever possessed to protect American lives and property from danger. It is a positive program for giving safety. This means less likelihood of incidents and controversies which tend to draw us into conflict, as they did in the last World War. There lies the road to peace.

The position of the executive branch of the Government is that the age-old and time-honored doctrine of international law, coupled with these positive safeguards, is better calculated than any other means to keep us out of this war. . . .

I should like to be able to offer the hope that the shadow over the world might swiftly pass. I cannot. The facts compel my stating, with candor, that darker periods may lie ahead. The disaster is not of our making; no act of ours engendered the forces which assault the foundations of our civilization. Yet we find ourselves affected to the core; our currents of commerce are changing, our minds are filled with new problems, our position in world affairs has already been altered.

In such circumstances our policy must be to appreciate in the deepest sense the true American interest. Rightly considered, this interest is not selfish. Destiny first made us, with our sister nations on this hemisphere, joint heirs of European culture. Fate seems now to compel us to assume the task of helping to maintain in the western world a citadel wherein that civilization may be kept alive. The peace, the integrity, and the safety of the Americas—these must be kept firm and serene. In a period when it is sometimes said that free discussion is no longer compatible with national safety, may you by your deeds show that we of the United States are one people, of one mind, one spirit, one clear resolution, walking before God in the light of the living.

Congressional Record. 76th Cong., 2d sess., vol. 85, pt. 1 (September 21, 1939): 10–12.

SENATOR WILLIAM E. BORAH (R-IDAHO) OPPOSES REVISION OF THE NEUTRALITY LAWS

... It is now fully recognized and very generally admitted that the pending bill is not a neutrality measure at all. It was not so designed. It is not so understood. And, if it becomes a law, it will not be so administered.... The bill is in fact legislation providing, in effect, for intervention in a great European struggle under such terms and conditions as will enable us to escape the more serious sacrifices of war. It is the theory of this bill and its supporters that we can furnish arms, munitions, and implements of war to one side and counsel and advise with them and yet avoid such involvement as will call for armies and navies.... If the bill becomes a law, the problem will no longer be how we can avoid intervention, how we can avoid taking sides—that will have been settled in the very fact of our furnishing arms, munitions, and implements of war to one of the groups of nations—but the problem will be can we, will we, be able to limit intervention so as to keep our young men out of Europe; will the demands of intervention be satisfied with arms, munitions, and implements of war, or will these demands call for armies?
[...]
Once we are a part of the conflict, however limited in the beginning ... is it not hazardous to suppose that we can stay the usual course of war or choose our own methods in waging it? Can we win in such a game? Is it worth while? Is there any justification for taking such a chance? If we take a gamble of that kind, the enemy should be our enemy, the war should be our war, it must be our Government which has been assailed, our country invaded, and our people whose lives are threatened.

Let us consider some of the powerful influences which are already unleashed and determined to take us into the European war should this war continue for any length of time and which influences will be greatly strengthened and greatly advantaged by the removal of the embargo. Do we so soon forget or so magnanimously overlook the fact that the British Government was opposed from the beginning to our embargo law and that from the hour of its passage until the present time the political forces of that Empire have exerted all possible influence to break it down and destroy it, a work in which they are even now actively engaged? These influences were determined that we should not establish a policy of neutrality as against European wars....

[. . .] So long as the embargo stands, we have done our utmost to invite the retaliation of no nation. We permit the shipment of arms to no people. But when the embargo is lifted, we permit the shipment of arms but permit the shipment to one group of nations only. No one longer disputes but that . . . the lifting of the embargo operates to the advantage exclusively of one group, and that that is the purpose of the bill. Nevertheless, men will grimly declare: Neutrality is untouched.

What is it we are shipping, or permitting to be shipped, to this one group? It is things fit for nothing on earth except to maim and to kill. We are shipping, or permitting to be shipped, among other things, poison gas and such things as are peculiarly fitted for the destruction of women and children. What does that mean? It means hate; it means retaliation; it means that in the hearts and minds of 80,000,000 people we are to be just as bitterly hated as are those who fire the guns upon the field or in the trenches. We are inviting trouble, such trouble as is most likely to rush our young men to the battlefield, as happened 20 years ago. . . . Why invite such a situation? Why take the chances? Why ask a million young men to commit their future, their health, their hopes and aspirations, their lives, to such chances thus aggravated by our own willingness to gamble on the question of whether we can keep out of the war after we are part of the way in? What, in the name of reason . . . drives us to take such chances with those whom fate and circumstances have for a brief season entrusted to our care and committed to our protection? [. . .]

It was the conviction of two of the greatest statesmen the world has ever known, Washington and Jefferson, that to involve this Nation in European political problems was to undermine and ultimately destroy the whole scheme of our free institutions. They made this conviction the basis of our foreign policy. They regarded such a foreign policy as essential to our independence and to the liberty of our people as the Federal Constitution itself. Give us an American policy, a policy suitable to American institutions and conforming at all times to American ideals. Within its scope and sublime purpose may be found one of the guaranties of independence and security for our own Nation and every duty and obligation we owe to every other nation.

Congressional Record. 76th Cong., 2d sess., vol. 85, pt. 2 (October 4, 1939): 461–63.

THE SELECTIVE SERVICE ACT (1940)

After the German conquest of Poland in the fall of 1939, the European war fell into a period of inactivity. Throughout the winter of 1940, neither the Germans nor the Allies attempted any offensive operations, leading some Americans to refer to the conflict as a "phony war." Some began to speculate that Britain and France had come to believe that their declarations of war had been a mistake, and that both sides would soon agree to a peace that would confirm German control of Poland.

All this was just so much wishful thinking. In April 1940, the German armed forces launched a combined land, sea, and air operation that over-ran Denmark and soon conquered Norway as well. Almost immediately afterward came the great blow—a massive Nazi invasion of France via the Netherlands, Belgium, and Luxembourg. Within days, the Low Countries had fallen, and in mid-June France sued for peace. Making matters worse was Italy's decision, made only days earlier, to enter the conflict as Germany's ally. Suddenly Great Britain stood without friends against an enemy that controlled most of Europe.

Americans received the news of the spring offensive with shock. Vir-tually no one expected Germany to be able to conquer France, and cer-tainly not in such a short space of time. Many began to believe that Great Britain would either have to make peace with Hitler or face invasion.

The German victory also caused many Americans to consider their own defensive capabilities. They had long felt invulnerable behind the Atlantic and Pacific Oceans; now they were far less certain. The U.S. Navy was a formidable force, but it was divided between the two oceans. If Hitler were capable of capturing the British fleet, then America itself would be in danger, particularly if the United States found itself at war with Germany and Japan at the same time. Even more ominous was the fact that the U.S. Army in 1940 was pitifully small—in fact, it was no more than one-third the size of the Belgian army!

In an effort to build up the armed forces quickly, Senator Edward Burke (D-Nebraska) and Representative James Wadsworth (R-New York) introduced a bipartisan bill in late June to introduce conscription; i.e., the draft. Entitled the Selective Service Act, it would be the first peace-time draft in U.S. history. It immediately generated vehement opposition from those who saw it as a threat to a free society and a step toward war. As Senator Burton K. Wheeler (D-Montana) claimed, "If this Bill passes—it will slit the throat of the last Democracy still living—it will accord to Hitler his greatest and cheapest victory. On the headstone of American Democracy he will inscribe—'Here Lies the Foremost Victim of the War of Nerves.' "[1]

Initially public opinion ran sharply against the measure, but the polls began to detect a shift as the Germans launched wave after wave of bombers against England in the summer of 1940. One man who watched these polls very carefully was President Roosevelt, who faced a tough reelection campaign in November. Although the Selective Service Act fit in well with his overall foreign policy goals, he feared that "even a lim-ited form of selective draft may very easily defeat the Democratic Na-tional Ticket."[2] Ultimately, however, the president decided to endorse the bill, as did his Republican opponent, Wendell Willkie. The bill passed by wide margins on September 16, 1940; at the insistence of anti-interventionists, however, the period of service for draftees was limited to one year, and deployment of troops outside the Western Hemisphere was strictly forbidden.

The Selective Service Act was designed to build the armed forces quickly, and it certainly succeeded in doing so. All young men between the ages of twenty-one and thirty-five were eligible for the draft, and within a month more than sixteen million had registered. The first name was drawn on October 29, and a total of 800,000 were soon enlisted.

However, the fight over peacetime conscription did not end there. The Burke-Wadsworth Act had only been a temporary, one-year measure, so that those who had been among the first wave of draftees were scheduled to return to civilian life in October 1941. In the summer of that year, therefore, the president asked Congress to extend the draftees' service by another eighteen months. The vote this time was far closer, but the measure was approved on August 12 by a margin of a single vote in the House. The prohibition on deployment beyond the Western Hemisphere remained in place, however, as it would until after the United States actually entered the war in December.

The first document in this section is Roosevelt's statement announcing the beginning of peacetime conscription. The second is an address by Senator Gerald P. Nye (R-North Dakota), a prominent anti-interventionist who claimed that the draft was not only unnecessary, but also a step toward dictatorship.

NOTES

1. William E. Leuchtenburg, *Franklin D. Roosevelt and the New Deal, 1932–1940* (New York: Harper & Row, 1963), 307–308.

2. David M. Kennedy, *Freedom from Fear: The American People in Depression and War* (New York: Oxford University Press, 1999), 459.

ROOSEVELT ANNOUNCES THE BEGINNING OF
PEACETIME SELECTIVE SERVICE

America has adopted Selective Service in time of peace, and, in doing so, has broadened and enriched our basic concept of citizenship. Beside the clear democratic ideals of equal rights, equal privileges, and equal opportunities, we have set forth the underlying other duties, obligations, and responsibilities of equal service.

In thus providing for national defense, we have not carved a new and uncharted trail in the history of our democratic institutions. On the contrary, we have merely reasserted an old and accepted principle of democratic government. The militia system, the self-armed citizenry with the obligation of military service incumbent upon every free man, has its roots in the old common law. It was brought to this continent by our forefathers. It was an accepted institution in colonial days. At the time of the adoption of the federal Constitution, nine of the thirteen states explicitly provided for universal service in their basic laws. . . .

Selective Service consists of four steps, which singly and in the group have been developed to operate with the fairness and justice characteristic of free, democratic institutions. These steps are: registration, classification, selection, and induction.

Wednesday, October 16, has been set aside, on which day every male between twenty-one and thirty-five, inclusive, will be expected to report to a neighborhood precinct to fill out a registration card and a registration certificate. The certificate issued to the individual will be carried by him as a testimonial to his acceptance of the fundamental obligation of citizenship. The registration card will be forwarded to the county clerk or similar official and will be delivered by him to the local Selective Service board. These boards, consisting of three men, each appointed by the president, upon recommendations of the state governors, will be set up in more than six thousand communities. When the states notify the national director of Selective Service that all the local draft boards have completed this work, a national drawing by lot will determine the order of priority of the registrants in each board area. The national priority list will be furnished to the local boards and the corresponding order of selection will be entered on the registration cards in their custody. . . .

The total number of individuals needed by the armed forces will be prorated among the several states. In this allocation due consideration will be given to the number of men already furnished by that state for our military forces. Within each state a quota, in a similar manner, will be divided among the local boards. Thus, each locality will be asked to furnish its fair share of individuals for induction into our armed forces. . . .

Following the tentative selection of these individuals, a local medical examiner will examine them physically. If they are accepted, they will be sent forward for final physical examination by medical officers of the army, navy, or Marine Corps. Those who pass will be inducted into the service.

In the military service they will be intelligently led, comfortably clothed, well fed, and adequately armed and equipped for basic training. By the time they get physically hardened, mentally disciplined, and properly trained in the fundamentals, the flow of critical munitions from factory to combat units will meet the full requirements for their advanced training.

In the military service, Americans from all walks of life—rich and poor, country-bred and city raised, farmer, student, manual laborer, and white-collar worker—will learn to live side by side, to depend upon each other in military drills and maneuvers, and to appreciate each other's dignity as American citizens.

Universal service will bring not only greater preparedness to meet the threat of war, but a wider distribution of tolerance and understanding to enjoy the blessings of peace.

Statement of the President on the Adoption of Peace Time Universal Selective Service, September 16, 1940, See *The Public Papers and Addresses of Franklin D. Roosevelt, 1940 Volume* (New York: Macmillan, 1941), pp. 431–34.

SENATOR GERALD P. NYE (R-NORTH DAKOTA) ATTACKS PEACETIME CONSCRIPTION

We have been and still are moving with terrific speed to that hour when there will be a forced and accepted American belief that the only way to successfully cope with foreign dictatorships is to make America a dictatorship.

Step by step we've moved of late years in surrendering powers to the Executive. The demands for more powers for the President have been constantly increasing. The President proclaims a limited emergency to exist and there automatically accrues to him still more of dictatorial powers. Now comes the proposal to grant to the President power to order a peace-time draft of men and boys for military training and service. It is asked in the name of an emergency, the emergency proclaimed by one man, the President. He hopes, of course, that this new power, the power to draft men for the military, will be thrust upon him. . . .

Every one of us ought to shudder about the direction which our government has been pursuing. No one can review its actions of the past year and then seriously believe that a continuation of the kind of leadership we have had is going to lead anywhere other than to our participation in war abroad and to the accomplishment of the highest degree of dictatorship for the United States. . . .

This newest advance, this peace-time conscription program, is an insult to every American. It is an insult particularly to our youth. It condemns them as cowardly, unwilling to defend their country, if the need should arise. Such is the inference of peace-time conscription as opposed to the voluntary system. No one can tell me our youth are cowardly or unwilling. They are, instead, as vigorous, as vital, as eager as the youth of any other time or period have been. They have had no chance to volunteer on any basis which can appeal to the average American young man. They have had no clear reason stated to them that would invite volunteering. But without any attempt at that we, instead, are proposing to shanghai them into service by force of arms and threat of terrible penalty. Conscription in peace-time, an insult to start with, is totalitarianism of the first water. . . .

We have every right to be disgusted with ourselves, with the ease with which we can be persuaded to run from our traditions and respond to fears, the perfect ease with which some influences can drive us away from service to our first obligations—obligations to our own country and our own people. We echo like parrots that an emergency exists upon the mere declaration of an emergency by the President, without even so much as asking what the emergency is. . . .

There is no proven need for conscription today. The voluntary response by men has had no real chance to succeed. And let me suggest that the administration will doubtless find a more than ready response by volunteers if only their base pay can be made equal to the pay now available to those on relief rolls.

I've been told that there is not need to fear that the President will invoke the draft even if the pending proposal is made law, that under the law he cannot proceed until and unless Congress appropriates the money necessary to provide for the draft. Such consideration is rather simple-minded. An authorization is an authorization. Time and again a Congress has been caused to see that having authorized a thing it MUST appropriate for it. And there can be a recitation of things our President has done without direct appropriations, sometimes even without authorizations. . . .

Let's not fool ourselves. Authorization now for a peace-time conscription means peace-time conscription, as un-American a thing as has ever yet been suggested. An open ear around the halls of Congress these days reveals that the cause of those who seek conscription grows more wobbly every hour. And I'm glad in conclusion to say to you that I believe the program to conscript American manhood in peace time can be and will be defeated by the vote of a Congress that will definitely want to respond to the public wish and mind on the dangerous subject.

Address by Senator Gerald P. Nye, August 1, 1940, Gerald P. Nye Papers, Box 57, Herbert Hoover Presidential Library, West Branch, Iowa.

LEND-LEASE (1941)

The presidential election campaign made it difficult for Roosevelt to suggest any bold new initiatives in the fall of 1940. Even though his

Republican opponent, Wendell Willkie, supported aid to Great Britain, it was still extremely dangerous to advocate anything that might suggest a willingness to enter the war. To alleviate the public's fears, he assured them that "Your boys are not going to be sent into any foreign wars."[1]

The good news for Roosevelt was that the economy was on the upswing, thanks largely to orders from Great Britain for weapons and other supplies. Unemployment was the lowest that it had been in ten years, and it promised to fall even further in the coming months. This recovery, naturally, was of great benefit to the president's chances for reelection, and he won with just under 55 percent of the popular vote.

At the same time, the situation in Great Britain was steadily growing more desperate. By the time Roosevelt had been reelected, German bombs had killed more than ten thousand London residents. And although Prime Minister Winston Churchill promised to fight to the bitter end, it was beginning to appear as though that end might come sooner rather than later. Particularly alarming was Britain's dwindling supply of American dollars, which was necessary in order to continue purchasing American supplies. By the beginning of December it was becoming apparent that the British would run out of money in a matter of weeks.

All of this was of grave concern to President Roosevelt. To be sure, he genuinely wanted to see Great Britain win the war, and believed that a German victory would threaten American security. But he also realized that British orders had been responsible for much of the economic growth of recent months. If Britain could no longer pay its bills, what would happen to the economy?

The president's options were limited. After all, the "cash-and-carry" provisions of the neutrality acts remained in place, and he was in no mood to reopen that issue in Congress. So he devised a plan by which the United States would "lend" weapons and other materials to the British. "Now, what I am trying to do," he told reporters on December 17, 1940, is to "get rid of the silly, foolish old dollar sign." He proposed providing the British with whatever they needed to resist Hitler, "with the understanding that when the show was over, we would get repaid something in kind, thereby leaving out the dollar mark . . . and substituting for it a gentleman's obligation to repay in kind."[2] He compared Britain to a neighbor's house that was on fire; if your neighbor needed your garden hose to put it out, he explained, you wouldn't charge him for it. You would simply lend him the hose, and he would return it after he had put out the fire.

Roosevelt put his case before Congress on January 6, 1941, in what has come to be called the "Four Freedoms" speech. The proposal came before the House of Representatives in the form of a bill cleverly labeled H.R. 1776—A Bill to Defend the United States, although it was more commonly known as "Lend-Lease." It maintained that the survival of certain countries (Britain was never specifically mentioned) was essential to national security, and that therefore the president could transfer anything to these countries that he deemed essential to their war effort. The initial congressional appropriation was for $7 billion.

What followed was the biggest debate of the entire Roosevelt presidency on an issue of foreign policy. A whole series of politicians, businessmen, journalists, and other public figures lined up in opposition to it. Some feared that it would inevitably draw the United States into the war; others claimed that it gave too much power to the president; still others argued that Britain was no better than Germany, and was therefore undeserving of help. The debate grew intense and heated. At one point, Senator Burton Wheeler (D-Montana) even went so far as to call Lend-Lease Roosevelt's Agricultural Adjustment Administration for foreign policy. It would, he claimed, "plow under every fourth American boy."[3]

Nevertheless, polls showed that most Americans supported the bill, and it enjoyed the backing of Wendell Willkie as well as most northeastern Republicans and southern Democrats. Lend-Lease passed both houses by comfortable margins, and Roosevelt signed it into law on March 11, 1941.

Lend-Lease was arguably the most important American foreign policy initiative of the interwar period. Winston Churchill called it "the most unsordid act in the history of any nation."[4] Aid began to flow to Britain almost immediately, and that summer, when German troops invaded the Soviet Union, Roosevelt announced that American weapons and other materials would be directed to that country as well. Over the next four years nearly $50 billion in U.S. aid would go to Britain, the USSR, and other nations fighting against Germany and its allies. While it is impossible to say whether Lend-Lease prevented a German victory in 1941, it is clear that it made Britain's burden far easier to bear.

The first document in this section comes from Roosevelt's message to Congress in January 1941, in which he lays out his plan for Lend-Lease. The second is a rebuttal from Senator Burton Wheeler (D-Montana), who claims that passage of the bill would draw the United States into the European war.

NOTES

1. Patrick J. Maney, *The Roosevelt Presence: A Biography of Franklin D. Roosevelt* (New York: Twayne Publishers, 1992), 125.

2. David M. Kennedy, *Freedom from Fear: The American People in Depression and War, 1929–1945* (New York: Oxford University Press, 1999), 468.

3. Michael E. Parrish, *Anxious Decades: America in Prosperity and Depression, 1920–1941* (New York: W.W. Norton, 1992), 471.

4. Warren F. Kimball, *The Most Unsordid Act: Lend-Lease, 1939–1941* (Baltimore: Johns Hopkins University Press, 1969), 236.

ROOSEVELT PROPOSES LEND-LEASE

I address you . . . at a moment unprecedented in the history of the Union. I use the word "unprecedented," because at no previous time has American security been as seriously threatened from without as it is today. . . .

Every realist knows that the democratic way of life is at this moment being directly assailed in every part of the world—assailed either by arms, or by secret spreading of poisonous propaganda by those who seek to destroy unity and promote discord in nations still at peace. During sixteen months this assault has blotted out the whole pattern of democratic life in an appalling number of independent nations, great and small. The assailants are still on the march, threatening other nations, great and small. . . .

Armed defense of democratic existence is now being gallantly waged in four continents. If that defense fails, all the population and all the resources of Europe, Asia, Africa and Australasia will be dominated by the conquerors. The total of those populations and their resources greatly exceeds the sum total of the population and resources of the whole of the Western Hemisphere—many times over. . . .

As long as the aggressor nations maintain the offensive they—not we—will choose the time and the place and the method of their attack. That is why the future of all American Republics is today in serious danger. That is why this Annual Message to the Congress is unique in our history. That is why every member of the Executive branch of the government and every member of the Congress face great responsibility—and great accountability. . . .

Our national policy is this:

First, by an impressive expression of the public will and without regard to partisanship, we are committed to all-inclusive national defense.

Second, by an impressive expression of the public will and without regard to partisanship, we are committed to full support of all those resolute peoples, everywhere, who are resisting aggression and are thereby keeping war away from our hemisphere. By this support, we express our determination that the democratic cause shall prevail; and we strengthen the defense and security of our own nation. . . .

New circumstances are constantly begetting new needs for our safety. I shall ask this Congress for greatly increased new appropriations and authorizations to carry on what we have begun.

I also ask this Congress for authority and for funds sufficient to manufacture additional munitions and war supplies of many kinds, to be turned over to those nations which are now in actual war with aggressor nations.

Our most useful and immediate role is to act as an arsenal for them as well as for ourselves. They do not need manpower, but they do need billions of dollars worth of the weapons of defense.

The time is near when they will not be able to pay for them all in ready cash. We cannot, and we will not, tell them that they must surrender, merely because of present inability to pay for the weapons which we know they must have.

I do not recommend that we make to them a loan of dollars with which to pay for these weapons—a loan to be repaid in dollars.

I recommend that we make it possible for those nations to continue to obtain war materials in the United States, fitting their orders into our own program. Nearly all their materiel would, if the time ever came, be useful for our own defense. . . .

For what we send abroad, we shall be repaid within a reasonable time following the close of hostilities, in similar materials, or, at our option, in goods of many kinds, which they can produce and which we need.

Let us say to the democracies: "We Americans are vitally concerned in your defense of freedom. We are putting forth our energies, our resources, and our organizing powers to give you the strength to regain and maintain a free world. We shall send you, in ever-increasing numbers, ships, planes, tanks, guns. This is our purpose and our pledge." [. . .]

In the future days, which we seek to make secure, we look forward to a world founded upon four essential human freedoms.

The first is freedom of speech and expression—everywhere in the world.

The second is freedom of every person to worship God in his own way—everywhere in the world.

The third is freedom from want—which, translated into world terms, means economic understandings which will secure to every nation a healthy peace time life for its inhabitants—everywhere in the world.

The fourth is freedom from fear—which, translated into world terms, means a worldwide reduction of armaments to such a point and in such a thorough fashion that no nation will be in a position to commit an act of physical aggression against any neighbor—anywhere in the world.

That is no vision of a distant millennium. It is a definite basis for a kind of world attainable in our own time and generation. That kind of world is the very antithesis of the so-called new order of tyranny which the dictators seek to create with the crash of a bomb.

To that new order we oppose the greater conception—the moral order.

A good society is able to face schemes of world domination and foreign revolutions alike without fear. . . .

This nation has placed its destiny in the hands and heads and hearts of its millions of free men and women; and its faith in freedom under the guidance of God. Freedom means the supremacy of human rights everywhere. Our support goes to those who struggle to gain those rights or keep them. Our strength is in our unity of purpose.

To that high concept there can be no end save victory.

Congressional Record. 77th Cong., 1st sess., vol. 87, pt. 1 (January 6, 1941):

SENATOR BURTON K. WHEELER (D-MONTANA) BLASTS LEND-LEASE

Today I would like to discuss House bill 1776—how ironical a designation. Ironical because in 1776 we, as a nation, gained our independence from Great Britain. Ironical because this bill would tend to destroy that independence and the Republic for which our forefathers fought. Ironical because the proponents of H.R. 1776 maintain that the safety of the United States and the preservation of our liberties are dependent upon Great Britain. . . .

During the past eight years we have gone far down the road toward one-man government. We have granted to President Roosevelt more power than was ever given to any peacetime President in the history of this Nation. The American people and the Congress have gratified the President's wish in order that he might solve our domestic problems.

But now—the American people are asked to give—in effect—to the President of the United States the power to wage undeclared war—not in the defense of our shores—our freedom—or our independence—but in defense of foreign powers.

Once given such vast powers—there will be no relinquishment—and against the will of the Executive a two-thirds vote of Congress is required to curtail—restrict—or repeal these powers. Further or future appropriations are not necessary to make effective this blanket authority. Last year the Congress voted billions and billions for defense equipment. That can be given away by the President—and then the Congress will of necessity appropriate further billions in the name of American defense—which can again be given away. The power in Congress to appropriate is indeed no check on the powers delegated to the President in H.R. 1776. . . .

In plain language, this bill means that the President can give to any foreign nation, our entire Navy, our entire air force, all our guns, all our tanks, all our munitions, and all our military secrets . . . to Russia, to

China, to Greece, to England, or to any country, though they are cautiously withheld from you, your Senators, and your Congressmen. In the name of a so-called crusade for world-wide freedom of speech, press, and religion, the Russians can be trusted, if the President says so, but you or I cannot be. . . .

This bill is not synonymous with aid to Britain, it is synonymous with war and it is synonymous with loss of our representative form of government.

If you taxpayers want to give five billion or fifty billion dollars of your money to Great Britain, to China, to Greece, and to any other nation the President may designate, that is your privilege. But I beg of you, do not demand the abdication of Congress, and above all else, do not be stampeded by the propaganda of England and a few international bankers, into sending your boys to fight and die in foreign wars.

We are hearing strange words and doctrines these days. Washington and Jefferson have gone out of style. It is unpatriotic to avoid the quarrels of Europe. It is dastardly to fight for the preservation of our form of government. . . .

This bill is wholly foreign to our conception of government. Its introduction followed months of careful ground-laying propaganda. Every agency of mass communication has been, and is being, utilized to excite the passions and emotions of the American people. Motion pictures constantly show the horrors visited on one of the belligerents—the one they would have us aid, Britain—even at the cost of war. Paid radio commentators editorialize the news and distort the facts to make American listeners believe this is an American and not a European war. Newspapers give banner headlines to polls which reputedly indicate that the deep sympathy we all feel for England is about to be translated into open warfare.

Despite this deluge of propaganda, and despite these brazen attempts to rush this country into another European blood bath, a little publicized but highly significant Gallup poll recently indicated that 88 percent of the American people still oppose a declaration of war.

Are we Americans to eternally dedicate ourselves and our children to the preservation of the British Empire? Are we to be called in twice in 25 years to save the British from a Frankenstein of their own creation? Are we, when we know the cost in blood, in tears, and in dollars, to meddle again in European affairs to satisfy the lust of warmongers? Or are we going to be practical as well as idealistic and build a nation so strong that no force will dare attack us from within or without?

Warmongers will label you appeaser, but be firm in your resolve to avoid the quarrels of Europe, be firm in your determination to save your boys from the hell that is Europe and Africa today, and take strength from the words of the Lord:

"Put up thy sword into its place for all they that take the sword shall perish with the sword."

Congressional Record. 77th Cong., 1st sess., vol. 87, pt. 10 (January 29, 1941): A296–97.

THE WAR LABOR DISPUTES ACT (1943)

In the weeks following Japan's attack on Pearl Harbor on December 7, 1941, leaders of all of the nation's major labor unions pledged that, in the interest of national unity, there would be no strikes as long as the war continued. But while this was a promise easily made, it was not as easy to deliver. The years 1940–1941 had been fruitful ones for organized labor. The economic recovery had put millions back to work, and many of these had been quick to join unions. Along with this new strength came new labor disputes—in 1941 roughly two million workers took part in more than 4,000 strikes.

Moreover, union workers had more reasons for concern now that war had arrived. Chief among them was inflation; they feared that prices would rise faster than wages, as had been the case during World War I. In the first months of 1942, the Roosevelt administration took steps to prevent this by freezing wages and prices, but while this kept things from getting as bad as they had gotten during World War I, inflation increased by about 28 percent during the course of the war. The average industrial worker, meanwhile, saw his income rise by 27 percent.

In 1943 the leader of the United Mine Workers union, John L. Lewis, opted to ignore the wage freeze and demand a two-dollar-a-day wage increase for his men in the coal industry. When the mine owners refused, he abandoned the "no strike" pledge and ordered his men onto the picket lines. As the nation's supply of coal dwindled, newspapers began to attack the miners as traitors. Some in Congress, meanwhile, demanded that Lewis be indicted for treason.

The attitude of Congress was key, because in the elections of 1942 Republicans had made further gains. The result was the most conservative Congress since the early years of the Hoover administration; for the first time in Roosevelt's presidency, Republicans and anti-New Deal Democrats together formed a majority. Ever since the National Labor Relations Act of 1935, conservatives had viewed organized labor as a threat to free enterprise. Now, pointing to the mine workers' strike, they saw it as jeopardizing national security as well.

In June, Congress passed the War Labor Disputes Act, sponsored by Representative Howard W. Smith (D-Virginia) and Senator Tom Connally (D-Texas), which gave the president broad authority to seize war plants where strikes were taking place. It also imposed a thirty-day "cooling off" period for strikes and required a majority vote among union members before a strike could be called. Finally, and most controversially, the act prohibited unions from making contributions to political campaigns in time of war.

Roosevelt and his supporters vigorously objected to the bill, particularly to its provision against union campaign contributions. Organized labor, after all, had played a key role in the president's reelection in 1936 and 1940. He therefore vetoed the bill, while insisting that he would continue to use all the power at his disposal to prevent strikes in war-related industries. He further suggested that the striking mine workers might find themselves drafted into the military.

During the 1930s, a veto by Roosevelt would have effectively killed any piece of legislation. However, these were very different times. Congress wasted no time in passing the War Labor Disputes Act a second time, with more than enough votes to override the veto.

Ultimately federal troops seized the coal mines; nevertheless, the mine owners gave in to the strikers and promised the two-dollar-a-day wage increase. But while this was a victory for Lewis and his union, it dealt a serious blow to the cause of organized labor. Public opinion turned vehemently against unions, particularly when disturbances spread to the railroads in December 1943. Never again would organized labor enjoy the kind of popular support that it had in the late 1930s. And not only did the War Labor Disputes Act remain part of federal law, but its anti-union provisions would be expanded further in the Taft-Hartley Act of 1947.

The first document in this section is Roosevelt's message to Congress indicating his veto of the War Labor Disputes Act. The second is an address by Representative Forrest A. Harness (R-Indiana) endorsing the bill.

ROOSEVELT VETOES THE WAR LABOR DISPUTES ACT

I am returning herewith, without my approval, S. 796, the so-called war labor disputes bill.

It is not a simple bill, for it covers many subjects. I approve many of the sections; but other sections tend to obscure the issues or to write into war legislation certain extraneous matter which appears to be discriminatory. In the form submitted to me the accomplishment of this avowed purpose—the prevention of strikes in wartime—could well be made more difficult instead of more effective.

Let there be no misunderstanding of the reasons which prompt me to veto this bill at this time.

I am unalterably opposed to strikes in wartime. I do not hesitate to use the powers of government to prevent them.

It is clearly the will of the American people that for the duration of the war all labor disputes be settled by orderly procedures established by law. It is the will of the American people that no war work be interrupted by strike or lock-out.

American labor as well as American business gave their "No strike, no lock-out" pledge after the attack on Pearl Harbor.

That pledge has been well kept except in the case of the leaders of the United Mine Workers. For the entire year of 1942, the time lost by strikes averaged only five one-hundredths of 1 percent of the total man-hours worked. The American people should realize that fact—that ninety-nine and ninety-five one hundredths percent of the work went forward without strikes, and that only five one-hundredths of 1 percent of the work was delayed by strikes. That record has never before been equaled in this country. It is as good or better than the record of any of our allies in wartime. . . .

Section 8 requires the representative of employees of a war contractor to give notice of a labor dispute which threatens seriously to interrupt war production to the Secretary of Labor, the National War Labor Board, and the National Labor Relations Board in order to give the employees the opportunity to express themselves by secret ballot whether they will permit such interruption of war production.

It would force a labor leader who is trying to prevent a strike in accordance with his no-strike pledge, to give the notice which would cause the taking of a strike ballot and might actually precipitate a strike.

In wartime we cannot sanction strikes with or without notice. . . .

The 30 days allowed before the strike vote is taken under Government auspices might well become a boiling period instead of a cooling period. The thought and energies of the workers would be diverted from war production to vote-getting. . . .

There should be no misunderstanding—I intend to use the powers of government to prevent the interruption of war production by strikes. I shall approve legislation that will truly strengthen the hands of government in dealing with such strikes, and will prevent the defiance of the National War Labor Board's decisions.

I recommend that the Selective Service Act be amended so that persons may be inducted into noncombat military service up to the age of 65 years. This will enable us to induct into military service all persons who engage in strikes or stoppages or other interruptions of work in plants in the possession of the United States.

This direct approach is necessary to insure the continuity of war work. The only alternative would be to extend the principle of selective service and make it universal in character.

I recognize that this bill has an entirely praiseworthy purpose to insure full war production. But I am convinced that section 8 will produce strikes in vital war plants which otherwise would not occur. Therefore, I could not properly discharge the duties of my office if I were to approve S. 796.

Congressional Record. 78th Cong., 1st sess., vol. 89, pt. 5 (June 25, 1943): 6487–88.

REPRESENTATIVE FORREST A. HARNESS (R-INDIANA) PRAISES THE WAR LABOR DISPUTES ACT

I believe this is one of the most important enactments of this Seventy-eighth Congress. I believe that with intelligent administration this act will do much to end wartime strikes and work stoppages, and will greatly help to restore the atmosphere of harmony and cooperation at home, which is so necessary for the successful prosecution of the war on a dozen battle fronts abroad. I am grateful, therefore, for this opportunity to help toward a national understanding of this new act and the purpose which Congress had in mind in its passage. . . .

Labor leadership will best serve the millions of common Americans it seeks to represent if it will abandon blind, bitter opposition to any regulation and sit calmly in conciliation on this question. For there is a safe, sane, reasonable middle ground which we must explore and occupy if we ever expect to reach a practical solution of this problem. . . .

Principal contribution by the house and, in my own opinion, the vitally important part of this act, is section 8, which provides for a 30-day period of conciliation before any strike or work stoppage in a war industry can be undertaken; and which provides that there shall be no interruption of production unless the employees so decide by secret ballot in an orderly election supervised by the National Labor Relations Board and held at the end of this 30-day period if conciliation fails to settle the dispute.

I want to say, and with all possible emphasis, that this is the most important provision of this entire act. It ought to be immediately apparent that by this provision Congress has demonstrated its implicit faith in the rank and file of American labor not only to maintain an uninterrupted production for war but to order its own affairs within its own organizations. Violent objection has been raised to this provision, both by labor leadership and by officials within the administration. . . .

I have no way of estimating labor's opinion in advance, but I am willing to stake my reputation that the average working man or woman will welcome and applaud this act; and will arise in a way we can all be proud of to this responsibility and this opportunity we are placing in their hands.

We think of this act first in terms of our war effort. We do desperately want to submerge all personal and group interests to the all-important job of winning the war at the last possible cost in blood and treasure, and at the earliest possible date. So the first problem is to deliver our maximum effort to this purpose, no matter whose toes may be trampled in the process. . . .

. . . [T]here is that group of labor leadership which strenuously opposes this whole measure, condemning, among other things, the right of individuals within the ranks of labor to make their own decisions in elections by secret ballot. Just one fact need be mentioned here to show how inconsistent this leadership is. There has been legislation in every recent session of Congress to outlaw State poll taxes which deprive the individual citizen of the right to vote in national elections. Certainly, a number of our States are guilty of abuses, against which I think labor has been absolutely right in protesting. I, too, have supported these proposals to outlaw poll-tax abuses.

But if labor leaders can cry out against these abuses by the several States which practice them, how can they consistently and reasonably oppose the provisions of this act which would give to every man and woman in labor a full voice in the conduct of his own organization?

There, my friends, may be the key to this whole situation. Possibly much of our labor problem arises from the ambitions for absolute power on the part of labor leadership. Possibly we have a labor problem at all only because the leadership insists that it, not the rank and file membership, shall rule and direct the destinies of labor.

I have steadfastly held that the Americans in the ranks of labor will quickly put an end to any labor problems if we will just give them the opportunity. I think that anyone who opposes this type of legislation either questions the intelligence of the average man and woman in labor, or deliberately tries to deprive them of their rights merely to cling to his own special privileges and advantages.

Congressional Record. 78th Cong., 1st sess., vol. 89, pt. 11 (June 17, 1943): A3050–51.

RECOMMENDED READINGS

Achenbaum, Andrew. *Social Security: Visions and Revisions.* New York: Cambridge University Press, 1986.

Badger, Anthony J. *The New Deal.* New York: Farrar, Straus and Giroux, 1989.

Bellush, Bernard. *The Failure of the NRA.* New York: Norton, 1975.

Best, Gary Dean. *Pride, Prejudice and Politics: Roosevelt versus Recovery, 1933–1938.* Westport, Conn.: Greenwood Press, 1991.

Brinkley, Alan. *The End of Reform: New Deal Liberalism in Depression and War*. New York: Knopf, 1995.

Burns, James MacGregor. *Roosevelt: The Lion and the Fox*. New York: Harcourt Brace, 1956.

Cole, Wayne S. *Roosevelt and the Isolationists, 1932–45*. Lincoln: University of Nebraska Press, 1983.

Dallek, Robert. *Franklin D. Roosevelt and American Foreign Policy, 1932–1945*. New York: Oxford University Press, 1979.

Freidel, Frank. *Franklin D. Roosevelt: A Rendezvous with Destiny*. Boston: Little, Brown, 1990.

Goodwin, Doris Kearns. *No Ordinary Time: Franklin and Eleanor Roosevelt: The Home Front*. New York: Simon & Schuster, 1994.

Leff, Mark H. *The Limits of Symbolic Reform: The New Deal and Taxation*. New York: Cambridge University Press, 1984.

Leuchtenburg, William E. *Franklin D. Roosevelt and the New Deal, 1932–1940*. New York: Harper Torchbooks, 1963.

———. *The Supreme Court Reborn: The Constitutional Revolution in the Age of Roosevelt*. New York: Oxford University Press, 1995.

Maney, Patrick. *The Roosevelt Presence*. New York: Twayne, 1992.

Marks, Frederick W. *Wind Over Sand: The Diplomacy of Franklin Roosevelt*. Athens: University of Georgia Press, 1988.

Miller, Nathan. *FDR: An Intimate Biography*. Garden City, N.Y.: Doubleday, 1983.

Patterson, James T. *Congressional Conservatism and the New Deal*. Lexington: University Press of Kentucky, 1967.

Romasco, Albert U. *The Politics of Recovery: Roosevelt's New Deal*. New York: Oxford University Press, 1983.

Internet Sources

Center for New Deal Studies—http://www.roosevelt.edu:80/newdeal/.

Fireside Chats of Franklin D. Roosevelt—http://www.mhrcc.org/fdr/fdr.html.

Franklin D. Roosevelt and the New Deal—http://www.geocities.com/Athens/4545.

Franklin D. Roosevelt Presidential Library and Museum—http://fdrlibrary.marist.edu/.

The New Deal Network—http://newdeal.feri.org/.

3

HARRY S. TRUMAN

(1945–1953)

Harry Truman was an unlikely president for the postwar world. He came into office by accident, through the death of Franklin Roosevelt, and the differences between the two men were stark. Roosevelt was born into a wealthy New York family; graduated from Harvard University and Columbia Law School, and moved easily among millionaires, intellectuals, and other East Coast elites. By contrast, Truman's origins lay in small-town Missouri, and he represented the simple values of hard work, plain speaking, and integrity that he shared with so many midwesterners of the time. He did not attend college (making him the only U.S. president in the twentieth century without a college degree), but rather tried his hand at farming after graduating high school. After serving in the artillery in World War I, he attempted a career in business, but soon met with failure. So instead he turned to politics, becoming a judge in Jackson County, Missouri and serving in that capacity until he was elected to the U.S. Senate in 1934.

There was little that was flashy about Truman's career in the Senate. He made a reputation for himself as a loyal Democrat, and a supporter of Roosevelt's New Deal, but his strength of character and his utter lack of pretentiousness made him popular among members of both parties. His greatest achievement came in 1941–1942, when as chairman of the Senate Special Committee to Investigate the National Defense Program he issued a series of recommendations that saved the federal government as much as $11 billion in military spending. The committee's results rocketed Truman into the public eye; in March 1943, he appeared on the cover of *Time* magazine, and in May 1944, a poll of fifty-two journalists named him one of the ten "most useful officials" in Washington, D.C.

Truman's image and popularity, as well as his midwestern origins, made him a good choice for vice president on the Democratic ticket in 1944. Roosevelt's current vice president, Henry Wallace, was widely seen as being too liberal at a time when most Americans wanted to shelve domestic reform in favor of winning the war. Truman was acceptable even to the most conservative Democrats, and he easily received the nomination. The Roosevelt-Truman ticket then went on to win the election with nearly 54 percent of the popular vote.

As Truman soon learned, the president was in ill health. In April, 1945, less than three months after the inauguration, Roosevelt died at his retreat in Warm Springs, Georgia. Harry Truman, who just a few years before had been an obscure senator from Missouri, was now president of the United States. In his first press conference, he asked reporters to pray for him—a request that would never have been heard coming from the lips of the ever-confident Roosevelt.

In Truman's first weeks as president, the country saw the end of the war in Europe, as well as the establishment of a new global peacekeeping organization—the United Nations. In July, Truman had his first and only meeting with Joseph Stalin, the premier of the Soviet Union. But fighting raged on in Asia and the Pacific, with Japan stubbornly refusing to surrender to the Allies. It was only upon becoming president that Truman learned of the atomic bomb, a new weapon which was tested for the first time in the New Mexico desert in mid-July. Less than two weeks later, he sent a personal message to the Japanese government—surrender unconditionally or face "prompt and utter destruction."[1] When no offer of surrender came, he ordered the first atomic bomb to be dropped on the city of Hiroshima on August 6, which killed 40,000 instantly. One hundred thousand more died of burns and radiation poisoning within days. Three days later, an American plane dropped a second bomb on Nagasaki, killing another 70,000. The Japanese surrendered the following day, bringing World War II to its final conclusion.

The United States emerged from World War II as the world's leading power, with a massive military establishment and a booming economy. For most Americans, however, the priority was to settle back into peacetime pursuits such as working in the private sector, getting married, and raising families. The birth rate saw a sharp increase throughout the late 1940s—the so-called "baby boom." There was an increasing lack of patience with the rationing and other controls imposed during the war, and even less enthusiasm over another round of New Deal reforms. Congress, now dominated by an alliance of Republicans and conservative Democrats, felt likewise, so all of Truman's efforts to expand the New Deal in 1945 and 1946 met with failure.

One issue that touched the lives of nearly all Americans was price controls. In an effort to curb inflation, wages and prices were frozen by law throughout the war, but once the fighting ceased there were growing demands by workers for higher pay. Employers countered that they could only afford to raise wages if they could also raise prices. As a result, a wave of labor unrest crossed the country, particularly in coal mining, the railroads, and the steel industry. Unable to agree with Congress on a continued price control strategy, Truman ended most price controls in the fall of 1946, leading to sharp increases in the cost of many consumer goods.

The president's first year and a half in the White House was an intensely frustrating period for Truman. Americans could not resist comparing him to his beloved predecessor and declaring that Truman came up short. Although Roosevelt had experienced equally vexing troubles with Congress since 1938, he at least had the war, which kept the country together. The midterm congressional elections of 1946 showed a deep dissatisfaction with the Democratic Party; for the first time since 1930, the Republicans took control of both the House and the Senate.

As was expected, the new Congress was even less willing to go along with Truman's domestic policy. The conservative high tide came with the passage of the Taft-Hartley Act, which sought to curb the power of labor unions. Truman vetoed it, claiming that it was anti-labor, but Congress passed it over his veto three days later. The same occurred with bills to reduce income taxes in 1947 and 1948. Virtually the only bold domestic initiative to come during these years was the president's executive order ending racial segregation in the armed forces in July 1948.

Truman had more luck with Congress when it came to foreign affairs, as relations deteriorated between the United States and the Soviet Union. Stalin had imposed Soviet-style satellite governments throughout Eastern Europe, leading many Americans to suspect that the USSR was just as bad as Nazi Germany had been. In March 1947 the president asked for $400 million to help resist the spread of communism in Greece and Turkey. Referring to the need to defend "free peoples who are resisting attempted subjugation," his speech (which became known as the "Truman Doctrine") won over Republicans and Democrats alike.[2] The request was approved, and soon afterward Congress also voted to establish a European Recovery Program (ERP) to help the nations of Europe get back on their feet economically. These measures mark the beginning of a long period of bipartisan cooperation in American foreign policy.

Despite these successes, however, Truman's chances for reelection in 1948 appeared slim. His bold stand on civil rights had infuriated southern Democrats, some of whom decided to bolt the party and support the "Dixiecrat" campaign of Governor Strom Thurmond of South Carolina. At the same time, certain left-wing Democrats, critical of Truman's anti-Soviet foreign policy, rallied to the independent candidacy of former vice president Henry Wallace. Given these divisions within the Democratic

Party, it seemed that little could prevent the election from going to Truman's Republican rival, New York Governor Thomas E. Dewey.

Nevertheless, Truman launched a spirited campaign. He called Congress into special session and challenged the Republicans to pass a series of bills establishing public housing, civil rights, and price controls. When none of these passed, the president began a 22,000-mile "whistle stop" campaign in which he denounced the "do-nothing" Congress in no less than 275 speeches. Ignoring Dewey altogether, he called the Republicans "gluttons for privilege" who cared only about the rich and big business, while claiming that he represented the true spirit of Franklin Roosevelt's New Deal.[3]

The strategy paid off. In the November elections, Truman overcame all of his challengers, returning to office with a convincing margin of victory. At the same time, the Democrats managed to regain control of both houses of Congress. Over the next several months, he laid out an ambitious program of reforms that included public housing, an increase in the minimum wage, an expansion of Social Security, civil rights legislation, and national health insurance. He called this package the "Fair Deal," emphasizing the relationship to Roosevelt's New Deal. Congress ultimately passed all of these measures except for civil rights legislation and national health insurance, which were blocked by an alliance of Republicans and southern Democrats.

Truman's second term also saw a continuation of the president's vigorous foreign policy. In the summer of 1949, Congress approved the North Atlantic Treaty, an alliance among the United States, Canada, and the countries of Western Europe. The president also won congressional support for Point Four, a vast program of foreign aid to poor countries. But that was the end of the good news for Truman. In September, it was announced that the Soviets had developed their own atomic bomb, thus ending the American monopoly on that powerful weapon. Soon afterward, communist forces took control of China after several years of civil war. Finally, in June 1950, troops from Soviet-backed North Korea invaded U.S.-supported South Korea. Truman quickly ordered U.S. forces to help defend South Korea, and the United Nations voted to send troops as well. General Douglas MacArthur, a World War II hero, was named overall commander of U.S. and UN units in Asia.

The arrival of MacArthur's forces halted the North Korean advance, and forced the enemy back toward the Chinese border. However, in November, China entered the war, leading Truman to proclaim a state of national emergency. The war eventually settled down to a stalemate— the Chinese advance was stopped, but no major offensive was planned for fear that a global war might result. When MacArthur publicly criticized the Truman administration for conducting a limited war—he insisted that there was "no substitute for victory"[4]—the president relieved him of his command.

All of these events had a crippling impact on Truman's popularity. The communist victory in China was seen as a particularly devastating loss for the United States, leading many in Congress to suggest that perhaps the U.S. State Department might have had some part in bringing it about. In particular, Senator Joseph McCarthy (R-Wisconsin) made a name for himself by claiming that the government was riddled with communists and communist sympathizers. Moreover, the Korean stalemate and the dismissal of the popular MacArthur opened Truman up to more criticism. Not only had the president involved the country in a war that it never wanted, but he had fired the one man who seemed capable of bringing that war to a successful conclusion.

The president attempted to fight back, but his defense often put him deeper in trouble. When he defended the State Department against charges of internal subversion, he faced accusations that he and other liberal Democrats were blind to the communist threat. Senator McCarthy stepped up his assault, claiming that the New Deal had allowed hundreds if not thousands of communists to infiltrate the federal government. In 1950 Congress passed the McCarran Internal Security Act, which required communist-backed organizations to register with the government. Truman vetoed it, claiming that it violated the right of free assembly, but his veto was promptly overturned.

By 1952 Truman's popularity was at an all-time low. On March 29 he announced that he would not be a candidate in the upcoming presidential election. He did, however, agree to campaign for the man who did get the Democratic nomination—Adlai Stevenson of Illinois. However, the president's support did him little good, and in November, Stevenson lost to the Republican candidate, General Dwight D. Eisenhower.

Truman retired to Independence, Missouri, where the Truman Presidential Library was eventually established in 1955. He remained active as a writer, both of newspaper articles and a book, *Mr. Citizen*, which was published in 1960. He also continued to involve himself in Democratic politics, campaigning actively for John F. Kennedy in 1960. He grew increasingly ill in the late 1960s, and died on December 26, 1972, at the age of eighty-eight.

NOTES

1. John Patrick Diggins, *The Proud Decades: America in War and Peace, 1941–1960* (New York: W. W. Norton, 1989), 48.

2. *Congressional Record*, 80th Cong., 1st Sess., vol. 93, pt. 2 (March 12, 1947): 1980–81.

3. Robert A. Donovan, *Conflict and Crisis: The Presidency of Harry S. Truman, 1945–48* (New York: Norton, 1977), 425.

4. U.S. Department of State, *Foreign Relations of the United States*, 1950, 7: 826.

THE DROPPING OF THE ATOMIC BOMB (1945)

Only weeks after having been sworn in as president, Harry Truman was faced with one of the most important decisions of his entire administration. The Manhattan Project, the country's top-secret project to develop and test an atomic bomb, had been kept from Truman, even when he was vice president. He first learned the details on April 25, 1945, in a meeting with Secretary of War Henry Stimson and General Leslie Groves, the director of the project. They informed him that considerable progress had been made, that the bomb could be expected to be powerful enough to destroy an entire city, and that one would probably be ready within four months. None of those present at this meeting—which lasted a mere forty-five minutes—expressed any doubts that the bomb should be used as soon as it was ready. As Truman later put it, "I regarded the bomb as a military weapon and never had any doubt that it should be used."[1]

In May Stimson appointed an eight-man Interim Committee of civilian officials to advise him and the president on the possible use of the bomb, but its role was of questionable importance. The committee's members had expected to deliberate the morality of using the new weapon against civilian targets, but Stimson and Truman seemed far more interested in hearing about how the bomb might be used in the postwar world. As one member of the committee put it, "It seemed to be a foregone conclusion that the bomb would be used" against Japan, which, since the surrender of Germany in May, was the only country still fighting the United States. An atomic attack, the secretary of war believed, would "carry convincing proof of our power to destroy the Empire," thus encouraging the Japanese to sue for peace rather than face complete destruction.[2]

That summer, Truman attended a conference with Winston Churchill and Joseph Stalin in Potsdam, just outside Berlin, Germany. By this time he was aware that an atomic bomb had been successfully tested at a proving ground in Alamagordo, New Mexico. He informed the Soviet leader that the United States possessed "a new weapon of unusual destructive force," to which Stalin responded that he hoped he would make "good use of it against the Japanese."[3] The Allied leaders then issued a proclamation to the Japanese government calling for "the unconditional surrender of all the Japanese armed forces." If they failed to do so, the document warned, Japan would face "prompt and utter destruction."[4]

In Tokyo at the time there was considerable debate about how to respond to the Potsdam Proclamation. Some—mainly the military leadership—wanted to reject it out of hand, but others were inclined to accept it, on the condition that the emperor of Japan would be allowed to remain on the throne. Faced with this bitter division, the Japanese finally agreed that their response would be *mokusatsu*, which meant "to ignore," but which could also be translated as "to kill with contempt." Either way, it was not the response the Allies wanted, and plans went ahead to use the atomic bomb.

On August 6, 1945, a B-29 bomber named the *Enola Gay* flew from an American airfield on Tinian Island carrying the first atomic bomb. The crew released the bomb over the city of Hiroshima, which was a staging area for Japanese forces preparing to resist an invasion of the home islands. The results were both impressive and horrifying—nearly 40,000 people were killed instantly, with 100,000 more dying within days from burns and radiation sickness.

The response of the Japanese was shock and disbelief. Many of those who had not been present at Hiroshima doubted the reports of devastation that were coming in; even those who were willing to accept that the Americans had developed an atomic bomb refused to believe that they could have more than one. The doubters were proven wrong on August 9, when the United States dropped a second bomb on the city of Nagasaki, killing another 70,000 people. Two days earlier, the Soviet Union had declared war on Japan and invaded the Japanese-held province of Manchuria, in China. After another round of debates among the Japanese leadership, the emperor himself made the decision to surrender.

The use of the atomic bomb was, and continues to be, a matter of debate. Some argued (and still do) that a weapon of such colossal destructive power should never have been used against population centers such as Hiroshima and Nagasaki. Truman responded that by forcing the Japanese to surrender, his decision saved the lives of as many as a half-million American soldiers who would have been killed in an attempted invasion of the Japanese home islands. Most Americans accepted this, and moreover saw the atomic bombings as an acceptable act of retaliation for the treacherous attack on Pearl Harbor. Public opinion polls at the time showed that roughly 75 percent approved of the decision to drop the bombs. Yet there is no doubt that the bombings ushered in a new era of military history, in which the threat of nuclear annihilation would loom over much of the world.

The first document in this section is the text of Truman's message to the American people announcing the bombing of Hiroshima. The second comes from an editorial in the conservative publication *Human Events*, which claims that the bombing illustrated the extent to which the administration had stooped to the enemy's tactics.

NOTES

1. John Lewis Gaddis, *The United States and the Origins of the Cold War, 1941–1947* (New York: Columbia University Press, 1972), 245.

2. David M. Kennedy, *Freedom from Fear: The American People in Depression and War, 1929–1945* (New York: Oxford University Press, 1999), 839–40.

3. Ibid., 843–44.

4. John Patrick Diggins, *The Proud Decades: America in War and Peace, 1941–1960* (New York: W. W. Norton, 1989), 48.

TRUMAN ANNOUNCES THE ATOMIC BOMBING OF HIROSHIMA

Sixteen hours ago an American airplane dropped one bomb on [Hiroshima] and destroyed its usefulness to the enemy. That bomb had more power than 20,000 tons of TNT. It had more than two thousand times the blast power of the British "Grand Slam" which is the largest bomb ever yet used in the history of warfare.

The Japanese began the war from the air at Pearl Harbor. They have been repaid many fold. And the end is not yet. With this bomb we have now added a new and revolutionary increase in destruction to supplement the growing power of our armed forces. In their present form these bombs are now in production and even more powerful forms are in development.

It is an atomic bomb. It is a harnessing of the basic power of the universe. The force from which the sun draws its power has been loosed against those who brought war to the Far East.

Before 1939, it was the accepted belief of scientists that it was theoretically possible to release atomic energy. But no one knew any practical method of doing it. By 1942, however, we knew that the Germans were working feverishly to find a way to add atomic energy to the other engines of war with which they hoped to enslave the world. But they failed. . . .

The battle of the laboratories held fateful risks for us as well as the battles of the air, land, and sea, and we have now won the battle of the laboratories as we have won the other battles. . . .

[. . .] We now have two great plants and many lesser works devoted to the production of atomic power. Employment during peak construction numbered 125,000 and over 65,000 individuals are even now engaged in operating the plants. Many have worked there for two and a half years. Few know what they have been producing. They see great quantities of material going in and they see nothing coming out of these plants, for the physical size of the explosive charge is exceedingly small.

We have spent two billion dollars on the greatest scientific gamble in history—and won.

But the greatest marvel is not the size of the enterprise, its secrecy, nor its cost, but the achievement of scientific brains in putting together infinitely complex pieces of knowledge held by many men in different fields of science into a workable plan. And hardly less marvelous has been the capacity of industry to design, and of labor to operate, the machines and methods to do things never done before so that the brain child of many minds came forth in physical shape and performed as it was supposed to do. Both science and industry worked under the direction of the United States Army, which achieved a unique success in managing so diverse a problem in the advancement of knowledge in an amazingly short time. It is doubtful if such another combination could be got together in the world. What has been done is the greatest achievement of organized science in history. It was done under high pressure and without failure.

We are now prepared to obliterate more rapidly and completely every productive enterprise the Japanese have above ground in any city. We shall destroy their docks, their factories, and their communications. Let there be no mistake; we shall completely destroy Japan's power to make war.

It was to spare the Japanese people from utter destruction that the ultimatum of July 26 was issued at Potsdam. Their leaders promptly rejected that ultimatum. If they do not now accept our terms they may expect a rain of ruin from the air, the like of which has never been seen on this earth. Behind this air attack will follow sea and land forces in such numbers and power as they have not yet seen and with the fighting skill of which they are already well aware. . . .

The fact that we can release atomic energy ushers in a new era in man's understanding of nature's forces. Atomic energy may in the future supplement the power that now comes from coal, oil, and falling water, but at present it cannot be produced on a basis to compete with them commercially. Before that comes there must be a long period of intensive research.

It has never been the habit of the scientists of this country or the policy of this Government to withhold from the world scientific knowledge. Normally, therefore, everything about the work with atomic energy would be made public.

But under the present circumstances it is not intended to divulge the technical processes of production or all the military applications, pending further examination of possible methods of protecting us and the rest of the world from the danger of sudden destruction.

I shall recommend that the Congress of the United States consider promptly the establishment of an appropriate commission to control the production and use of atomic power within the United States. I shall give further consideration and make further recommendations to the Congress as to how atomic power can become a powerful and forceful influence towards the maintenance of world peace.

"Statement by the President of the United States," August 6, 1945, http://www.whistlestop.org/study_collections/bomb/small/mb10.htm.

JOURNALIST FELIX MORLEY LAMENTS THE ATOMIC BOMBINGS

According to Japanese experts, accepted in Washington as probably truthful, some 30,000 human beings were blasted into eternity by the first atomic bomb, exploded over the city of Hiroshima on August 6.

Of the 160,000 who were injured by this act of annihilation, directed at a community of a quarter of a million persons, additional thousands are said to have died in subsequent agony from the delayed cremation of the neutron rays. The same report on after-effects comes from Nagasaki, where on August 9 the second atomic bomb caused a somewhat smaller number of casualties.

If December 7, 1941, is "a day that will live in infamy," what will impartial history say of August 6, 1945?

At Pearl Harbor the target was an isolated naval base; the material destruction was virtually limited to warships and military installations; the relatively small loss of life was for the most part confined to men who had voluntarily enlisted in the armed services.

At Hiroshima the target was the heart of a teeming city. The great majority of those obliterated were civilians, including thousands of children trapped in the thirty-three schools that were destroyed. It was pure accident if a single person slain at Hiroshima had any personal responsibility for the Pearl Harbor outrage. These victims, like ourselves, were merely the helpless instruments of the ruthless Moloch of Totalitarian Government.

Pearl Harbor was an indefensible and infamous act of aggression. But Hiroshima was an equally infamous act of atrocious revenge. Because perpetrated by a nation that calls itself Christian, on a people with less lofty spiritual pretensions, eventual judgment may call our action ethically the more shameful, morally the more degrading, of the two. . . .

Undoubtedly Hiroshima shortened the war. The atomic bomb may well have saved more lives than it has destroyed to date. But to say that is to excuse rather than to explain.

The price we have paid for victory is terribly high. And perhaps the cost of this last installment, at Hiroshima, is even heavier for us than for the Japanese. For its measurement is the loss of ideals which, far more than our material strength, have made America great and distinctive in the long human story. The measurement of our loss may be seen, for instance, in the miserable farce put on by those who try to reconcile mass murder of "enemy children" with lip service to the doctrine that God created all men in his image.

We tend to forget, also, that under our system of government each of us must carry individual responsibility for the decisions of our rulers, civilian or military. The brilliant scientists who designed, the intrepid flyers who released, the atomic bomb are actually less responsible than the rest of us for its effects. They were our servants, paid by us to do what we wanted done.

The German people, we have decreed, have corporate responsibility for the acts of the National Socialist State. So, at Nazi concentration camps, we have paraded horrified German civilians before the piled bodies of tortured Nazi victims. We have drafted German women to bury these pitiful dead. We have forced German prisoners in this country to witness pictures of these abominable deeds.

It would be equally salutary to send groups of representative Americans to blasted Hiroshima. There, as at Buchenwald, are many unburied dead. There are many towards whose bereavement we can scarcely feel vindictive. There is a spiritual desolation for which we cannot dodge responsibility. . . .

Great effort has been made to picture the atomic bomb as an eminently laudable achievement of American inventiveness, ingenuity and scientific skill. On the day of the destruction of Hiroshima the floodgates of official publicity were swung wide. Rivers of racy material prepared in our various agencies of Public Enlightenment poured out to the press and radio commentators whose well-understood duty it is to "condition" public opinion. Puddles of ink confusedly outlined the techniques whereby we have successfully broken the laws of God.

Never has any totalitarian propaganda effort fallen more flat. Instead of the anticipated wave of nationalistic enthusiasm, the general reaction was one of unconcealed horror. Even the immediate Japanese surrender, even the joy of "going places" on unrationed gas, even the universal sense of relief over the ending of the war, has not concealed an apprehension which reflection does less than nothing to diminish. Many who cannot voice their thoughts are none the less conscious of the withdrawal of the Governing Hand, are well aware that at the crossroads we have chosen the turning which leads back to Nothingness. . . .

So a country dedicated by its founders to individual enlightenment now controls a secret which makes the individual look as does the insect in response to D.D.T. Quite naturally our new scale of values loses its moral grandeur and shifts to insect values—"full employment" or "security" within the meticulously organized anthill of the expanding State.

We have won the war. Now what is our purpose for the Power we control?

Felix Morley, "The Return to Nothingness," *Human Events* 2:35 (August 29, 1945).

PRICE CONTROLS (1946)

The most pressing domestic problem facing Harry Truman in late 1945 and 1946 was the need to readjust the economy to peacetime priorities. Ever since late 1939—when large-scale orders for American military hardware started coming in from Great Britain and France—weapons and armaments had been the single most important segment of the industrial economy. After the United States actually entered the war, American industry turned almost exclusively to the manufacture of products for the military; ordinary consumer goods such as automobiles and kitchen appliances began to disappear from store shelves, as tanks and airplanes took priority.

But while consumer goods were becoming harder to find, the income of the average American was soaring. Unemployment, the scourge of the depression years, virtually disappeared as millions of men and women entered the military or took jobs in factories or offices. Suddenly finding themselves with more income than they had enjoyed since the 1920s, the American people wanted to shop. This combination—high demand for consumer goods that were in short supply—was a recipe for high prices, as virtually everyone in Washington knew. Therefore, mere months after Pearl Harbor, President Roosevelt established the Office of Price Administration, which issued regulations stipulating that wages and prices be frozen at the level they had been in March 1942.

At the end of the war, the future of price controls became a matter for debate. Manufacturers and farmers argued that, with the war over, controls should be removed. The American people, having had more money during the war than they were able to spend, had accumulated quite a bit of savings, and businesses hoped to capitalize on this. At the same time, industrial workers were beginning to demand higher wages, while management insisted that any wage hikes were impossible as long as price controls remained in effect. The result was a wave of strikes occurring in early 1946, involving millions of workers, particularly in the coal, steel, railroad, and automobile industries.

Others, including Truman, advised proceeding with caution. It would take months, perhaps years, for industry to gear itself back to the production of consumer goods. Until that time, such products would remain scarce, and that fact, combined with the millions of returning soldiers and sailors who were eager to spend their hard-earned pay, might lead to rampant inflation if controls were lifted. The Office of Price Administration had to remain intact, at least for the time being.

Congress attempted to steer a middle course between these two arguments. In June 1946, a bill was passed that kept the OPA alive, but which placed severe limitations on its operations, and exempted many products from any sort of price control. Truman vetoed the bill, arguing that it would be better to have no OPA at all than one that was subject to so many restrictions.

Since the president and Congress failed to agree on price control strategy, the existing price controls expired on June 30. Prices began to soar immediately, and by the end of July, the average price of groceries and consumer goods had risen by roughly 25 percent. Recognizing that the midterm elections were only a few months away, Congress quickly passed a compromise bill that Truman signed, but it proved too weak to stop the rising prices, which increased by another 5 percent during the month of August. But for certain commodities, the return of price controls led to shortages; meat in particular virtually vanished from stores in September, leading Truman to lift controls on meat on October 15.

Frustration over prices and shortages played a considerable role in the outcome of the 1946 elections, in which Republicans won control of both houses of Congress. Days after the election, Truman signed an executive order ending all wage and price controls except on rents, sugar, and rice. Prices rose sharply once again, and continued to do so until early 1949, when production caught up to demand for most commodities. The whole affair was quite damaging to the president, whose approval rating fell to an abysmal 32 percent. Truman had flip-flopped repeatedly on price controls, contributing to a widespread view of him as a weak leader, and certainly a poor successor to Roosevelt.

The first document in this section is a radio address by Truman, explaining why he chose to veto the 1946 price control bill. The second is a rebuttal by Senator Robert Taft, who defends the bill as representing a "reasonable transition" from a wartime to a peacetime economy.

TRUMAN EXPLAINS HIS VETO OF THE PRICE CONTROL BILL

[. . .] You have all heard a great deal about inflation. Its seriousness cannot be overestimated. It would affect every individual in our country. Inflation would cause an increase in the price of every article you buy. As prices soared with inflation, your money would buy fewer and fewer of the necessities of life. Your savings, your insurance, your war bonds—all would decrease in value.

For five years we have proved to this country and to the world that inflation can be prevented. Those of you who remember the First World War will recall the wild inflation and the collapse that followed. You will remember how farmers were ruined, how businessmen went bankrupt, how wage earners suffered.

This time we have succeeded in preventing such a calamity. We have done this largely through price control. It was not done by a miracle. It was done because the American people had the wisdom and the courage and the restraint to know that they had to submit to restrictions and controls or be overcome by the force of inflation. This is as important now and in the months to come as it was during the war. Time and again I have stated and restated this proposition.

I wanted to sign a price-control bill. I gave this bill long and careful study. I came to the conclusion that the bill which the Congress sent me was no price-control bill at all. It gave you no protection against higher and higher prices. . . .

It would have been much easier for me to sign this bill. But the American people would have soon realized that real price control was at an end in spite of the law. If I had signed the bill the people would have seen their prices going up, day by day. You would have realized soon that the bill which had passed and called a price-control law was not price control at all. . . .

I know how weary you all are of these restrictions and controls. I am also weary of them. I spend a good deal of my time listening to complaints. I know how eager everyone of you is for the day when you can run your own affairs in your own way as you did before the war. I know, therefore, how strong the temptation is to remove too quickly the safeguards which we have built up for ourselves and our children.

The bill which the Congress sent me yielded to that temptation. . . .

I do not have time this evening to comment on all the provisions of the bill. There are many objections to it, but my most fundamental objection is the price-raising amendment for manufacturers which was introduced by Senator Taft.

Under this amendment there would be thousands of needless price increases amounting to many billions of dollars. The Taft amendment provides that the manufacturer shall receive for each article the profit which he made on that article in 1941 and that he may add to the 1941 selling price all increases in cost which have occurred since that time. In 1941 the manufacturer received a much greater profit out of each dollar in sales than at any time in the five preceding years or in any of the five following wartime years. In fact, profit margins in 1941 were 50 percent greater than in the banner year 1929. . . .

I believe in the profit system and desire that profits should be ample to provide the incentive for full production. The Taft amendment, however, provides for higher prices and higher profits even where production is already going at full blast and profits are wholly satisfactory. . . .

I have submitted to the Congress in my veto message a plan for price control legislation for the comparatively short period of time that it is still needed. The will of the people is still the supreme law of our land. Your determination to retain price controls and so prevent inflation must be made known to the Congress. The Congress is the only branch of our Government which has the power to pass a law providing for proper price control. . . .

I also request every employee of the OPA to stay at his battle station. The fight is not over. I am counting on all employees of the OPA to continue to serve in the future as they have in the past and to finish the job. I urge these loyal civil servants and the thousands of volunteers who are giving their time to make price control a success to see this fight through.

And, finally, my fellow citizens, I say to you that we as a Nation have it within our hands to make this postwar period an era of the greatest opportunity and prosperity in our Nation's history. But if short-sightedness and impatience, if partisanship and greed are allowed to triumph over the efforts to maintain economic stability, this grand opportunity will have been sacrificed.

Congressional Record. 79th Cong., 2nd sess., vol. 92, pt. 6 (July 1, 1946): 8023–25.

SENATOR ROBERT A. TAFT (R-OHIO) DEFENDS THE PRICE CONTROL BILL

Yesterday President Truman vetoed the bill to extend his own power to fix prices and rents, so that OPA expires at midnight tonight. Last night he defended his curious action by what amounted to a long personal attack on me, because I had some part in drafting one of the various amendments to the bill. His whole broadcast had the aspect of a partisan political attack. . . .

As a matter of fact, I have always supported price control as essential in the war period. I believe we would be better off to continue it for 6 months longer, although like every other person who believes in the American system, I think it should be ended at the earliest possible moment. I assisted in drafting the original Price Control Act and all the amendments. . . .

My own position and that of Congress is perfectly logical. We think the time has not quite come to take off basic price controls, but we do think the administration of OPA must be improved. The bill provides for the gradual liquidation of OPA over the next 12 months, the ending of subsidies on April 1, 1947, and reasonable pricing in the interval so that we can stimulate production and get rid of all the shortages and injustices that exist today. . . .

The President's attack on the amendment which I offered in the Senate is utterly unfair. All that the Taft amendment provides is that producers, including farmers, mining concerns, and manufacturers, shall be allowed to charge prices which reflect the increased cost of labor and material which they now have to pay. This is done by permitting them to charge for each major product a price equal to their 1941 prices plus the average increase in the cost of labor, materials, et cetera since 1911. After all, this is peacetime again. Why shouldn't the producer be placed in the same position he was in before the war? No producer is guaranteed any profit. There is no question of a freeze any more, because the OPA itself has put over 500 price increases into effect since March 1. All we want to prevent during the next 6 months are the speculative rises in price over and above the increase in costs. The danger I am concerned about is taking the roof off, as the President does by his veto. But how can anyone hope to get production if we don't allow the producers to charge enough for their products to pay for the increased cost of labor and material? Even the President admits in his message that this principle has a superficial reasonableness. There is nothing superficial about it except to the master minds among the New Deal economists at the OPA. . . .

In short, in the act passed by Congress, the President received complete power to prevent speculation and speculative increases in price and all increases in rents. We merely reaffirm more vigorously the original principles of the Price Control Act to secure production, yet the President has chosen to plunge the economy of this country into chaos. In such a controversial field where feelings already run high, we cannot hope that the Senate will act without debate, and it should not do so, because the issues to be settled are vital to the welfare of the country. I hope price control will be continued, and I should vote to reenact the bill the President has vetoed, but I am afraid the bill which he will get the next time, if he gets any, may go further toward decontrol than the one he has vetoed. In the meantime there are no price controls. No businessman knows what he should do or what price he should charge. I hope that everyone will exercise the reasonable restraint which Americans always exhibit in a crisis.

The President has a choice between a reasonable transition from price control back to the free enterprise system, on the one hand, and the ending of all OPA powers by veto, on the other. He chose to take all the chances of chaos, followed by speculative rises in price. He chose this course, having been warned by his own Democratic leaders of the necessary result of his policy. He has repudiated their leadership and assumed to write a law for Congress, although the Constitution of the United States gives the Congress power to state the conditions on which price control shall be continued.

Congressional Record. 79th Cong., 2d sess., vol. 92, pt. 6 (July 1, 1946): 8025–26.

THE TRUMAN DOCTRINE (1947)

Not long after the end of World War II, Americans realized that the wartime alliance between the United States and the Soviet Union was not going to last. Stalin seemed intent upon strangling democracy in Eastern Europe in an attempt to create a series of satellite states. Soviet spy rings were soon uncovered in the United States and Canada, suggesting that the Russians had been spying upon their allies throughout the war. Even more importantly, it appeared that America and the Soviet Union were too ideologically different to get along; after all, Americans valued individual freedom, religion, and private property, while Soviet orthodoxy called for world revolution to abolish property and destroy religion.

In February 1947, the British ambassador requested an emergency meeting with Secretary of State George C. Marshall. Great Britain, the ambassador explained, could not afford to defend its traditional interests in the eastern Mediterranean, and wanted to know if the United States would help. Of particular concern were Greece and Turkey. Greece was in the midst of a civil war, with government forces fighting against a communist-backed insurgency. Turkey was under heavy pressure from the Soviet Union to allow passage for Soviet ships through the straits that separated the Black Sea from the Mediterranean. The British estimated that the two countries would need at least $400 million to resist their current threats, and postwar Britain simply did not have it, particularly after Truman ordered an end to Lend-Lease in 1946.

Truman decided to ask Congress to provide the necessary funds. He realized that he faced an uphill battle. Americans were extremely concerned about inflation and other domestic problems, and would be reluctant to bail out other countries. Moreover, Congress was now in Republican control for the first time since 1930, and the GOP was demanding deep cuts in both taxes and federal spending.

Before proceeding, Truman met with Under Secretary of State Dean Acheson and the chairman of the Senate Foreign Relations Committee, Arthur Vandenberg (R-Michigan). Acheson told the president and the senator that "Soviet pressure" on the Middle East had reached a point where further penetration could "open three continents to Soviet penetration." If Greece and Turkey were allowed to fall, communist influence would "infect Iran and all the East," and eventually overwhelm Europe and Africa as well. Only American assistance stood between Stalin and a Soviet-dominated world. After a long silence, Vandenberg told the president that if he would "say that to the Congress and the country, I will support you and I believe most of its members will do the same."[1]

This is exactly what the president did. On March 12, 1947, he addressed a joint session of Congress in which he outlined the Soviet threat not only to Greece and Turkey, but to the entire world. Truman concluded that "it must be the policy of the United States to support free people who are resisting attempted subjugation by armed minorities or by outside pressures."[2] The speech, and the sentiments it expressed, soon came to be known as the "Truman Doctrine."

The speech had the desired effect. There was, to be sure, some opposition. Certain Republicans, such as Senator Robert A. Taft of Ohio, argued that the bill would needlessly provoke the Soviet Union, and would lead to potentially endless commitments. Some on the Left, such as former vice president Henry Wallace and Senator Glen Taylor (D-Idaho) made similar arguments. Nevertheless, the bill passed with strong support from both parties, marking the beginning of a period of bipartisanship in foreign policy that would last until the 1960s.

The Truman Doctrine was one of the most important public utterances of the early cold war, and it marked a sharp break from earlier foreign policy. Americans in the 1930s had shown little interest in what happened overseas; indeed, it had taken an actual Japanese attack on U.S. territory to draw the nation into World War II. Now, however, Americans were committing themselves to supporting "free people," no matter where they might be. The country had taken its first step toward a world struggle against communism.

This section features excerpts from Truman's 1947 message to Congress, as well as a rejoinder by Henry Wallace, who claims that the Truman Doctrine will commit the United States to the defense of "reactionary" regimes all over the world.

NOTES

1. Daniel Yergin, *Shattered Peace: The Origins of the Cold War and the National Security State* (Boston: Houghton Mifflin, 1977), 281–82.

2. *Congressional Record*, 80th Cong., 1st sess., vol. 93, pt. 2 (March 12, 1947): 1980–81.

TRUMAN ASKS FOR LOANS FOR GREECE AND TURKEY

[. . .] The United States has received from the Greek Government an urgent appeal for financial and economic assistance. Preliminary reports from the . . . American Ambassador in Greece corroborate the statement of the Greek Government that assistance is imperative if Greece is to survive as a free nation.

I do not believe that the American people and the Congress wish to turn a deaf ear to the appeal of the Greek Government. . . .

The very existence of the Greek state is today threatened by the terrorist activities of several thousand armed men, led by Communists, who defy the Government's authority at a number of points, particularly along the northern boundaries. A commission appointed by the United Nations Security Council is at present investigating disturbed conditions in northern Greece and alleged border violations along the frontier between Greece on the one hand and Albania, Bulgaria, and Yugoslavia on the other.

Meanwhile, the Greek Government is unable to cope with the situation. The Greek Army is small and poorly equipped. It needs supplies and equipment if it is to restore the authority of the Government throughout Greek territory.

Greece must have assistance if it is to become a self-supporting and self-respecting democracy.

The United States must supply this assistance. . . . There is no other country to which democratic Greece can turn. . . .

The Greek Government has been operating in an atmosphere of chaos and extremism. It has made mistakes. The extension of aid by this country does not mean that the United States condones everything that the Greek Government has done or will do. We have condemned in the past, and we condemn now, extremist measures of the right or the left. We have in the past advised tolerance, and we advise tolerance now.

Greece's neighbor, Turkey, also deserves our attention. . . .

Since the war, Turkey has sought financial assistance from Great Britain and the United States for the purpose of effecting that modernization necessary for the maintenance of its national integrity.

That integrity is essential to the preservation of order in the Middle East. . . .

As in the case of Greece, if Turkey is to have the assistance it needs, the United States must supply it. We are the only country able to provide that help.

I am fully aware of the broad implications involved if the United States extends assistance to Greece and Turkey, and I shall discuss these implications with you at this time.

One of the primary objectives of the foreign policy of the United States is the creation of conditions in which we and other nations will be able to work out a way of life free from coercion. This was a fundamental issue in the war with Germany and Japan. Our victory was won over countries which sought to impose their will, and their way of life, upon other nations.

To insure the peaceful development of nations, free from coercion, the United States has taken a leading part in establishing the United Nations. The United Nations is designed to make possible lasting freedom and independence for all its members. We shall not realize our objectives, however, unless we are willing to help free peoples to maintain their free institutions and their national integrity against aggressive movements that seek to impose upon them totalitarian regimes. This is no more than a frank recognition that totalitarian regimes imposed on free peoples, by direct or indirect aggression, undermine the foundations of international peace and hence the security of the United States. . . .

At the present moment in world history nearly every nation must choose between alternative ways of life. The choice is too often not a free one.

One way of life is based upon the will of the majority, and is distinguished by free institutions, representative government, free elections, guaranties of individual liberty, freedom of speech and religion, and freedom from political oppression.

The second way of life is based on the will of a minority forcibly imposed upon the majority. It relies upon terror and oppression, a controlled press and radio, fixed elections, and the suppression of personal freedoms.

I believe that it must be the policy of the United States to support free peoples who are resisting attempted subjugation by armed minorities or by outside pressures. . . .

The world is not static and the status quo is not sacred. But we cannot allow changes in the status quo in violation of the Charter of the United Nations by such methods as coercion, or by such subterfuges as political infiltration. In helping free and independent nations to maintain their freedom, the United States will be giving effect to the principles of the Charter of the United Nations. . . .

The seeds of totalitarian regimes are nurtured by misery and want. They spread and grow in the evil soil of poverty and strife. They reach their full growth when the hope of a people for a better life has died.

We must keep that hope alive.

The free peoples of the world look to us for support in maintaining their freedoms.

If we falter in our leadership, we may endanger the peace of the world—and we shall surely endanger the welfare of our own Nation.

Great responsibilities have been placed upon us by the swift movement of events. I am confident that the Congress will face these responsibilities squarely.

Congressional Record. 80th Cong., 1st sess., vol. 93, pt. 2 (March 12, 1947): 1980–81.

HENRY A. WALLACE DENOUNCES THE TRUMAN DOCTRINE

March 12, 1947, marked a turning point in American history. It is not a Greek crisis that we face, it is an American crisis. It is a crisis in the American spirit.... Only the American people fully aroused and promptly acting can prevent disaster.

President Truman, in the name of democracy and humanitarianism, proposed a military lend-lease program. He proposed a loan of $400,000,000 to Greece and Turkey as a down payment on an unlimited expenditure aimed at opposing Communist expansion. He proposed, in effect, that America police Russia's every border. There is no regime too reactionary for us provided it stands in Russia's expansionist path. There is no country too remote to serve as the scene of a contest which may widen until it becomes a world war.

President Truman calls for action to combat a crisis. What is this crisis that necessitates Truman going to Capitol Hill as though a Pearl Harbor has suddenly hit us? How many more of these Pearl Harbors will there be? How can they be foreseen? What will they cost? [...]

One year ago at Fulton, Mo., Winston Churchill called for a diplomatic offensive against Soviet Russia. By sanctioning that speech, Truman committed us to a policy of combating Russia with British sources. That policy proved to be so bankrupt that Britain can no longer maintain it. Now President Truman proposes we take over Britain's hopeless task. Today Americans are asked to support the Governments of Greece and Turkey. Tomorrow we shall be asked to support the Governments of China and Argentina.

I say that this policy is utterly futile. No people can be bought. America cannot afford to spend billions and billions of dollars for unproductive purposes. The world is hungry and insecure, and the peoples of all lands demand change. President Truman cannot prevent change in the world any more than he can prevent the tide from coming in or the sun from setting. But once America stands for opposition to change, we are lost. America will become the most-hated nation in the world.

Russia may be poor and unprepared for war, but she knows very well how to reply to Truman's declaration of economic and financial pressure. All over the world Russia and her ally, poverty, will increase the pressure against us. Who among us is ready to predict that in this struggle American dollars will outlast the grievances that lead to communism? I certainly don't want to see communism spread. I predict that Truman's policy will spread communism in Europe and Asia. You can't fight something with nothing. When Truman offers unconditional aid to King

George of Greece, he is acting as the best salesman communism ever had. In proposing this reckless adventure, Truman is betraying the great tradition of America and the leadership of the great American who preceded him. . . .

When President Truman proclaims the world-wide conflict between East and West, he is telling the Soviet leaders that we are preparing for eventual war. They will reply by measures to strengthen their position in the event of war. Then the task of keeping the world at peace will pass beyond the power of the common people everywhere who want peace. Certainly it will not be freedom that will be victorious in this struggle. Psychological and spiritual preparation for war will follow financial preparation; civil liberties will be restricted; standards of living will be forced downward; families will be divided against each other; none of the values that we hold worth fighting for will be secure. . . .

This is the time for an all-out worldwide reconstruction program for peace. This is America's opportunity. The peoples of all lands say to America: Send us plows for our fields instead of tanks and guns to be used against us. . . . The dollars that are spent will be spent for the production of goods and will come back to us in a thousand different ways. Our program will be based on service instead of the outworn ideas of imperialism and power politics. It is a fundamental law of life that a strong idea is merely strengthened by persecution. The way to handle communism is by what William James called the replacing power of the higher affection. In other words, we must give the common man all over the world something better than communism. I believe we have something better than communism here in America. But President Truman has not spoken for the American ideal. It is now the turn of the American people to speak.

Common sense is required of all of us in realizing that helping militarism never brings peace. Courage is required of all of us in carrying out a program that can bring peace. Courage and common sense are the qualities that made America great. Let's keep those qualities now.

Congressional Record. 80th Cong., 1st sess., vol. 93, pt. 10 (March 27, 1947): A1328–29.

THE TAFT-HARTLEY ACT (1947)

The labor troubles of early 1946 grew worse as the year went on. Rising prices for consumer goods led to demands for wage hikes in a variety of industries, and when these were not forthcoming, millions went out on strike. Steel, electrical, coal, shipping, timber, and railroads were particularly hard hit, and altogether more than 4.5 million workers participated in nearly five thousand strikes across the country. When John L.

Lewis announced that his United Mine Workers were again going on strike, the nation braced for the worst.

Truman first tried to mediate, and he managed to settle a major strike in the steel industry on the basis of an 18 ½-cent-per-hour wage increase. He then approached the railroads, and secured management approval of an across-the-board 15 percent pay raise. The unions balked at this, however, insisting that they deserved no less than 30 percent to make up for lost overtime pay and the rising cost of living. The president, unwilling to see the nation's rail system paralyzed, threatened a government seizure of the railroads if the workers failed to return to work. The threat was effective, and the strike ended after only two days.

Finally, Truman moved to stop the coal strike. When Lewis failed to obey a government injunction to return to work, the president ordered that contempt charges be brought against the union leader. When a federal district court fined the union $3.5 million, and ordered that Lewis personally pay a $10,000 fine, the mine workers returned to the pits.

The net result of this wave of unrest was a growing hostility on the part of the American public toward organized labor, and much of this was tied to a growing fear of communism. A number of admitted communists had joined unions in the 1930s, and there was a rising concern that they secretly controlled many unions. The wave of strikes in 1946, some suspected, was only the first step toward a revolution.

The Republican Congress needed little encouragement along these lines. The GOP had consistently fought against the labor legislation of the New Deal, and had been looking for an opportunity to curb the power of the unions ever since. In June 1947, it capitalized on the prevailing antiunion sentiment by passing the Labor-Management Relations Act, better known as the Taft-Hartley Act after its two principal sponsors, Senator Robert A. Taft (R-Ohio) and Representative Fred Hartley (R-New Jersey). The main feature of the bill was that it prohibited the so-called "closed shop," in which only union members could be hired. However, it continued to permit the operation of "union shops," in which employees were required to join a union once hired. In other respects the bill expanded upon the 1943 War Labor Disputes Act by providing for federal injunctions against strikes that endangered national security, and by extending to sixty days the "cooling-off period" before a strike could be called. Finally, it required that all union leaders take an oath upon taking office swearing that they were not communists.

Truman disliked the Taft-Hartley Act from the start, calling it "a shocking piece of legislation" that would "take fundamental rights away from our working people," but he recognized that it had passed by such wide margins that any veto would be quickly overturned.[1] Nevertheless, after two weeks of deliberation he sent it back to Congress with a stinging veto message. He argued that it would make strikes more, not less likely, and would actually increase the federal government's involvement in labor disputes. Most importantly, he argued that it would reverse the gains made by labor in the 1930s, depriving workers of protections that had been extended in the Wagner Act and similar legislation.

Although Republicans and southern Democrats combined to pass the bill over his veto three days later, the president's fight against it would eventually work to his political benefit, as it caused unions to rally to him as they had to Franklin Roosevelt. Indeed, the labor vote would be a key factor in Truman's surprisingly successful campaign for reelection in 1948. But despite the fact that unions made repeal of Taft-Hartley a priority, all efforts to do so failed. Contrary to the predictions of many union leaders, the law did not destroy organized labor, or even seriously harm it. Unions would continue to flourish, and would reach the height of their influence in the 1950s.

The first document in this section comes from Truman's message to Congress explaining his veto of the Taft-Hartley Act. The second is a defense of the bill delivered by Taft.

NOTE

1. Alonzo L. Hamby, *Man of the People: A Life of Harry S. Truman* (New York: Oxford University Press, 1995), 424.

TRUMAN VETOES THE TAFT-HARTLEY ACT

[. . .] I share with the Congress the conviction that legislation dealing with the relations between management and labor is necessary. I heartily condemn abuses on the part of unions and employers, and I have no patience with stubborn insistence on private advantage to the detriment of public interest.

But this bill is far from a solution of those problems. . . .

The bill taken as a whole would reverse the basic direction of our national labor policy, inject the Government into private economic affairs on an unprecedented scale, and conflict with important principles of our democratic society. Its provisions would cause more strikes, not fewer. It would contribute neither to industrial peace nor to economic stability and progress. It would be a dangerous stride in the direction of a totally managed economy. It contains seeds of discord which would plague this Nation for years to come.

Because of the far-reaching import of this bill, I have weighed its probable effects against a series of fundamental considerations. In each case I find that the bill violates principles essential to our public welfare. . . .

1. The bill would substantially increase strikes. . . .

2. The bill arbitrarily decides, against the workers, certain issues which are normally the subject of collective bargaining, and thus restricts the area of voluntary agreement. . . .

3. The bill would expose employers to numerous hazards by which they could be annoyed and hampered. . . .

4. The bill would deprive workers of vital protection which they now have under the law. . . .

5. The bill abounds in provisions which would be unduly burdensome or actually unworkable. . . .

6. The bill would establish an ineffective and discriminatory emergency procedure for dealing with major strikes affecting the public health and safety. . . .

7. The bill would discriminate against employees. . . .

The most fundamental test which I have applied to this bill is whether it would strengthen or weaken American democracy in the present critical hour. This bill is perhaps the most serious economic and social legislation of the past decade. Its effects—for good or ill—would be felt for decades to come.

I have concluded that the bill is a clear threat to the successful working of our democratic society.

One of the major lessons of recent world history is that free and vital trade-unions are a bulwark against the growth of totalitarian movements. We must, therefore, be everlastingly alert that in striking at union abuses we do not destroy the contribution which unions make to our democratic strength.

This bill would go far toward weakening our trade-union movement. And it would go far toward destroying our national unity. By raising barriers between labor and management and by injecting political considerations into normal economic decisions, it would invite them to gain their ends through direct political action. I think it would be exceedingly dangerous to our country to develop a class basis for political action.

I cannot emphasize too strongly the transcendent importance of the United States in the world today as a force for freedom and peace. We cannot be strong internationally if our national unity and our productive strength are hindered at home. Anything which weakens our economy or weakens the unity of our people—as I am thoroughly convinced this bill would do—I cannot approve. . . .

There is still a genuine opportunity for the enactment of appropriate labor legislation this session. I still feel that the recommendations which I expressed in the state of the Union message constitute an adequate basis for legislation which is moderate in spirit and which relates to known abuses.

For the compelling reasons I have set forth, I return H.R. 3020 without my approval.

Congressional Record. 80th Cong., 1st sess., vol. 93, pt. 6 (June 20, 1947): 7485–88.

SENATOR ROBERT A. TAFT (R-OHIO) DEFENDS THE TAFT-HARTLEY ACT

... [I]t is now approximately 6 months since this Congress returned to Washington to consider the task which lay before it. Regardless of the issues in the election, there was unquestionably a demand at that time, as there is now, for labor legislation, for a reform of the abuses which had become apparent to the American people. They had been deluged with a series of strikes. They had been deluged with strikes ordered for men who did not desire the strikes. They had been deluged with strikes against companies which had settled all difference with their own men. They had been deluged with strikes in violation of existing collective-bargaining agreements. They know of mass picketing. They knew that in those strikes men had been excluded from their own plants by force and violence. They knew that the men in the unions themselves had been arbitrarily treated by the leaders, and that unless they chose to please the leaders they lost their jobs. They were fired from the union and lost their jobs with the company, and in many cases they found it impossible to continue their own trade.... They knew of the limitation on the freedom of employers, and they knew of the many unjust provisions of the Wagner Act as administered by the National Labor Relations Board.

... [W]e have drafted his bill and it is based on the theory of the Wagner Act.... It is based on the theory that the solution of the labor problem in the United States is free, collective bargaining—a contract between one employer and all of his men acting as one man. That is the theory of the Wagner Act, that they shall be free to make the contract they wish to make....

... The truth is that originally, before the passage of any of the laws dealing with labor, the employer had all the advantage. He had the employees at his mercy, and he could practically in most cases dictate the terms which he wished to impose. Congress passed the Clayton Act [of 1914], the Norris-LaGuardia Act [of 1931] and the Wagner Act. The latter act was interpreted by a completely prejudiced board in such a way that it went far beyond the original intention of Congress, until we reached a point where the balance had shifted over to the other side, where the labor leaders had every advantage in collective bargaining and were relieved from any liability in breaking the contract after they had made the bargain. That was a condition under which strikes actually were encouraged and protected, no matter what the purpose or the character of the particular strike.

All we have tried to do is to swing that balance back, not too far, to a point where the parties can deal equally with each other and where they have approximately equal power. I think the largest companies today can deal with their employees throughout the Nation, but the smaller companies are practically at the mercy of the labor-union bosses. Whatever they have insisted upon in the last 4 or 5 years the employers have practically had to give to them. We want to get the situation back to the point where it is fair. If a man does not have the power to enforce and obtain an unreasonable demand, he is much less likely to make an unreasonable demand. Strikes have largely been brought about by unreasonable demands to which the employer finally felt he could not possibly yield and at the same time maintain the integrity and independence of his business.

This is a perfectly reasonable bill in every respect. If we are to have free collective bargaining it must be between two responsible parties. Some of the provisions of this bill deal with the question of making the unions responsible. There is no reason in the world why a union should not have the same responsibility that a corporation has which is engaged in business. So we have provided that a union may be sued as if it were a corporation. We have provided that the union must file statements as corporations have had to file them, setting up their methods of doing business and making financial reports to the members and to the Secretary of Labor. That sort of reform actually strengthens the members in their collective bargaining. There will be no collective bargaining until both sides are equally responsible. . . .

So we face here the problem of whether, the Senate and the House of Representatives having agreed upon a constructive labor measure, we are going to put that through or whether we are going to say to the labor-union leaders, "No; there is no Congress of the United States, there is no President of the United States, who dares to stand up against your power." Certainly the power they exercise today is a threat to the welfare of the people of the United States. . . .

I appeal to the Senate of the United States to stand up to the work of the legislative body. This is a case of legislation. It is a case in which the President never should have intervened. It is a case in which the President could well have taken the position that, regardless of whether he liked or did not like the work that had been done, the public desire for equity between employer and employee should prevail, no matter what his personal opinion might be.

... I trust that the President's veto will be overridden.

Congressional Record. 80th Cong., 1st sess., vol. 93, pt. 6 (June 23, 1947): 7536–38.

TRUMAN'S LOYALTY PROGRAM (1947)

During the 1930s, communism reached an unprecedented level of acceptability in the United States, mainly due to the severity of the Great Depression. Many intellectuals came to believe that the free enterprise system had failed, and looked toward the Soviet Union as an example of how future crises could be avoided. Hundreds of Americans traveled to the USSR and participated in Soviet-sponsored tours. They did not see the thousands interned in labor camps, or the millions of starving peasants in the Ukraine; instead they returned to the United States with glowing accounts of prosperous farms and efficient factories. As one prominent intellectual put it, "I have seen the future, and it works."

By the early 1940s, many communists had found a home in the American labor movement, and some in the federal government. During World War II, of course, the United States and the Soviet Union were allies, so there was a greater willingness to tolerate communists in such positions. All this changed, however, after the war ended and relations with the USSR began to sour. The communists now appeared to be a threat to national security, fomenting revolution under orders from Moscow. Particularly disturbing were revelations that the Soviets had been using communist sympathizers in the United States to carry out espionage. Classified documents were discovered in the office of the magazine *Amerasia*, whose editorial staff was known to have pro-Soviet leanings. Even more ominous was the announcement by the Canadian government in June 1946 that it had uncovered a spy ring made up of Canadian citizens who had passed atomic secrets to the Soviets.

The issue of domestic security became a campaign issue in the 1946 congressional elections, and although Truman personally thought too much was being made of what he called "the Communist bugaboo," he was well aware that the new Republican Congress would continue to play on this theme.[1] Just weeks after the election, therefore, he appointed the temporary Commission on Employee Loyalty to study existing loyalty standards and make recommendations on how they might be strengthened. He was much encouraged in this by the director of the FBI, J. Edgar Hoover, who sought the authority to remove from federal employment anyone who even appeared sympathetic to communism. Hoover believed that the State Department was infested with communists, and urged the president to develop a program to determine the loyalty of government employees.

On March 21, 1947, Truman bowed to Hoover's request by issuing executive order 9835, establishing the Federal Employees Loyalty and Security Program. Under its provisions, all federal employees were to be subject to investigation by a specially created Loyalty Review Board made up of twenty prominent citizens. Those deemed to be disloyal—which could mean everything from participation in acts of espionage to membership in any organization that the attorney general designated as subversive—would be dismissed from their jobs. In an effort to mollify Congress, Truman named Seth Richardson, a conservative Republican lawyer in Washington, to head the board.

The loyalty program quickly proved a disappointment. Hoover saw this as the green light he needed, and over the next few months, the FBI began running "name checks" on each of the more than two million employees of the federal government. But by 1950, only 212 had been dismissed on grounds of disloyalty (although several thousand others resigned rather than face possible dismissal). Liberals accused Truman of drumming up anticommunist hysteria, and claimed that the loyalty program violated civil liberties. At the same time, conservatives of both parties in Congress argued that it did not go far enough. Given that in the next few years more and more revelations of treason emerged, many Americans believed that they were right. Public fears about communist infiltration of government only grew stronger in the late 1940s, and would become an even more potent Republican issue after Truman's 1948 reelection.

This section features a press statement by the president explaining the details of his loyalty program, and an address by California Democrat, Representative Chester Holifield, who claims that the plan poses grave risks to civil liberties.

NOTE

1. David McCullough, *Truman* (New York: Simon & Schuster, 1992), 550–51.

TRUMAN EXPLAINS HIS LOYALTY PROGRAM

[. . .] I believe I speak for all the people of the United States when I say that disloyal and subversive elements must be removed from the employ of the Government. We must not, however, permit employees of the Federal Government to be labeled as disloyal or potentially disloyal to their Government when no valid basis exists for arriving at such a conclusion. The overwhelming majority of Federal employees are loyal citizens who are giving conscientiously of their energy and skills to the United States. I do not want them to fear they are the objects of any

"witch hunt." They are not being spied upon; they are not being restricted in their activities. They have nothing to fear from the loyalty
program, since every effort has been made to guarantee full protection
to those who are suspected of disloyalty. Rumor, gossip, or suspicion
will not be sufficient to lead to the dismissal of an employee for disloyalty.

Any person suspected of disloyalty must be served with a written
notice of the charges against him in sufficient detail to enable him to
prepare his defense. In some unusual situations security considerations
may not allow full disclosure.

It would have been possible for the Government to remove disloyal
persons merely by serving them with the charges against them and giving them an opportunity to answer those charges. I realize fully, however, the stigma attached to a removal for disloyalty. Accordingly, I have
ordered the agencies of the Government, except where a few agencies
find it necessary to exercise extraordinary powers granted to them by
Congress, to give hearings to persons who are charged with disloyalty.

Loyalty boards are being set up in each agency for this purpose. They
are definitely not "kangaroo" courts. The personnel of these boards is
being carefully selected by the head of each agency to make sure that
they are judicious in temperament and fair-minded. Hearings before the
boards will be conducted so as to establish all pertinent facts and to
accord the suspected employee every possible opportunity to present his
defense. The employee is to be given the right to be accompanied by
counsel or a representative of his own choosing.

After the hearing has been completed the loyalty board in each department can recommend the retention or the dismissal of an employee.
But the matter does not rest there. The employee may appeal the findings
of the loyalty board to the head of the department, who can either approve or disapprove the board's recommendations.

If the head of the department orders the dismissal of the employee,
he has still another avenue of appeal: namely, to the Loyalty Review
Board within the Civil Service Commission. This Board is composed of
outstanding citizens of the United States. These citizens have no ax to
grind. They will not be concerned with personalities. Their judgment will
be as detached as is humanly possible. . . .

The question of standards is of deep concern to me. Under the Executive order inaugurating this program, provision has been made, for
example, for furnishing to the Loyalty Review Board by the Attorney
General the name of each foreign or domestic organization, association,
movement, group, or combination of persons which he, after appropriate
investigation and determination, has designated as totalitarian, fascist,
communist, or subversive. The Executive order in turn provides that the

Loyalty Review Board shall disseminate such information to all departments and agencies.

This provision of the order has been interpreted by some to mean that any person who at any time happened to belong to one of these organizations would automatically be dismissed from the employ of the Federal Government.

This interpretation completely overlooks the fact that, under the provisions of the Executive order, "the standard for the refusal of employment or the removal from employment in an executive department or agency on grounds relating to loyalty shall be that, on all the evidence, reasonable grounds exist for belief that the person involved is disloyal to the government of the United States."

Membership in an organization is simply one piece of evidence which may or may not be helpful in arriving at a conclusion as to the action which is to be taken in a particular case.

The Government has a great stake in these loyalty proceedings. The Government, as the largest employer in the United States, must be the model of a fair employer. It must guarantee that the civil rights of all employees of the Government shall be protected properly and adequately. It is in this spirit that the loyalty program will be enforced.

Statement by the President on the Government's Employee Loyalty Program, November 14, 1947, *Public Papers of the Presidents: Harry S. Truman* (Washington, D.C.: United States Government Printing Office, 1963), pp. 489–91.

REPRESENTATIVE CHESTER E. HOLIFIELD (D-CALIFORNIA) DENOUNCES TRUMAN'S LOYALTY PROGRAM

. . . I wish to express today my deep concern over a new and dangerous tendency in American life, which I think threatens the very existence of the United States as a free nation.

I do not refer to any growth of communism or fascism as such, but I do refer to the conduct of those who are most vocal in their efforts to—they say—"defend us against communism and fascism."

These people, while castigating individuals and organizations as being Communists or Fascists, deny these same individuals or organizations the right of a fair trial, the right of self-defense, the right of equal opportunity, to publicize their defense, against their accusers. . . .

. . . [W]e all know that the very root of our democracy is in the freedom and opportunity for each American to think for himself, to speak his thoughts to his neighbor, and that his ability to do so depends, most importantly of all, upon the freedom of his neighbors to speak their minds, upon any subject, without fear of reprisal or oppression.

If the expression of all points of view is in any respect curtailed, or citizens are to that extent deprived of the opportunity to reach their own conclusions, they are deprived of the founding fathers' principle of free speech, and free assembly, and therefore the play and interplay of free ideas among free men. . . .

Let us then review some of the dangerous practices of today. During the 1946 campaign, the red-smearing technique of Hitler was used, and used successfully, to retire many progressive men from public life. Men whose patriotism was unquestioned, men who stood for the best principles of American democracy.

But they found themselves helpless against the insidious technique of character assassination. . . . In too many instances, there was no opportunity for the accused to face his accuser on an equal basis before the bar of public attention. . . .

Candidates for public office were defeated. Their civil rights had been violated, and they paid the penalty.

But the process which the victors used, holds within it a danger of which we should all be aware—that technique of character assassination continues. It continues in the press. It continues in the radio. . . .

As a result of this hysteria, this panic against communism, President Truman has issued a so-called loyalty order. I believe that President Truman is sincere in issuing such an order. I question the wisdom of the methods proposed, however, . . . of determining loyalty, or disloyalty, the provisions for defense against one's accuser. I do not question the sincerity of the President, nor the desirability of his purpose. I realize that we do not want either Communists or Fascists taking part in confidential positions in our National Government. However, many imminently conservative, reputable people . . . think that certain terms of the order, and the loose method of determining disloyalty, are dangerously broad and lacking in safeguards for the freedom of the individual. The order bestows on the Attorney General arbitrary judicial power regarding civil liberties heretofore reserved to the courts. . . .

It is only the police states that desire the growth of fear in the hearts of their abject subjects. If we continue these practices, people will fear that their jobs will be jeopardized, or that their security will be threatened, or that they will be publicly attacked, and have no means of answering that attack.

They will be afraid to express or to listen to any ideas, whether radical or conservative. The totalitarian states purposely encouraged the growth of fear to control their people. They believe in both tyranny of the body and tyranny of the mind. . . .

We know that neither Hitler, Stalin, nor Mussolini could rise to power until they had established the pattern for suppressing dissenting ideas. . . . They established it through the suppression of civil liberties and the persecution of the opposition. They created fear, panic, and hysteria in the minds of the people.

These are the things, therefore, that we must guard against.

We must guard against the suppression of civil liberties.

We must guard against intemperance and intolerance, whether it be of ideas or of minority groups.

If we do not guard against these insidious practices and methods, our best efforts to combat communism and fascism will fail.

These are the methods which destroy democracy. And when democracy is destroyed, either fascism or communism rushes in to fill the vacuum. . . .

Let me conclude my remarks by reminding you of the oft-quoted statement of Voltaire. "I do not believe a word that you say, but I will defend with my life, if need be, your right to say it."

That is the spirit of democracy, and that attitude of heart and mind must be our guide and compass in the perilous days that lie ahead.

Congressional Record. 80th Cong., 1st sess., vol. 93, pt. 6 (June 27, 1947): 7846–48.

THE MARSHALL PLAN (1948)

Soon after Congress passed the legislation authorizing funds for Greece and Turkey, the administration made a study to determine what other "free peoples" should receive assistance under the Truman Doctrine. The State Department quickly decided that China, which had been in the midst of a civil war since the end of World War II, was a lost cause. The Nationalist regime of Chiang Kai-Shek, it was believed, was thoroughly corrupt and enjoyed virtually no public support. The Communist insurgents were bound to win sooner or later, but this would be of no great loss, since China was believed to be far too underdeveloped to become an important industrial power.

But if the administration were to write off Asia, where could it turn instead? The answer seemed clear—Europe. Much of the continent had been devastated during the war, and at a time when the American economy was booming, the countries of Europe were experiencing massive unemployment. To make matters worse, an unusually severe winter in 1946–1947 created serious shortages of coal and food. Former president Herbert Hoover warned that the population was on the verge of starvation, and that in desperation they might turn to communism to solve their problems. Already the communist parties of France and Italy had shown considerable strength in national elections. If the misery continued, they might well win control of those countries through free elections.

The State Department soon designed a European Recovery Program (ERP) that was announced in a speech by Secretary of State George C. Marshall in June 1947. The goal, Marshall said, was to bring about "the revival of a working economy . . . so as to permit the emergence of political and social conditions in which free institutions can exist." He denied that it was directed against the Soviet Union or communism; indeed, the speech did not rule out the possibility of aid going to the USSR and its satellites. The real targets, Marshall claimed, were "hunger, poverty, desperation and chaos."[1]

The idea of sending taxpayer dollars to the Soviet Union would have no doubt been rejected out of hand by Congress. It was fortunate, therefore, that the Soviet foreign minister Vyacheslav Molotov announced that the "Marshall Plan" (as it was now being called) was just another example of U.S. imperialism, and that neither his country nor its Eastern European allies would be participating. Communist parties in Western Europe soon followed Moscow's lead in denouncing the proposal.

But if the Marshall Plan was not popular among the Soviet leadership, it quickly gained public support in both the United States and Western Europe. In mid-July, while the Truman administration prepared to put its case before Congress, representatives of sixteen European nations gathered in Paris to determine their precise needs. This group, the Committee of European Economic Cooperation, outlined a four-year program of reconstruction at an estimated cost of $22.3 billion. They warned that such aid would have to come soon, otherwise conditions would grow so severe that the program would be of little use.

On December 19, Truman formally asked Congress to pass the Foreign Assistance Act, which would appropriate $17 billion between 1948 and 1952. The president had already done a good job of laying the groundwork by selling the proposal to the congressional leadership, so it already had the endorsement of Senator Arthur Vandenberg (R-Michigan) and other high-ranking Republicans. The fact that the program was named for the widely-respected Marshall (who had been chief of staff of the U.S. Army during World War II) instead of Truman no doubt made it easier for the GOP to swallow.

Despite the bipartisan support for the bill, there was nevertheless opposition, mainly among those who had attacked the aid package to Greece and Turkey. Senator Robert A. Taft (R-Ohio) spoke for many midwestern conservatives when he charged that the plan would be ruinously expensive, and would go to support socialist programs in Europe. Meanwhile Henry Wallace, who had just announced that he would challenge Truman for the presidency on the Progressive Party ticket, claimed that it would needlessly provoke the Soviet Union. Nevertheless, both houses of Congress voted overwhelmingly in favor of the Marshall

Plan, and Truman signed the bill into law on April 3, 1948. It was, he said, "a striking manifestation of the fact that a bipartisan foreign policy can lead to effective action."[2]

The Marshall Plan was perhaps the most successful single initiative of the Truman administration. More than $13 billion in American aid flowed into Europe between 1948 and 1951, which greatly facilitated economic recovery. In addition, the experience of working together to determine needs led to greater cooperation among the nations of Western Europe, leading first to the European Coal and Steel Community (1952) and eventually to the European Union of today. Finally, the opposition to the plan by European communist parties seriously undermined their public support, thus ending for the moment any chance that communism might take hold in Western Europe through free elections.

The first document in this section is a message by Truman to Congress, urging the legislature to appropriate the necessary funds to launch the Marshall Plan. The second is an address by Illinois Republican, Representative Charles Vursell, who claims that the money would be better spent in building up the country's military forces.

NOTES

1. Barton J. Bernstein and Allen J. Matusow, eds., *The Truman Administration: A Documentary History* (New York: Harper & Row, 1966), 256–59.

2. Donald R. McCoy, *The Presidency of Harry S. Truman* (Lawrence: University Press of Kansas, 1984), 127–28.

TRUMAN PROPOSES THE EUROPEAN RECOVERY PROGRAM

A principal concern of the people of the United States is the creation of conditions of enduring peace throughout the world. In company with other peace-loving nations, the United States is striving to insure that there will never be a World War III. In the words of the Charter of the United Nations, we are "determined to save succeeding generations from the scourge of war."

We seek lasting peace in a world where freedom and justice are secure and where there is equal opportunity for the economic well-being of all peoples. . . .

We must now make a grave and significant decision relating to our further efforts to create the conditions of peace. We must decide whether or not we will complete the job of helping the free nations of Europe to recover from the devastation of the war. Our decision will determine in large part the future of the people of that continent. It will also determine in large part whether the free nations of the world can look forward with hope to a peaceful and prosperous future as independent states, or whether they must live in poverty and in fear of selfish totalitarian aggression.

It is of vital importance to the United States that European recovery be continued to ultimate success. The American tradition of extending a helping hand to people in distress, our concern for the building of a healthy world economy which can make possible ever-increasing standards of living for our people, and our overwhelming concern for the maintenance of a civilization of freemen and free institutions, all combine to give us this great interest in European recovery. . . .

Considered in terms of our own economy, European recovery is essential. The last two decades have taught us the bitter lesson that no economy, not even one so strong as our own, can remain healthy and prosperous in a world of poverty and want. . . .

Our deepest concern with European recovery, however, is that it is essential to the maintenance of the civilization in which the American way of life is rooted. It is the only assurance of the continued independence and integrity of a group of nations who constitute a bulwark for the principles of freedom, justice, and the dignity of the individual.

The economic plight in which Europe now finds itself has intensified a political struggle between those who wish to remain freemen living under the rule of law and those who would use economic distress as a pretext for the establishment of a totalitarian state.

The next few years can determine whether the free countries of Europe will be able to preserve their heritage of freedom. If Europe fails to recover, the peoples of these countries might be driven to the philosophy of despair—the philosophy which contends that their basic wants can be met only by the surrender of their basic rights to totalitarian control.

Such a turn of events would constitute a shattering blow to peace and stability in the world. It might well compel us to modify our own economic system and to forego, for the sake of our own security, the enjoyment of many of our freedoms and privileges.

It is for these reasons that the United States has so vital an interest in strengthening the belief of the people of Europe that freedom from fear and want will be achieved under free and democratic governments. . . .

In proposing that the Congress enact a program of aid to Europe, I am proposing that this Nation contribute to world peace and to its own security by assisting in the recovery of 16 countries which, like the United States, are devoted to the preservation of free institutions and enduring peace among nations.

It is my belief that United States support of the European recovery program will enable the free nations of Europe to devote their great energies to the reconstruction of their economies. On this depend the restoration of a decent standard of living for their peoples, the development of a sound world economy, and continued support for the ideals of individual liberty and justice.

In providing aid to Europe we must share more than goods and funds. We must give our moral support to those nations in their struggle to rekindle the fires of hope and strengthen the will of their peoples to overcome their adversities. We must develop a feeling of teamwork in our common cause of combating the suspicions, prejudices, and fabrications which undermine cooperative effort, both at home and abroad.

This joint undertaking of the United States and a group of European nations, in devotion to the principles of the Charter of the United Nations, is proof that free men can effectively join together to defend their free institutions against totalitarian pressures, and to promote better standards of life for all their peoples. . . .

I recommend this program of United States support for European recovery to the Congress in full confidence of its wisdom and necessity as a major step in our Nation's quest for a just and lasting peace.

Congressional Record. 80th Cong., 1st sess., vol. 93, pt. 9 (December 19, 1947): 11749–54.

REPRESENTATIVE CHARLES W. VURSELL (R-ILLINOIS) ATTACKS THE MARSHALL PLAN

. . . This Congress is faced with grave decisions. We are being asked to take from the American people in money and supplies at a critical time of shortages on every hand, $597,000,000 for immediate emergency relief. Later we are being asked by the administration to enter into a 4-year contract to furnish some $20,000,000,000 or more in money and supplies to implement the Marshall plan. In the interest of our own people and Nation, we must not approach them in an atmosphere of hysteria and emotion; we must think as realists. . . .

. . . [B]y holding up the false specter of starvation, the administration and the thousands of bureau propagandists and friendly commentators, over the air, seek to influence the American people and the Congress by the biggest barrage of propaganda ever turned loose on the public, to support the $20,000,000,000 Marshall plan. . . .

. . . [T]hose who favor the Marshall plan will tell you that we must rebuild western Europe to stop communism. We all want to retard or stop communism if we can, but we must be honest with ourselves and honest with the American people we represent. We cannot stop communism taking western Europe unless we have the power to stop Russia and her armies. We held a serious conference with a group of high-ranking military men while in Europe whose duty it is to know what Russia can and may do. We asked the question as follows: "Suppose, under the Marshall plan or some other plan, we spend from $10,000,000,000 to $20,000,000,000 rebuilding western Europe and get those countries going in good shape in 4 or 5 years, is there anything then to stop Russia from moving in and taking a much richer prize after we have spent our money to build it up?" The answer was "No." I do not believe any top military man in the Nation will make the statement that we can land and maintain in western Europe sufficient military forces to prevent Russia, if she so desires, from taking over western Europe. Germany will have no army. Italy, France, Belgium and Holland will have no military strength capable of putting up any serious resistance if Russia should make such a move. You just as well quit trying to deceive the American people by telling them you can stop communism if you put over the Marshall plan. . . .

. . . We should kill the Marshall plan which provides that we enter into a 4-year contract with 16 nations to shore up their financial difficulties to the extent of some $20,000,000,000. We should kill this plan because we cannot supply the food, oil, steel, and hundreds of other products that would be required.

. . . Now, if you want to exert the strongest influence possible by the United States to retard, or stop the encroachment of communism on western Europe, take some of these $20,000,000,000 that you would waste in the Marshall plan, and spend them here at home in building the strongest air force with the greatest striking power of any air force in the world. Give more attention to cooperation in hemispheric defense with South America, strengthen our military departments where necessary to enable us in any emergency to strike promptly with power and effect. Mr. Stalin and his warlords, if they knew we were making such moves, would probably hesitate to move further into western Europe for fear they might precipitate a war with a powerful Nation that is prepared.

I would rather risk this course for the long pull future, and for the immediate effect it would have on Russia, than to tempt them by setting before them a $20,000,000,000 banquet table through the Marshall plan of rebuilding western Europe. Force is the only thing Russia understands.

. . . [I]f we weaken ourselves by shipping away our resources, causing the cost of living to go higher and higher, and spending our Nation into bankruptcy, such action will bring smiles and great satisfaction to Stalin, Molotov, and Russia. Twenty billion dollars spent on our part in western Europe now, plus the efforts of the European nations should be worth

$50,000,000,000 in a few years. It is too great a temptation to place before the Russian warlords. . . .

. . . The first responsibility of the Members of this Congress is to protect the interests of our own people and preserve the financial solvency of our own Nation. The greatest contribution we can make for the future peace of the world, is to keep America strong.

Congressional Record. 80th Cong., 1st sess., vol. 93, pt. 13 (December 4, 1947): A4500–502.

CIVIL RIGHTS (1948)

Harry Truman was the first U.S. president since Abraham Lincoln to make civil rights for African Americans an important part of his political agenda, although he managed to accomplish little along these lines. He was motivated to embrace civil rights at least in part by personal conviction. Truman seems to have genuinely believed that blacks were being treated unfairly in American society. He was particularly bothered by stories of black soldiers being attacked by whites both during and after the war.

At the same time, there were powerful political reasons for embracing a civil rights agenda. Blacks had turned out in large numbers to support Franklin Roosevelt, but by 1947 there were indications that they had grown sour on the Democratic Party. Certainly, the attitude of most southern Democrats—who staunchly defended racial segregation and opposed federal laws against the lynching of blacks—did nothing to make African Americans feel welcome in the party. When the liberal Henry Wallace declared his candidacy for president in December 1947, there were growing fears that blacks might abandon the Democrats in favor of Wallace's Progressive Party.

Truman therefore made a point of raising civil rights as an issue in his State of the Union address of February 2, 1948. He put forth a series of proposals, such as the abolition of the poll tax, a practice used mainly in the South to prevent blacks from voting. He called for federal antilynching laws and an end to discrimination in federal employment (including in the armed services), and promised the creation of a permanent Commission on Civil Rights, as well as a civil-rights division in the Department of Justice.

The president predicted that this stand would be controversial, and it was. Democrats from across the South claimed that the proposals amounted to an attack on their traditions and heritage, and promised to fight any part of Truman's civil rights program that reached the House or the Senate. However, southern Democrats represented a minority in Congress; had the Republican majority joined with northern Democrats to press for Truman's agenda, they would almost certainly have passed. But Republicans, unwilling either to associate themselves with any of Truman's domestic programs or to offend the southern Democrats who had so often allied with them in the past, chose to ignore civil rights. A bill to create a Fair Employment Practices Commission never reached the Senate floor, while anti-lynching legislation suffered a similar fate. An anti-poll tax bill did come up for a vote, but was defeated by a filibuster by southern Democrats that the Republicans did nothing to stop.

The civil rights issue came up again at the 1948 Democratic National Convention, when northern liberals managed to have a plank adopted into the party platform advocating anti-discrimination laws. Outraged southerners walked out of the convention, then met two days later in Birmingham, Alabama, where they announced the formation of the States Rights' Party (often referred to as the "Dixiecrats") and endorsed for president South Carolina governor Strom Thurmond. While most southern Democrats remained true to their party, the presence of Thurmond on the ballot made Truman wary about making civil rights a major campaign issue. In only one speech—significantly, in Harlem—did the president go into detail on the subject.

There were, however, two concrete actions that Truman did take on civil rights. On July 26, 1948, he issued two executive orders, the first establishing a Fair Employment Board to investigate cases of discrimination in federal hiring, the second desegregating the armed forces. These measures alone were enough to convince most African Americans that the president cared about their concerns. The *Chicago Defender* praised the orders as "unprecedented since the time of Lincoln."[1] More importantly, blacks would turn out in large numbers to support Truman's reelection in November.

The president included civil rights in the Fair Deal program that he embraced during his second term. Many of the same bills that had been defeated in the last Congress came forward again in 1949 and 1950. But although the Democrats had majorities in both houses of Congress, southerners were often in positions of leadership. As a result, virtually no progress on civil rights occurred during Truman's second term. The president would continue to speak out on issues of importance to African Americans, but very little of substance was accomplished. Most blacks gave Truman credit for at least trying, and remained loyal to the Democratic Party despite the attitude of its southern contingent. However, meaningful civil rights legislation would have to wait until the 1960s.

This section's documents include excerpts from Truman's 1948 message to Congress calling for civil rights legislation, and the text of a rebuttal by Senator James Eastland, a conservative Democrat from Mississippi.

NOTE

1. Donald R. McCoy, *The Presidency of Harry S. Truman* (Lawrence: University Press of Kansas, 1984), 109.

TRUMAN CALLS FOR CIVIL RIGHTS LEGISLATION

[. . .] This Nation was founded by men and women who sought these shores that they might enjoy greater freedom and greater opportunity than they had known before. The founders of the United States proclaimed to the world the American belief that all men are created equal, and that governments are instituted to secure the inalienable rights with which all men are endowed. In the Declaration of Independence and the Constitution of the United States, they eloquently expressed the aspirations of all mankind for equality and freedom. . . .

Today, the American people enjoy more freedom and opportunity than ever before. Never in our history has there been better reason to hope for the complete realization of the ideals of liberty and equality.

We shall not, however, finally achieve the ideals for which this Nation was founded so long as any American suffers discrimination as a result of his race, or religion, or color, or the land of origin of his forefathers.

Unfortunately, there still are examples—flagrant examples—of discrimination which are utterly contrary to our ideals. Not all groups of our population are free from the fear of violence. Not all groups are free to live and work where they please or to improve their conditions of life by their own efforts. Not all groups enjoy the full privileges of citizenship and participation in the government under which they live.

We cannot be satisfied until all our people have equal opportunities for jobs, for homes, for education, for health, and for political expression, and until all our people have equal protection under the law. . . .

The protection of civil rights is the duty of every government which derives its powers from the consent of the people. This is usually true of local, State, and national governments. There is much that the States can and should do at this time to extend their protection of civil rights. Wherever the law enforcement measures of State and local governments are inadequate to discharge this primary function of government, these measures should be strengthened and improved.

The Federal Government has a clear duty to see that constitutional guarantees of individual liberties and of equal protection under the laws are not denied or abridged anywhere in our Union. That duty is shared by all three branches of the Government, but it can be fulfilled only if the Congress enacts modern, comprehensive civil-rights laws, adequate to the needs of the day, and demonstrating our continuing faith in the free way of life.

I recommend, therefore, that the Congress enact legislation at this session directed toward the following specific objectives:

1. Establishing a permanent Commission on Civil Rights, a Joint Congressional Committee on Civil Rights, and a Civil Rights Division in the Department of Justice.

2. Strengthening existing civil-rights statutes.

3. Providing federal protection against lynching.

4. Protecting more adequately the right to vote.

5. Establishing a Fair Employment Practice Commission to prevent unfair discrimination in employment.

6. Prohibiting discrimination in interstate transportation facilities. . . .

The legislation I have recommended for enactment by the Congress at the present session is a minimum program if the Federal Government is to fulfill its obligation of insuring the constitutional guaranties of individual liberties and of equal protection under the law.

Under the authority of existing law, the Executive branch is taking every possible action to improve the enforcement of the civil-rights statutes and to eliminate discrimination in Federal employment, in providing Federal services and facilities, and in the armed forces. . . .

The position of the United States in the world today makes it especially urgent that we adopt these measures to secure for all our people their essential rights.

The peoples of the world are faced with the choice of freedom or enslavement, a choice between a form of government which harnesses the state in the service of the individual and a form of government which chains the individual to the needs of the state.

We in the United States are working in company with other nations who share our desire for enduring world peace and who believe with us that, above all else, men must be free. We are striving to build a world family of nations—a world where men may live under governments of their own choosing and under laws of their own making. . . .

To be effective in these efforts, we must protect our civil rights so that by providing all our people with the maximum enjoyment of personal freedom and personal opportunity we shall be a stronger nation— stronger in our leadership, stronger in our moral position, stronger in the deeper satisfactions of united citizenry.

We know that our democracy is not perfect. But we do know that it offers a fuller, freer, happier life to our people than any totalitarian nation has ever offered.

If we wish to inspire the peoples of the world whose freedom is in jeopardy, if we wish to restore hope to those who have already lost their civil liberties, if we wish to fulfill the promise that is ours, we must correct the remaining imperfections in our practice of democracy.

We know the way. We need only the will.

Congressional Record. 80th Cong., 2nd sess., vol. 94, pt. 1 (February 2, 1948): 927–29.

SENATOR JAMES EASTLAND (D-MISSISSIPPI) BLASTS TRUMAN'S CIVIL RIGHTS PROGRAM

Civil rights is a term that appeals to all Americans. The program of the President, however, is not a civil-rights program, but a program which will create a police state in America, destroy our economic system, and usurp the basic rights that make men free. . . .

Southern opposition to this so-called civil-rights program is not an attempt to hold the Negro down. All decent southerners believe in economic equality and better educational opportunities and health facilities for all, regardless of race. The South has made tremendous strides in this direction, in spite of the obstacles which have been placed against us by the Federal Government. By the protective tariff and freight rate discriminations the South has been systematically impoverished. This, more than anything else, has held the Negro down, and it was placed on the statute books by Senators and Congressmen from Northern States. . . .

. . . [T]he crux of the whole program is the destruction of all segregation in America. There is no way to force such a program on Southern people. We have pride of race and will not permit the Federal Government to tamper with our social structure.

. . . [T]he social structure of the South is best for all concerned. We have less inter-racial crime and less racial friction than any section of the country. On the subject of race and segregation there is practically no difference between the views of Southern and Northern people. You of the North believe in and practice segregation for yourselves and families. You, like Southern people, live segregated lives. You are guilty of racial discrimination in the newspaper business. There are thousands of Negro reporters in this country, yet a proportionate 10 percent of your reporters do not come from this race. Ten percent of your executives are not Negroes. You are not to be condemned. It is your civil right to associate with, employ, and work with whom you please. Liberty is dead when you are deprived of this right. . . .

We of the South believe in the equality of the administration of the law for all citizens of every race. We do insist upon the right which we regard as sacred to choose our own associates. Before other sections condemn our views, you must realize that it is an entirely different problem in a community where the population is 5 percent Negro and 95 percent white, and where the population is 50–50. Editors from New York know that in the past few weeks there have been news items in the New York papers which describe conditions in the public schools in New York where the races are mixed in schools in approximately even numbers, and city police are stationed in the corridors to maintain order and discipline in the public schools. Is this an educational pattern that the advocates of the civil rights report desire to foster upon other areas where harmony and good will now prevail?

Our views are not caused by bigotry and intolerance. We have had experience; we know which is best. The whole question was analyzed by General Eisenhower a few days ago when he told a congressional committee which was discussing segregation in the Army, "You can never make people love each other by passing a law."

. . . [T]his program, if enacted, will destroy the inalienable rights of all Americans and will destroy our private enterprise system. Where is the justice in depriving the majority of their inalienable traditional rights to enable members of minority groups to enjoy newly created rights which are in reality nothing but special privileges? The interest and welfare of the United States and all her people of every section are best served by retaining the American economic system and her system of government with all its guarantees of liberty and freedom. That, simply, is the issue here. The South will use every resource to maintain our system and liberties inviolate. In so doing we will best serve our country as a whole.

Congressional Record. 80th Cong., 2d sess., vol. 94, pt. 10 (April 19, 1948): A2337–38.

THE HOUSING ACT (1949)

The Great Depression and World War II brought new construction of housing to a virtual standstill, so that by 1945 a serious housing shortage had developed. Truman made solving the crisis one of his top priorities. As early as September 1945, he asked Congress to consider "the redevelopment of large areas of the blighted and slum sections of our cities so that . . . they may be remade to accommodate families not only of low-income groups as heretofore, but every income group. . . ." [1]

The situation was made more serious by the huge numbers of returning soldiers and sailors, many of whom were eager to settle down and raise families of their own. As a result, by October the United States was facing the biggest housing shortage in its history. Some estimates suggested that as many as ten million Americans were in the market for homes, and the construction industry found it impossible to keep up with demand. Reports indicated that there were 100,000 homeless veterans in Chicago alone. A Los Angeles man wrote to Truman relating how he had met one such veteran, a former medical sergeant, accompanied by his pregnant wife and small child. He had taken them in for the night, as they had nowhere else to go; "Do *something*," he implored the president.[2]

Truman did take some steps toward solving the crisis, asking Congress in 1946 to authorize subsidies to encourage construction of more than two and a half million homes in the next two years. This goal proved too much for the construction industry to handle, however, and the president began to turn toward the idea of having the federal government itself enter the housing business. By the time Truman prepared legislation to this end, however, the 1946 elections had taken place, and the president was forced to work with the Republican majority. Senators Robert A. Taft (R-Ohio), Allen J. Ellender (D-Louisiana), and Robert Wagner (D-New York) eventually put together a bipartisan bill to encourage the construction of hundreds of thousands of inexpensive houses. But while the bill managed to pass the Senate, it ran into opposition in the House. The real estate industry, concerned that government competition would seriously hurt their business, lobbied hard against the bill, and the chairman of the House Banking and Currency Committee, Jesse P. Wolcott (R-Michigan) successfully kept it from coming to a floor vote. Instead, the House passed a substitute bill that placed price ceilings on new homes for veterans and extended more subsidies to homebuilders. Truman signed the bill, but made no secret of the fact that it did not go far enough to suit him.

After the president's successful reelection in 1948, he revisited the issue of housing, which had been one of his major campaign promises. Again he chose to cooperate with Senator Taft, who by this time had emerged as the Republican Party's leading champion of public housing. The result was the Housing Act of 1949, which provided for the construction of more than one million low-cost housing units over the next seven years. It also offered loans and grants for the clearance of inner-city slums, as well as the construction of rural housing.

The bill encountered little opposition in the Senate, but ran into resistance in the House, from largely the same forces that had blocked the Taft-Ellender-Wagner bill the previous year. This time they tried a new tactic by proposing an amendment prohibiting racial discrimination in public housing—they realized that southern Democrats would reject any bill containing such an amendment. However, the proposed amendment failed, the bill passed the House without it, and Truman signed it into law on July 15, 1949.

At the time, the Housing Act was hailed as a great accomplishment, but its actual results were rather disappointing. Far from leading to the construction of a million homes in seven years, only 156,000 had been started by 1952, and only 356,000 were built by 1964. Moreover, many of the units constructed under the bill were of very poor quality, and within a generation would end up quite similar to the slums that the Housing Act had originally promised to clear away. Fortunately, however, private enterprise managed to solve the housing shortage without large-scale government intervention; by 1949, housing made up 62 percent of all new construction, and by 1950, the building trades were putting up more than one and a half million new homes every year.

This section includes a speech by Senator Taft in which the Ohio Republican endorses the housing legislation which he has helped to draft. It also features an address by Representative Herbert A. Meyer (R-Kansas), calling the plan "socialist," and insisting that private enterprise is able to provide adequate housing at lower cost.

NOTES

1. Barton J. Bernstein and Allen J. Matusow, *The Truman Administration: A Documentary History* (New York: Harper & Row, 1966), 93.
2. David McCullough, *Truman* (New York: Simon & Schuster, 1992), 470.

SENATOR ROBERT A. TAFT (R-OHIO) BACKS PUBLIC HOUSING

[. . .] Regardless of all the measures taken, one thing is certain: we have not solved the housing problem. On top of the permanent problem, we have now an emergency situation arising out of the very low construction in the thirties, and the inadequate construction during the war. Undoubtedly, this temporary situation will cure itself in a few years. It takes nearly half a million units a year to provide for new families. Last year we provided 800,000 units and this year about a million units, all through private industry and with little slum elimination, so there has been a net gain of some 700,000 units. In many locations we seem to have caught up; in others, there is a shortage. . . .

The difficulty with the housing problem as compared to food, clothing, medicine, and the like is that shelter is absolutely essential for every family, and yet the cost is out of line with the income of most of the population. Only about half the families in the United States can afford to buy a new house, even of the simplest type. The other half can only buy or live in second-hand houses. . . . [A]s these houses are handed down to families with still less income, they get older and older and finally reach families which can only pay a minimum rent. In 1940, the 6,000,000 substandard homes were rented by 6,000,000 low-income fam-

ilies at rent averaging less than $15 a month. The rent paid is not suffi-
cient to keep the houses in good condition, and they deteriorate further.

Until the cost is reduced, . . . I see no way in which to cure the situation, except by some direct Government action at the lowest income levels to replace slum dwellings with public housing, thereby
supplementing efforts to get more new houses built by private builders
for those with adequate income. . . .

. . . I believe that the Federal Government does have a responsibility
for preventing the suffering and hardship resulting from extreme poverty at any point in the United States. I believe the Federal Government
has an interest in seeing that every child in every State has substantially
equal opportunity, regardless of how poor his parents may be. Under
American principles of freedom, we have built up the highest standard
of living in the history of the world—on the average. But its success is
based on adequate reward for those who are more intelligent, better
workmen, more diligent, or superior in other ways. Some must necessarily fall behind, either from misfortune or lack of ability or their own
fault. . . .

It is said that if we once admit the principle of public housing, we will
have to build a total of from three to six million homes. This I certainly
do not admit. As I have said, the reduction of costs might make all public
housing unnecessary. Other methods of dealing with the housing situation may be developed. Many low-income families have found homes
at low cost or low rental which are satisfactory for their children, particularly in the environs of cities since the automobile has spread the
population over a wide area.

My belief is that if we take the edge off the problem at the bottom,
destroy many of the existing slums and set an example in many neigh-
borhoods, it will not be necessary to extend the public housing program
beyond a total of perhaps a million homes in the course of the next 10
years. I have seen public housing projects in Cleveland, and elsewhere,
which have changed the whole character of the neighborhood. Private
owners have come in and improved all the homes in the neighboring
section, new stores have been built and a standard established extending
far beyond the number of homes covered by public housing. . . .

. . . There is no reason why the public-housing program should compete with or interfere in any way with the private-housing industry, any
more than general hospitals interfere with the practice of the private
physician. I know of no one who does not feel that the major problem
of providing shelter can only be solved by private industry.

I believe that those who are opposed to public housing have done their
own industry a disservice by their indiscriminate and unreasoning opposition. They should promote the plan and spend their energy and their
funds in confining it to its proper scope in making it more of a local

enterprise clearly devoted to the lower-income problem. They have invited more radical housing measures and have assisted the critics of free enterprise in the United States. The American people, in my opinion, are determined to adopt a housing plan which will substantially provide for every child who is born in the United States decent home surroundings, so that he may actually enjoy the freedom and equality of opportunity [for] . . . which our forefathers came to America.

Congressional Record. 81st Cong., 1st sess., vol. 95, pt. 12 (January 27, 1949): A343–45.

REPRESENTATIVE HERBERT A. MEYER (R-KANSAS) ATTACKS "SOCIALIZED HOUSING"

[. . .] This socialized housing bill provides that there will be built in the next 7 years 1,050,000 low-rental family units of public housing, paid for by Federal funds, at a total cost to the Federal taxpayers of $16,000,000,000.

The socialized housing idea arose from the housing shortages that developed during the war when workers and materials were channeled into war work and no new housing was built.

It totally ignores the fact that in 1947 and 1948 private builders constructed 1,785,000 new homes, the greatest number of housing units in 2 years in the history of the country. This construction, incidentally, was encouraged by and built under the Republican Eightieth Congress. . . .

It is well to keep in mind that Government does not make money. Every time the Government issues a check for anything, the money to cover that check must come out of your, the taxpayer's pocket.

. . . [T]his public housing will be owned perpetually by the Government and the local housing authorities. None of these houses or apartments will be sold to private owners. They will be rented at a probable $30 per month for four or five rooms. This rental, in most cases, will be far less than the rental value of the properties.

And so we have a new subsidy, this time to tenants. If past experience means anything, it will cost the Government, which means you, the taxpayer, more to erect this public, socialized housing than if the same work was done by private business. . . .

And so, in my opinion, one of the greatest mistakes this Congress can make is to put the Government into the housing and rental business. It is the same step France took after the First World War when she socialized housing to such an extent that the investment of private funds in building construction practically stopped, with the result today that French cities are largely slums. . . .

Frankly, I don't believe this housing program if it goes through, will greatly increase the number of houses that will be built. Instead, if this socialized-housing bill does go through, housing will cost more money and, in my judgment, we will get less units of housing.

You just can't get housing by legislation. Houses are built by carpenters, painters, bricklayers, and other workmen. Practically every workman in the building trades industry who wants to work, can work every day at the present time in the building of new houses or the repairing of old ones. When the Federal Government goes into the housing business, it will slow down private investment capital which would otherwise go into housing. That has been proven in the past. I repeat, in 1947 and 1948, even with the shortage of material we had then, private builders built 1,785,000 homes, the greatest number of housing units ever built in the history of our country.

If the Government will stay out of this housing business, I predict within a short space of time the housing needs of the people will be met. And, as the cost of materials drops, at prices the people can afford to pay.

This bill would provide homes or apartments for about 4,000,000 people. They would be securing their rent at approximately 50 percent less than normal rentals. In addition, the contracts which must be let, the commissions paid, the jobs created, will work to the benefit of political leaders, both national and local. If you get housing well into politics, it will be a gold mine . . . for the politicians. And there will be additional hordes of political bureaucrats hired out of the taxpayers' money to administer this program. Public housing has already made itself felt in the political field. Where it exists today it is used politically. . . .

I feel the people in my district should not be compelled to pay the rentals of citizens in Chicago, New York, or Jersey City, for instance, and continue to pay it for the next 40 years. Take a look at France and at England where the socialistic government is taxing the people more and more. We don't want that nor do we need it here.

Congressional Record. 81st Cong., 1st sess., vol. 95, pt. 14 (June 21, 1949): A3883–84.

THE NORTH ATLANTIC TREATY (1949)

In the late 1940s, Western Europeans were growing increasingly concerned about the intentions and capabilities of the Soviet Union. When the Soviets refused Marshall Plan aid for themselves and their Eastern European satellites, they created a clear breach between East and West. In late 1947, negotiations over the future of Germany—by this time divided and occupied by U.S., British, French, and Soviet troops—seemed to be going nowhere, while Russian propaganda against the Allies grew more virulent and bitter. The final straw came in February 1948, when a Soviet-backed coup overthrew the democratic government of Czechoslovakia and established a communist state.

These events led several Western European nations to discuss some sort of formal agreement for collective security in the face of a perceived Soviet threat. After some weeks of negotiation, Britain, France, Belgium, the Netherlands, and Luxembourg signed the Brussels Pact, a fifty-year agreement for economic and military cooperation, on March 17, 1948. On that same day, Truman addressed a joint session of Congress in which he denounced the Soviet Union as an enemy of peace, praised the Brussels Pact, and promised to take action that would "extend to the free nations the support which the situation requires."[1]

Senator Arthur Vandenberg (R-Michigan), Truman's ally on questions of foreign policy, applauded the speech and proposed a resolution recommending the creation of regional defense arrangements similar to the Brussels Pact. It further called for "[a]ssociation of the United States by constitutional process, with such regional and other collective arrangements as are based on continuous and effective self-help and mutual aid, and as affect its national security."[2] The Vandenberg Resolution appealed to Democrats and Republicans alike, and when it came before the Senate on June 11, 1948 it passed by a vote of sixty-four to four.

Truman saw the Vandenberg Resolution as a clear sign that the Senate would support participation by the United States in collective security arrangements with Canada and Western Europe. Talks with these nations got underway in July, and although they were put on hold during the 1948 election campaign, they resumed soon after. On March 18, 1949, the terms of the North Atlantic Treaty were made public, and in a ceremony in Washington representatives from Belgium, Canada, Denmark, France, Great Britain, Iceland, Italy, Luxembourg, the Netherlands, Norway, Portugal, and the United States signed the treaty on April 4. It obligated all the signatories to provide assistance if any of them were attacked, but it also contained promises to promote economic development and to settle disputes among the signatories peacefully.

The North Atlantic Treaty came before the Senate for ratification that summer, and met with resistance from many of the same individuals who had opposed aid to Greece and Turkey and the Marshall Plan. Senator Robert A. Taft (R-Ohio) argued that it would commit the United States to fight a war in which there might be no vital national interest at stake. Henry Wallace, still smarting from his overwhelming defeat in the 1948 election, claimed that the pact would be an intolerable insult to the Soviet Union. Nevertheless, theirs were isolated voices by mid-1949, and the treaty passed by a vote of eighty-two to thirteen. Bipartisanship in foreign policy had triumphed yet again.

The fight over the North Atlantic Treaty Organization (or NATO, as it came to be better known), however, did not stop there. In January 1951 Senator Taft, upset over the Truman administration's handling of the war in Korea, proposed legislation requiring congressional authorization before U.S. forces could be sent out of the country. He specifically hoped to minimize the military commitment to NATO, for which he thought the Western Europeans should bear the largest responsibility. He hoped that, in any war with the Soviet bloc, the United States could limit its involvement to naval and air support. Taft and his allies, who included Senator William F. Knowland (R-California), Senator John Bricker (R-Ohio), Senator Kenneth Wherry (R-Nebraska), and former president Herbert Hoover, feared that the cold war was growing too expensive, and that it was concentrating too much authority over foreign policy in the hands of the executive branch.

The battle over Taft's proposal soon became known as the Great Debate, and it would last throughout much of the remainder of Truman's presidency. Ultimately the Senate adopted a resolution sponsored by Wherry, which gave the president the power to dispatch up to four divisions of U.S. troops to Europe without congressional approval. President Truman accepted this as a compromise, hailing it as "further evidence that the country stands firm in its support of the North Atlantic Treaty."[3]

NATO stands as one of the Truman administration's most enduring legacies; indeed, it has even managed to outlive the Soviet threat that it was designed to resist. And while it is debatable how much value it had in deterring the Soviet Union from attacking the West, it has served to create a sense of community among its member nations. Before 1949, war was a regular feature of European politics, but since then, the thought of armed conflict among the nations of Western and Central Europe has been practically unimaginable. For that happy outcome, the North Atlantic Treaty can take at least some of the credit.

This section features excerpts from Truman's message urging the Senate to ratify the North Atlantic Treaty, and a radio address by Taft in which the Ohio Republican explains why he voted against ratification.

NOTES

1. Susan M. Hartmann, *Truman and the 80th Congress* (Columbia: University of Missouri Press, 1971), 173.

2. Barton J. Bernstein and Allen J. Matusow, *The Truman Administration: A Documentary History* (New York: Harper & Row, 1966), 274–75.

3. Donald R. McCoy, *The Presidency of Harry S. Truman* (Lawrence: University Press of Kansas, 1984), 260.

TRUMAN ASKS THE SENATE TO RATIFY THE NORTH ATLANTIC TREATY

[...] This treaty is an expression of the desire of the people of the United States for peace and security, for the continuing opportunity to live and work in freedom.

Events in this century have taught us that we cannot achieve peace independently. The world has grown too small. The oceans to our east and west no longer protect us from the reach of brutality and aggression.

We have also learned—learned in blood and conflict—that if we are to achieve peace we must work for peace.

This knowledge has made us determined to do everything we can to insure that peace is maintained. We have not arrived at this decision lightly or without recognition of the effort it entails. But we cannot escape the great responsibility that goes with our stature in the world. Every action of this nation in recent years has demonstrated the overwhelming will of our people that the strength and influence of the United States shall be used in the cause of peace, justice, and freedom.

In this determination, our people wholeheartedly accepted the Charter of the United Nations in 1945. Since then, we have worked unceasingly to reach international agreement through the United Nations and to make the United Nations a more effective instrument for its mighty task.

In the last year we have embarked on a great cooperative enterprise with the free nations of Europe to restore the vitality of the European economy—so important to the prosperity and peace of our country and the world.

The North Atlantic treaty is further evidence of our determination to work for a peaceful world. It is in accord with the action of the Senate last June when it signified its approval of our country's associating itself in peace time with countries outside the Western Hemisphere in collective arrangements, within the framework of the United Nations Charter, designed to safeguard peace and security.

The twelve nations which have signed this treaty undertake to exercise their right of collective or individual self-defense against armed attack, in accordance with Article 51 of the United Nations Charter, and subject to such measures as the Security Council may take to maintain and restore international peace and security. The treaty makes clear the determination of the people of the United States and of our neighbors in the North Atlantic community to do their utmost to maintain peace with justice and to take such action as they may deem necessary if the peace is broken.

The people of the North Atlantic community have seen solemn agreements, designed to assure peace and the rights of small nations, broken one by one and the people of those nations deprived of freedom by terror and oppression. They are resolved that their nations shall not, one by one, suffer the same fate.

The nations signing this treaty share a common heritage of democracy, individual liberty and the rule of law. The American members of the North Atlantic community stem directly from the European members in tradition and in love of freedom. We have joined together in the progressive development of free institutions, and we have shared our moral and material strength in the present task of rebuilding from the devastation of war.

The security and welfare of each member of the community depend upon the security and welfare of all. None of us alone can achieve economic prosperity or military security. None of us alone can assure the continuance of freedom.

Together, our joint strength is of tremendous significance to the future of free men in every part of the world. For this treaty is clear evidence that differences in language and in economic and political systems are no real bar to the effective association of nations devoted to the great principles of human freedom and justice.

This treaty is only one step—although a long one—on the road to peace. No single action, no matter how significant, will achieve peace. We must continue to work patiently and carefully, advancing with practical, realistic steps in the light of circumstances and events as they occur, building the structure of peace soundly and solidly.

I believe that the North Atlantic treaty is such a step, based on the realities of the situation we face today and framed within the terms of the United Nations charter and Constitution of the United States.

In the conviction that the North Atlantic treaty is a great advance toward fulfillment of the unconquerable will of the people of the United States to achieve a just and enduring peace, I request the advice and consent of the Senate to its ratification.

Congressional Record. 81st Cong., 1st sess., vol. 95, pt. 4 (April 12, 1949): 4354–55.

SENATOR ROBERT A. TAFT (R-OHIO) CRITICIZES THE NORTH ATLANTIC TREATY

[. . .] Why did I vote against the Atlantic Pact? I wanted to vote for it—at least I wanted to vote to let Russia know that if she attacked western Europe, the United States would be in the war. I believe that would be a deterrent to war. . . . We issued just this warning in the Monroe Doctrine, and though we were a much less powerful nation, it prevented aggression against Central and South America. That was only a President's message to Congress, and there were no treaty obligations, and no arms for other nations. But it was one of the most effective peace measures in the history of the world. I would favor a Monroe Doctrine for western Europe.

But the Atlantic Pact goes much further. It obligates us to go to war if at any time during the next 20 years anyone makes an armed attack on any of the 12 nations. Under the Monroe Doctrine we could change our policy at any time. We could judge whether perhaps one of the countries had given cause for the attack. Only Congress could declare a war in pursuance of the doctrine. Under the new pact the President can take us into war without Congress. But, above all the treaty is a part of a much larger program by which we arm all these nations against Russia. . . . A joint military program has already been made. . . . It thus becomes an offensive and defensive military alliance against Russia. I believe our foreign policy should be aimed primarily at security and peace, and I believe such an alliance is more likely to produce war than peace. A third world war would be the greatest tragedy the world has ever suffered. Even if we won the war, we this time would probably suffer tremendous destruction, our economic system would be crippled, and we would lose our liberties and free system just as the Second World War destroyed the free systems of Europe. It might easily destroy civilization on this earth. . . .

There is another consideration. If we undertake to arm all the nations around Russia from Norway on the north to Turkey on the south, and Russia sees itself ringed about gradually by so-called defensive arms from Norway and Denmark to Turkey and Greece, it may form a different opinion. It may decide that the arming of western Europe, regardless of its present purpose, looks to an attack upon Russia. Its view may be unreasonable, and I think it is. But from the Russian standpoint it may not seem unreasonable. They may well decide that if war is the certain result, that war might better occur now rather than after the arming of Europe is completed. . . .

How would we feel if Russia undertook to arm a country on our border; Mexico, for instance?

Furthermore, can we afford this new project of foreign assistance? I think I am as much against Communist aggression as anyone, both at home and abroad; certainly more than a State Department which has let the Communists overrun all of China. . . . But we can't let them scare us into bankruptcy and the surrender of all liberty, or let them determine our foreign policies. We are already spending $15,000,000,000 on our armed forces and have the most powerful Air Force in the world and the only atomic bomb. That, and our determination to go to war if Europe is attacked, ought to be sufficient to deter an attack by armed force.

We are spending $7,000,000,000 a year on economic aid to build up those countries to a condition of prosperity where communism cannot make internal progress. Shall we start another project whose cost is incalculable, at the very time when we have a deficit of 1,800,000,000 dollars and a prospective deficit of three to five billion? The one essential defense against communism is to keep this country financially and economically sound. If the President is unwilling to recommend more taxes for fear of creating a depression, then we must have reached the limit of our taxpaying ability and we ought not to start a new and unnecessary building project. . . .

But, finally, I believe there is only one real hope of peace in the world to come—an association of nations binding itself to abide by a law governing nations and administered by a court of legal justice. Such a judicial finding must not be subject to veto by any nation and there must be an international force to enforce the court's decree. Such a plan can only succeed if the public opinion of the world is educated to insist on the enforcement of justice.

The United Nations looks in this direction but it can be improved and should be. This pact might have set up such a system between the nations of western Europe. It unfortunately did not do so. We should undertake to make it a model to which the United Nations may later conform. But as set up, it is a step backward—a military alliance of the old type where we have to come to each others' assistance no matter who is to blame, and with ourselves the judges of the law.

Congressional Record. 81st Cong., 1st sess., vol. 95, pt. 15 (July 26, 1949): A4785–86.

NATIONAL HEALTH INSURANCE (1949)

The modern health care debate has its origins in World War II and its immediate aftermath. During the war, the Office of Price Administration's wage and price controls prevented most employers from raising the pay of their workers. At the same time, the shortage of manpower (due to the fact that most able-bodied young men were in the armed forces) often forced employers to compete for a limited pool of employees. But since they couldn't offer higher wages, they had to find other ways to attract new workers. Pension plans and stock options were popular methods, but perhaps the most common benefit extended to employees during the war was health insurance. Companies would pay their workers' insurance premiums, allowing them to see their doctors or stay in hospitals for a fraction of what they would pay if they had to assume the cost of their own health care.

Health insurance was a tremendous help to those who had it, but it also had negative effects on those who did not. The increased affordability of medical care for those with insurance raised the demand, and therefore drove up costs for everyone, whether they had insurance or not. Demand further increased with the return of millions of military personnel at the end of the war. Thanks to the GI Bill of 1944, the federal government picked up the cost of their health care, which also caused the prices of doctors' appointments and hospital stays to rise. Combined with the general inflation of the post–World War II period, the situation seemed quite serious.

Truman recognized that rising costs were making it difficult for millions of Americans to receive quality medical care. He was also shocked at the numbers of those deemed unfit for service in the armed forces due to illness—as many as 30 percent, according to the Selective Service Administration. Therefore, in November 1945, he told the Congress that he hoped to expand on Roosevelt's New Deal by instituting a comprehensive program to improve the nation's health. He proposed new federal spending to build hospitals and attract doctors to poorer parts of the country, to expand public health programs, and to subsidize medical research. More controversially, he called for a system of compulsory medical insurance to be funded through payroll deductions. Under this system, all citizens would be provided with medical and hospital service regardless of their ability to pay.

While the speech attracted substantial press attention at the time, Congress did not seem particularly interested in taking up the issue of health care. Senators Robert Wagner (D-New York) and James E. Murray (D-Montana) sponsored a bill that embodied most of Truman's program, but it never made it beyond the Senate Committee on Education and Labor.

Health care remained on the back burner for a year and a half, as more pressing matters occupied the president's attention. However, in May 1947, Truman sent a message to Congress urging that it give immediate consideration to his plan of national health insurance. He must have realized that the chances of the Republican-dominated Congress of 1947–1948 adopting the measure were slim. However, he also knew that he could derive political benefit from attacking the GOP for failing to address the issue. He was particularly concerned because a group of Republican senators—Robert A. Taft (R-Ohio), Joseph H. Ball (R-Minnesota), and Forrest C. Donnell (R-Missouri)—had only recently introduced a measure that would have provided federal assistance for health care to the poor only. Truman hoped to convince the voters that his own plan—which was for a truly national system—was a better solution to rising medical costs.

Had Congress passed the Taft-Ball-Donnell plan, it is likely that much of the force behind the president's proposals would have been depleted.

As it stood, however, no action was taken on it. At the same time, the Republican leadership loudly denounced Truman's plan as "socialized medicine," arguing that it would ultimately place doctors and hospitals under government control. They were seconded in this by the American Medical Association, which lobbied long and hard to stop national health insurance.

The Republican failure to adopt any health care measure in 1947 and 1948 handed Truman a powerful campaign issue, and he spent much of his time in the fall of 1948 attacking the "do-nothing" Congress. While it is impossible to say whether health care had any real impact on the presidential election, it is certain that his anti-Republican strategy helped return him to office for a second term. In any case, national health insurance was a major element in the Fair Deal program that he laid out in early 1949. Yet, although Democrats now controlled both houses of Congress, there was little enthusiasm for Truman's plan. The American Medical Association redoubled its efforts to block it, and enough Democrats joined the Republicans in opposition that it stood no chance.

By the time the Korean War broke out in June 1950, the president had to admit that compulsory national health insurance would not be enacted during his presidency. However, he did make some effort to ensure that future administrations might take up the idea. At the end of 1951, he created the Commission on the Health Needs of the Nation, and a year later it released its findings in a five-volume report. The commission concluded that the federal government should take steps to ensure that all Americans had access to decent and reasonably priced health care. This report would ultimately play a role in the passage of Medicare and Medicaid in 1965, during the presidency of Lyndon Johnson.

This section features excerpts from Truman's message to Congress calling for the creation of a federal health insurance system. It also includes a response by Representative A. L. Miller, a Nebraska Republican who labels the Truman proposal "socialized medicine."

TRUMAN ASKS CONGRESS FOR A NATIONAL HEALTH INSURANCE PROGRAM

[. . .] We are in an era of startling medical progress. The technical resources available to the physician are tremendously greater than a generation ago. But to make these resources effective, he must use much more complicated, more exact equipment. He must turn to specialized laboratories and technicians for help. He must apply new techniques and must secure more effective drugs and appliances.

As a Nation we have not yet succeeded in making the benefits of these scientific advances available to all those who need them. The best hospitals, the finest research laboratories, and the most skillful physicians are of no value to those who cannot obtain their services.

Now that we have the medical knowledge that can bring good health within our reach to a degree heretofore undreamed of, we must improve the means for putting that knowledge to practical use. Good health is the foundation of a Nation's strength. It is also the foundation upon which a better standard of living can be built for individuals. To see that our people actually enjoy the good health that medical science knows how to provide is one of the great challenges to our democracy. . . .

The traditional method of paying for medical care cannot meet the health needs of today. As medical education and practice have become better, they have become more specialized and at the same time more expensive. As treatment has become more expensive, families have found it more and more difficult to meet the extraordinary costs of accidents, serious illness, or major surgery. Thus, at the same time that our knowledge of how to provide medical care is at its highest point, more and more people are unable to afford it. It is no longer just the poor who are unable to pay for all the medical care they need—such care is now beyond the means of all but the upper income groups.

This is an anomalous situation. It can and should be met through social insurance. Under such a system, regular contributions to the insurance fund will replace irregular, often overwhelming, family outlays for medical care. . . .

The only fair and effective means to assure adequate medical care through insurance is to build on the pattern of our existing social-insurance plans. As in the case of those plans, we should seek to include as many persons as possible within the health-insurance system, so that more may benefit and costs can be more widely shared.

Health insurance is a method of paying for medical care. It will not require doctors to become employees of the Government. It will not disturb the freedom of doctors and hospitals to determine the nature and extent of treatment to be given. It will not interfere with the personal relationship between doctor and patient. Under such a plan, patients will remain free to choose their own doctors, and doctors will remain free to accept or reject patients. Moreover, patients, doctors, and hospitals will remain free to make their own arrangements for care outside the insurance system if they so choose. . . .

Many people are concerned about the cost of a national health program. The truth is that it will save a great deal more than it costs. We are already paying about 4 percent of our national income for health care. More and better care can be obtained for this same amount of money under the program I am recommending. Furthermore we can and should invest additional amounts in an adequate health program—for the additional investment will more than pay for itself.

The real cost of our present inadequate medical care is not measured merely by doctors' bills and hospital bills. The real cost to society is in unnecessary human suffering and the yearly loss of hundreds of millions of productive working days. To the individual the real costs are the shattering of family budgets, the disruption of family life, the suffering and disabilities, the permanent physical impairments left by crippling diseases, and the deaths each year of tens of thousands of persons who might have lived. This is the price we are now paying for inadequate medical care.

It is plain common sense that we should not permit these needless costs to continue when we have it within our power to reduce them with a practical health program. Where there are differences remaining as to the details of the program we should not permit these differences to stand in the way of our going forward. They should be threshed out with honesty and tolerance, as is our democratic fashion. We should enact the best possible program and then all of us should get behind it to make it work.

We are striving in this country to see that the strength and flexibility of our political and economic institutions are used to bring the greatest possible good to our people. I consider this health program as part of that endeavor—to adjust to modern conditions without losing traditional values, to bring to the people of this country the full enjoyment of the benefits which our freedom makes possible.

Congressional Record. 81st Cong., 1st sess., vol. 95, pt. 4 (April 22, 1949): 4936–38.

REPRESENTATIVE A. L. MILLER (R-NEBRASKA) ATTACKS COMPULSORY HEALTH INSURANCE

[. . .] Compulsory health insurance is socialized medicine pure and simple and it would mean nationalizing the health services of the country.

Compulsory health insurance is political distribution of the health services. It is an old nostrum done up to look like an attractive package. It would put Federal Government bureaucrats and all of their bungling inefficiency into the sick rooms and the hospitals of the Nation. . . .

The cost of administering a compulsory health plan would be enormous. It would mean the creation of another gigantic Government agency which would have regional administrators in every city, town and village, to be appointed like a postmaster. These local czars, appointed from far-away Washington, would function much like OPA directors did during the war. Thus it would be impossible to keep politics out of the medical care system. Inevitably private information on a patient's health would become public records available for the scrutiny of the type of politician who hangs around the courthouse. . . .

We all know that America today enjoys the highest standards of medical care in the world. In relation to our total population we have more doctors, dentists, nurses, and hospital technicians than any other nation. We have more hospital beds than any other nation. Our hospital equipment and laboratory machinery is the finest in the world. The type of research being carried on in this country has no equal in any part of the world. It will continue to progress if unhampered by Government regulation.

Today there are some 60,000,000 Americans participating in various voluntary medical-care plans. In addition to this there are industrial, fraternal, and labor health plans, and private-group clinics. There are approximately 100 nonprofit, prepaid medical-care plans operating in the United States. The people participating in these plans buy as much protection as they wish to pay for. They have written contracts telling them exactly what they are entitled to receive for their voluntary insurance payments. Prepaid voluntary insurance plans have been growing rapidly. This is the traditional American way of thrift and honest acceptance of responsibility for one's family. Our Socialist planners would wipe out all this great advance toward solvent prepayment medical insurance.

Advocates of this compulsory health plan allege that 325,000 persons die needlessly every year. They ignore the fact that most of these people do not die because of the lack of the best medical care in the world but in spite of it.

Every physician has seen many people die of conditions that are easily curable in others and are at a loss to explain why they did not respond to treatment that proved effective in other cases.

They do not tell you that 40,000 died of accidents which any form of health insurance could not prevent. Nor did they say that 120,000 died of communicable diseases, although this cause of death is being reduced every year by the outstanding accomplishments of American medicine. . . .

America today enjoys better health than the people of any other country on the face of the globe. The average span of life in the United States has increased from 49 years in 1900 to 67 years in 1948. Our mortality rate established an all time low in 1948, less than 10 for each 1,000 population. We are blessed with more resources for scientific research than any other nation. Up to date we have enjoyed a freedom which has kept the medical profession and scientific development unfettered by political machines and their handcuffs.

Now I ask, why change all this, why toss overboard the American health way in favor of a foreign plan with its record of consistent failure in every country it has been tried?

I am going to be told that the compulsory health insurance scheme is not socialized medicine. I say it is. It is because the Government proposes to collect the tax, control the money, determine the services, maintain the records, and lay down the regulations for the patient and the doctor to participate in the program. The Government would control not only the medical and dental professions but all the hospitals, clinics, nursing and all allied professions.

When the Government dominates the medical affairs of every citizen from the Central Government in Washington down to the grass roots, then it is socialism and I challenge any one to honestly call it anything else. . . .

Compulsory health insurance would make an assembly line of medical care. It might be fine for automobile production but it is scarcely the way to tend to the health of our people. Government control of medicine with its consequent OPA means of operation would find the fingers of the Nation's doctors covered with ink instead of iodine. . . .

I say to you again that socialized medicine is political medicine. It would regiment not only the medical profession but would regiment the sick and the suffering. It would force the patient into a mechanical goose step automatically following the tune being played in Washington. It is not for America.

Congressional Record. 81st Cong., 1st Sess., vol. 95, pt. 9 (August 22, 1949): 12003–5.

POINT FOUR (1949)

Foreign policy was the focus of Truman's second inaugural address in January 1949. In that speech, he stressed the danger of global communism, and laid out four basic elements of his strategy for meeting that threat. The first was unfailing support for the United Nations; the second a continuation of programs (such as the Marshall Plan) aimed at global economic recovery; the third a mutual security agreement (the North Atlantic Treaty) to protect the free world.

So far, the speech had offered little that was new. However, the president then discussed the final component to the strategy—"a bold new program for making the benefits of our scientific advances and industrial progress available for the improvement and growth of underdeveloped areas."[1] Scientists, technicians, and other experts would be sent to poor countries to share advanced technologies. The government would also encourage capital investment in less-developed nations. Since it was listed as the fourth element of his four-point plan, the press quickly dubbed the proposal "Point Four."

The idea behind "Point Four" originated with Benjamin Hardy, who worked in the Office of Public Affairs in the State Department. When his own office failed to show any interest in the plan, he discussed it with Clark Clifford, one of Truman's closest and most trusted advisors. Clifford was enthusiastic about the plan, mainly because he had been looking for some dramatic new initiative that could be included in the inaugural address. The president also liked it, as did his audience at the speech—the proposal met with sustained applause. The press praised it as well, hailing it as a " 'Fair Deal' Plan for the World." The *New York Times* claimed that not only Franklin Roosevelt would have approved, but also Woodrow Wilson, Theodore Roosevelt, and even Abraham Lincoln.[2]

Nevertheless, to make a good speech was one thing; to design an effective program quite another. Point Four ran into immediate resistance from the new secretary of state, Dean Acheson, who only heard about it when Truman gave his speech. He, as well as many other high-ranking diplomats, did not see the transfer of technology as the proper function of the State Department. The result was a battle within the administration that went on throughout the winter and spring of 1949. It was only in June that the president asked Congress to pass specific legislation embodying the plan's goals. Moreover, even that bill seemed far more modest than the inaugural speech had suggested, appropriating only $45 million to promote technical, scientific, and economic self-help programs in poor countries.

Congress realized that the administration was not united behind Point Four, and as a result they did not proceed particularly quickly in considering it. In addition, its support in Congress was lukewarm at best; to Republicans, and even to many Democrats, it seemed like a waste of money. Finally, in the spring of 1950—well over a year after Truman first proposed it—the program appeared as part of the Foreign Economic Assistance Act of 1950, a bill designed to continue a number of other foreign aid measures. Truman dutifully signed the legislation in June, despite the fact that it authorized only $27 million for the program.

Yet Point Four remained unpopular in Congress, as senators and congressmen of both parties claimed to be unable to see how it benefited the country militarily or diplomatically. Two months after Truman signed the Foreign Economic Assistance Act, therefore, Congress reduced the funding for the program to a mere $10 million. However, the president made a personal appeal to key members, writing Speaker of the House Sam Rayburn that he could imagine "no more tragic blunder" than to eviscerate Point Four.[3] His appeal proved effective, for Congress eventually authorized $34.5 million.

The program finally began to function in 1951, under the direction of Henry G. Bennett of the Oklahoma Agricultural and Mechanical College.

Bennett administered it enthusiastically and intelligently, but after a promising start he was killed in an airplane crash later that year. Thereafter Point Four stagnated, faced with an indifferent State Department and an occasionally hostile Congress. It never really achieved the ambitious goals that Truman had laid out for it in 1949, although some aspects of the program would find their way into the plan for the Peace Corps, established during the Kennedy administration.

This section includes excerpts from a 1950 speech by Truman in which he emphasizes the importance of aiding foreign countries. It also features an address by Spruille Braden, formerly U.S. ambassador to Argentina and Cuba, who claims that the program is too costly, and that the United States should solve its domestic problems before extending aid to less developed countries.

NOTES

1. Donald R. McCoy, *The Presidency of Harry S. Truman* (Lawrence: University Press of Kansas, 1984), 192.
2. David McCullough, *Truman* (New York: Simon & Schuster, 1992), 731.
3. McCoy, *Presidency*, 210.

TRUMAN ARGUES FOR AID TO UNDERDEVELOPED COUNTRIES

[. . .] It is hard for us to realize just how bad economic conditions are for many peoples of the world. Famine, disease, and poverty are the scourge of vast areas of the globe. Hundreds of millions of people in Asia, for example, have a life expectancy of 30 years or less. That's what this country had when the people landed at Jamestown. Many of these people live on in adequate diets, unable to perform the tasks necessary to earn their daily bread. Animal plagues and plant pests carry away their crops and their livestock. Misuse of natural resources exposes their land to flood and drought.

Conditions such as this are the seedbed of political unrest and instability. They are a threat to the security and growth of free institutions everywhere. It is in areas where these conditions exist that communism makes its greatest inroads. The people of these areas are eagerly seeking better living conditions. The Communists are attempting to turn the honest dissatisfaction of these people with their present conditions into support for Communist efforts to dominate their nations.

In addition to these attempts at persuasion, the Communists in these countries use the weapon of fear. They constantly threaten internal violence and armed aggression. . . .

It is essential that we do everything we can to prevent such aggression and to enforce the principles of the United Nations Charter. We must and we shall give every possible assistance to people who are determined to maintain their independence. We must counteract the Communist weapon of fear.

But we must not be misled into thinking that our only task is to create defenses against aggression. Our whole purpose in creating a strong defense is to permit us to carry on the great constructive tasks of peace. Behind the shield of a strong defense we must continue to work to bring about better living conditions in the free nations.

Particularly in the underdeveloped areas of the world we must work cooperatively with local governments which are seeking to improve the welfare of their people. We must help them to help themselves. We must aid them to make progress in agriculture, in industry, in health, and in the education of their children. Such progress will increase their strength and their independence.

The growing strength of these countries is important to the defense of all free nations against Communist aggression. It is important to the economic progress of the free world. And these things are good for us as well as good for them.

For these reasons I recommended in my inaugural address the program that has become known as point 4. The Congress authorized technical assistance to underprivileged areas under this program. This new law marked the congressional endorsement of a practical and sensible course of action that can have tremendous benefits for the future of the world. . . .

Point 4 is not new—and should not become a matter for partisan differences of opinion. However, some critics have attempted to ridicule point 4 as a do-good measure; others have said it is a waste of money. This is the most foolish kind of shortsightedness. If we fail to carry out a vigorous point 4 program we run the risk of losing to communism, by default, hundreds of millions of people who now look to us for help in their struggle against hunger and despair. . . .

Point 4 is a successor to the old colonialism idea, the exploiting idea of the middle seventeenth, eighteenth, and nineteenth centuries. We want to have a prosperous world that will be interested in buying the immense amount of surplus things that we are going to have to sell. And now to do that they have got to have something to give back to us in order that they can buy our goods. I want to keep this factory organization of ours going at full tilt.

In order to do that we must help these people to help themselves.

Point 4 is an investment in a peaceful and prosperous world. It is a program which will bring increasing results over the years. It will bring about a chain reaction in economic development. It will serve to create economic health where poverty existed, and to equip the people of underdeveloped areas to carry forward their economic gains and preserve their independence. . . .

All our citizens must play a part in making the point 4 program a success. Our missionary groups, our philanthropic, and charitable agencies, must continue the efforts they have been making over the years for the improvement of conditions in foreign lands.

Our young people can find careers in the pioneering work of bringing technical assistance to these countries. Our unions and our business organizations should enlarge their foreign contracts and bring the benefits of their experience to less developed countries. . . .

Our point 4 program and the work of the United Nations are constructive ways to build the kind of world where all nations can live in peaceful prosperity, dedicated to the purpose of creating better lives for their people. We support this program because we seek a peaceful world, and a free world, where all men can live as good neighbors.

Congressional Record. 81st Cong., 2nd sess., vol. 96, pt. 16 (June 29, 1950): A4785–87.

FORMER AMBASSADOR SPRUILLE BRADEN QUESTIONS THE POINT FOUR PROGRAM

[. . .] [W]ith the world in its desperate economic and political straits, this is no time for our Government to dash forth in pursuit of utopias, otherwise to indulge in misguided endeavors or to heap further taxes on an already overspent Nation in order to finance global panaceas. Yet, in effect, that is exactly what the American people from a relatively small beginning may gradually, perhaps unwittingly, slip into doing, led astray by their emotions and by the glittering enticements attributed to the so-called bold new program. . . .

Before waxing overbold in aspiration by devising methods and expedients for the alleviation of ills common to all humanity, would it not be wise first to cure our own ailments? In this way we might set a good example for others to follow, we could better learn how later on effectively to assist our neighbors, and, after all, charity does begin at home.

Everything the point IV program proposes to do for the undeveloped areas of the earth should also be done in and for this country. Millions of our fellow citizens need and wish to realize their yearnings for a better life; to have more and better food, clothing, housing and more mechanical power to lighten their burdens; in short, to raise substantially their standards of living.

In contrast with the manifold divergencies, obstacles and risks which will be encountered in trying to spread our industrial and scientific techniques abroad, it would be easier first to attack this huge job to be done at home. Here we have a more or less homogeneous population, already possessing technical know-how or, at least, a ready adaptability thereto. We enjoy general uniformity of laws, customs and principles and, above all, a firm belief in our way of life—in the private competitive enterprise system. . . .

It is pertinent to observe that American enterprises cannot afford to give away their scientific and industrial knowledge, experience, and techniques for nothing; payment must be made for patents and know-how. Nor can they permit these things to be misused by reason of ignorance or for improper ends.

On the other hand, the United States Government mostly does not possess those things and, therefore, cannot supply them. To the extent that foreigners, unaware of this fact, are disappointed in their expectations, they will accuse Washington of bad faith. However, this probably won't stop the bureaucrats, since no government organ, I ever heard of, has yet abstained from any function because it acknowledged itself to be ignorant or incompetent.

Therefore, unless Congress rigidly circumscribes governmental operations under point IV, there is grave danger that the appropriations required for the program, within a surprisingly short time, will become enormous. Frequently they will be of a speculative nature. To employ United States taxpayers' money in such ventures would be unprincipled and unsound; it would be counter to our democratic-capitalistic tenets; it would involve us in the worst sort of dollar diplomacy; it would turn over the investment of our savings to bureaucrats, ill-equipped for the task and whose responsibilities for the errors they may commit would be blurred; and it would deprive our citizens of their fundamental right to choose their own investments. . . .

In the development of the Truman program, it is imperative at all times to bear certain verities in mind:

(a) It is dangerous to generalize. Each country and area must be studied separately and plans adjusted to the specific conditions prevailing therein, before an attempt is made to formulate a coordinated general plan.

(b) It is a common error to attribute unlimited resources to so-called undeveloped areas, as for instance Latin America, when actually extensive investigations in each country have already proven that the alleged riches are not readily at hand.

(c) Our scientific advances and industrial or technical procedures are not universally applicable. A small mine in the Andes may be worked profitably by local methods; whereas it would be a losing proposition for American operators.

(d) The exploration, development, and working of such large natural resources as do exist can be performed successfully only by private enterprise. Government, and still more international government, is incapable of doing the job.

(e) As previously noted, no attempts should be made to industrialize areas which are unsuitable by reason of scarcity of raw materials, inadequate or incompetent labor, meager markets, or other adverse conditions.

(f) Any positive program to succeed must be premised on the proposition that private property rights are human rights and if they are lost all freedoms will perish. . . .

If I have sounded several notes of caution, it is precisely because President Truman's idea—his ultimate objective—is so splendid that we must not . . . fail by being overbold in aspiration or building castles in the air. Nothing can be so foolish as empty boldness.

The most inspiring incentive which can be given toward forwarding this program would be for the United States itself to stop the insidious drift toward a collectivist economy which now threatens to smother the American way of life; to put our own house in order; to restrict Government to its proper functions; and to return to the free private competitive enterprise system which respects economic rights and rewards honesty, hard work, and intelligence with profits, higher standards of living, and general well-being.

Congressional Record. 81st Cong., 1st sess., vol. 95, pt. 15 (August 23, 1949): A5486–88.

INTERVENTION IN KOREA (1950)

In the closing days of World War II in Asia, Soviet armies quickly overran Manchuria, a part of China that had been occupied by the Japanese since 1931. They then approached Korea, which had once been an independent country but had been part of the Japanese Empire since the turn of the century. The United States and the Soviet Union agreed that Korea would return to its independent status after the war, but the speed of the Russian advance was disturbing. If the Soviets managed to liberate Korea from the Japanese, would they continue to dominate the country as they appeared ready to do in Eastern Europe?

In an effort to stabilize the situation, the State Department offered the Soviets a deal. The country would be temporarily divided into zones of occupation, with the Russians in the North and the Americans in the

South. Eventually there would be free elections held under the super-vision of the United Nations, the country would be reunited, and both sides would withdraw their forces. The Soviets accepted, and halted their advance at the forty-ninth parallel. However, over the next several years, they grew increasingly unwilling to work with the United States, and they set up their own "People's Republic" in North Korea under the leadership of Kim Il-Sung. When the time for elections arrived in spring 1948, the Soviet premier, Joseph Stalin, refused to participate, so they were held in the South alone. Syngman Rhee became the president of the new American-backed Republic of Korea.

Over the next two years, relations between North and South Korea grew increasingly strained, as each side called for the reunification of the country, but only on its own terms. The U.S. Congress voted to send economic and military aid to the South, while the Soviets helped North Korea to develop a modern army. Kim Il-Sung repeatedly sought per-mission from Stalin to launch an invasion of the South, but the Russian leader only gave his approval after learning of a speech by U.S. Secretary of State Dean Acheson which seemed to suggest that the United States would not fight to defend South Korea.

On June 24, 1950, North Korean forces crossed the border into South Korea. Americans immediately believed that Stalin had masterminded the attack. Nevertheless, it came as a complete surprise, since few be-lieved that Korea was important enough to Stalin for him to risk starting a global war. On the following day, the United Nations Security Council voted to demand an immediate cease-fire and a North Korean with-drawal from the South. Ordinarily, the Soviets would have vetoed such a proposal, but at the time their delegation was boycotting the UN's proceedings.

Back in Washington, Truman and his advisors all agreed that Stalin was using Korea as a test. If the West failed to stop the conquest of South Korea, then this would suggest that he might try similar "pinprick" at-tacks elsewhere in Asia, or perhaps even in Europe. To prevent this, the United States and its allies would have to meet the aggression with a strong response, so on June 27, Truman ordered American troops stationed in Japan to move to South Korea to resist the attack. The pres-ident then successfully pressed the United Nations to send troops as well.

Truman's quick response to the invasion met with initial support from Republicans and Democrats on Capitol Hill; even Senator Robert Taft (R-Ohio), who often opposed Truman's initiatives, indicated his approval. In early July, the president named General Douglas MacArthur as overall commander of UN forces in Asia, and by the end of the year no less than sixteen countries had committed troops to the defense of Korea. In September, MacArthur engineered a brilliant amphibious attack at Inchon that virtually destroyed the North Korean army and ended the threat to South Korea.

However, by this time congressional support for the war had begun to waver. Truman at no point consulted Congress on any of the actions he had taken thus far, which annoyed members of both parties. Some began to argue that Secretary of State Acheson's address had incited the North Koreans to attack, so that ultimately the administration was to blame for the war. Criticism grew even more intense when units of the Chinese army charged over the border into North Korea in late November. UN and South Korean forces were soon in full retreat. Republicans began talking about using the atomic bomb, or making use of Chinese Nationalist troops stationed on Taiwan.

By the following spring, the situation had become fairly stabilized, and the war settled into a stalemate with little movement on either side. The conflict grew increasingly unpopular at home, as many began to question what exactly they were fighting for. Korea seemed very far away, and it appeared that victory was nowhere in sight. Republicans, and even some Democrats, were declaring the Truman foreign policy in Asia a complete failure, and charging that communist sympathizers in the State Department were to blame. Nineteen-fifty-one would not be a good year for the president.

The first document in this section is Truman's first message to Congress on the Korean situation, in which he officially informs the legislature of the North Korean attack and his administration's response. The second comes from an address by Senator Joseph McCarthy (R-Wisconsin), who blames the administration, and particularly Secretary of State Dean Acheson, for the invasion of South Korea.

TRUMAN REPORTS TO CONGRESS ON THE KOREAN SITUATION

[. . .] At 4 o'clock in the morning, Sunday, June 25, Korean time, armed forces from north of the thirty-eighth parallel invaded the Republic of Korea. . . .

. . . [W]ithin a few hours after the invasion was launched from the north, the [United Nations] Commission reported to the United Nations that the attack had come without warning and without provocation.

The reports from the Commission make it unmistakably clear that the attack was naked, deliberate, unprovoked aggression, without a shadow of justification.

This outright breach of the peace, in violation of the United Nations Charter, created a real and present danger to the security of every nation.

This attack was, in addition, a demonstration of contempt for the United Nations, since it was an attempt to settle, by military aggression, a question which the United Nations had been working to settle by peaceful means.

The attack on the Republic of Korea, therefore, was a clear challenge to the basic principles of the United Nations Charter and to the specific actions taken by the United Nations in Korea. If this challenge had not been met squarely, the effectiveness of the United Nations would have all but ended, and the hope of mankind that the United Nations would develop into an institution of world order would have been shattered. . . .

United States forces, as they have arrived in the area, have fought with great valor. The Army troops have been conducting a very difficult delaying operation with skill and determination, outnumbered many times over by attacking troops, spearheaded by tanks. Despite the bad weather of the rainy season, our troops have been valiantly supported by the air and naval forces of both the United States and other members of the United Nations.

In this connection, I think it is important that the nature of our military action in Korea be understood. It should be made perfectly clear that the action was undertaken as a matter of basic moral principle. The United States was going to the aid of a nation established and supported by the United Nations and unjustifiably attacked by an aggressor force. Consequently, we were not deterred by the relative immediate superiority of the attacking forces, by the fact that our base of supplies was 5,000 miles away, or by the further fact that we would have to supply our forces through port facilities that are far from satisfactory.

We are moving as rapidly as possible to bring to bear on the fighting front larger forces and heavier equipment, and to increase our naval and air superiority. But it will take time, men, and material to slow down the forces of aggression, bring those forces to a halt, and throw them back. . . .

The hard facts of the present situation require relentless determination and firm action. The course of the fighting thus far in Korea shows that we can expect no easy solution to the conflict there. We are confronted in Korea with well-supplied, well-led forces which have been long trained for aggressive action. We and the other members of the United Nations who have joined in the effort to restore peace in Korea must expect a hard and costly military operation.

We must also prepare ourselves better to fulfill our responsibilities toward the preservation of international peace and security against possible further aggression. In this effort, we will not flinch in the face of danger or difficulty.

The free world has made it clear, through the United Nations, that lawless aggression will be met with force. This is the significance of Korea—and it is a significance whose importance cannot be over-estimated. . . .

The United States can be proud of the part it has played in the United Nations action in this crisis. We can be proud of the unhesitating support of the American people for the resolute actions taken to halt the aggression in Korea and to support the cause of world peace.

The Congress of the United States, by its strong, bipartisan support of the steps we are taking and by repeated actions in support of international cooperation, has contributed most vitally to the cause of peace. The expressions of support which have been forthcoming from the leaders of both political parties for the actions of our Government and of the United Nations in dealing with the present crisis, have buttressed the firm morale of the entire free world in the face of this challenge.

The American people, together with other free peoples, seek a new era in world affairs. We seek a world where all men may live in peace and freedom, with steadily improving living conditions, under governments of their own free choice.

For ourselves, we seek no territory or domination over others. We are determined to maintain our democratic institutions so that Americans now and in the future can enjoy personal liberty, economic opportunity, and political equality. We are concerned with advancing our prosperity and our well-being as a Nation, but we know that our future is inseparably joined with the future of other free peoples.

We will follow the course we have chosen with courage and with faith, because we carry in our hearts the flame of freedom. We are fighting for liberty and for peace—and with God's blessing we shall succeed.

Congressional Record. 81st Cong., 2nd sess., vol. 96, pt. 8 (July 19, 1950): 10626–630.

SENATOR JOSEPH MCCARTHY (R-WISCONSIN) BLAMES THE ADMINISTRATION FOR THE WAR IN KOREA

. . . America is facing the greatest military disaster in its entire history. Day by day and hour by hour the situation grows blacker, blacker for the world, blacker for the United States, and more particularly it is painfully blacker for over 100,000 American young men in Korea.

At this very moment the mothers and wives of the young men are treading deeply into the valley of darkness and despair. It is not necessary to use high-sounding words to describe the situation to our men in Korea. Those men, their mothers, fathers, and wives, see the situation in its elemental ugliness. They are face to face with facts—facts that cannot be escaped with pious platitudes. It is high time for all, including those responsible for administration policy, to get down to rugged reality, to look at conditions as they actually are today, and not as we wish them to be. . . .

Now let us look briefly at the State Department's plan for Asia insofar as it affects the life and death of this Nation and the life and death of 100,000 of our young men in Korea—the plan to turn all of Asia over to international communism. . . . This plan was proceeding according to schedule until Truman on June 26 ordered MacArthur to defend South Korea. This, of course, was directly contrary to Acheson's previous public statements in which he publicly assured the Chinese Communists that neither Formosa nor Korea was within our defense perimeter, thereby inviting the Communists to move into Korea and Formosa. . . . While it appeared upon the surface on June 26 that Truman was scrapping the disastrous . . . plan, actually the reversal and the scrapping did not go deep. It can now be seen that the Communists sustained only a temporary, minor loss, that is, temporary and minor unless—unless at this late date we scrap the entire Acheson plan, lock, stock, and barrel, and scrap the men who were responsible for the plan.

For example, as we all recall, part of Truman's order to the Seventh Fleet was that it prevent the Republic of China from taking any military action against the Chinese Communists on the mainland. Truman's orders to the Seventh Fleet also were to break Chiang Kai-shek's blockade of the Communist mainland. This released over a quarter of a million Communist troops which were stationed upon the mainland of China opposite Formosa. . . .

As a result of this Acheson-inspired Truman order, at this moment a quarter of a million troops which had been immobilized on the China coast by Chiang Kai-shek's forces are now surrounding and cutting to pieces American forces in North Korea. Those Chinese Communists are using equipment which would not have gotten to them had the American fleet not been ordered to break Chiang Kai-shek's blockade of the China coast. This double-barreled action to aid the Chinese Communists was not United Nations action. It was action taken by President Truman under the advice of Dean Gooderham Acheson. . . .

Let us keep that part of the picture clearly in mind. While the President was ordering our young men to fight and die in the battle against Communists in Korea, Acheson was saying to his Chinese Communist friends . . . : "Don't worry, the Acheson hand will be quicker than the Truman brain. I will have him sign an order under which the Seventh Fleet will make it unnecessary for you to guard the China mainland from Chiang Kai-shek's 500,000 troops on Formosa. I will insert in that order a provision forbidding the continuance of the blockade of the China coast by Chiang Kai-shek. Then you can get the necessary war materiel and oil which Chiang has prevented reaching your armies."

But that was only one of the major services which our State Department has rendered the Chinese Communists. With half a million Chinese Communists in Korea—I believe it is now 1,000,000—killing American men, Acheson says, "Now let's be calm; let's not take hasty action; let's do nothing to alienate the friendship of the Chinese Communists who are killing our men. Let's keep them friendly."

With the rim of the world on fire, with the death toll of American men mounting by the hour, the great Red Dean asks us to be calm and patient. It is like advising a man whose home is being pillaged and burned, whose family is being killed, to be calm and not take hasty action for fear that he might alienate the affection of the murderers.

Such has been the blueprint for disaster. It doesn't take a military or diplomatic expert to tell the American people that if we continue with the same plans and the same planners 100,000 men will be sacrificed on Acheson's altar of double dealing, and western civilization will have been dealt a staggering blow. . . .

Congressional Record. 81st Cong., 2d sess., vol. 96, pt. 12 (December 6, 1950): 16177–79.

McCARTHYISM (1950)

Truman's loyalty program for federal employees was launched in 1947 in an effort to deflect congressional criticism that the administration was not taking seriously the question of communists in government. However, domestic and foreign events from 1948 to 1950 conspired to make the president's efforts appear insufficient, and to give Republicans a ready-made campaign issue in the elections of 1950 and 1952.

The House Un-American Activities Committee (HUAC) had been established before World War II to investigate organizations and individuals suspected of harboring pro-Nazi and pro-Soviet sympathies. With the end of the war the committee came to focus exclusively on communism. After the Republicans won the House and Senate in 1946, it took on a more partisan character, seeking to identify communist sympathizers connected with Roosevelt's New Deal. The committee accomplished little before 1948, aside from identifying a number of "subversives" in the motion picture industry. However, beginning in 1948, a series of former communists—some of whom had confessed to spying for the Soviet Union—appeared before the committee to claim that a number of high-ranking government officials were secretly working for the Soviets. Among those so identified were Lauchlin Currie, one of Roosevelt's closest wartime advisors, former assistant treasury secretary Harry Dexter White, and Alger Hiss, a former director of political affairs in the State Department. Republicans began to claim that communists had infiltrated the federal government even at its highest levels.

Truman and his administration responded defensively to such charges. In a particularly poor choice of words, he labeled the issue of communists in government a "red herring," and charged HUAC with being only interested in getting publicity.[1] Moreover, after Alger Hiss was convicted of perjury for denying that he had been a Soviet spy (the statute of limitations for espionage having expired by this time), Secretary of State Dean Acheson promised that he did "not intend to turn his back" on his friend Hiss.[2] Republicans interpreted this as an administration attempt to minimize Hiss's crimes.

Foreign events also served to strengthen in the public mind the idea that communists had infiltrated the government. Republicans blamed the State Department for the communist victory in China in 1949, since leading American diplomats had decided that the nationalists were a lost cause and pushed to cut off aid to them. The successful Soviet test of an atomic bomb led to further recriminations, since it was assumed that the Russians had only succeeded in doing so thanks to their espionage efforts during the war. Finally, the State Department came under fire over Korea when it was revealed that Acheson had made a speech which seemed to suggest that the United States would not come to South Korea's defense. The net effect of these developments suggested to some a conspiracy within the federal government—perhaps at its very highest levels—to advance the cause of international communism.

One ambitious young politician who successfully capitalized on this notion was Senator Joseph McCarthy (R-Wisconsin). In February 1950, McCarthy made a speech at a Republican rally in Wheeling, West Virginia, in which he claimed to "have here in my hand a list of 205 that were known to the Secretary of State as being members of the Communist party, and who nevertheless are still working and shaping policy in the State Department."[3] Truman angrily denied the charges, calling the Wisconsin senator unfit "to have a hand in the operation of the Government of the United States," but Republicans, frustrated by their defeat in 1948, eagerly seized on McCarthy's accusations.[4] Moreover, a number of Democrats proved willing to go along. In September 1950, Congress passed an internal-security bill proposed by Senator Patrick McCarran (D-Nevada) that required communist organizations to register with the federal government, and authorized the imprisonment of suspected communists if a national emergency occurred. Truman vetoed that bill, arguing not only that it was unnecessary but that it would "greatly weaken our liberties and give aid and comfort to those who would destroy us."[5] However, Congress quickly voted to override the veto by overwhelming margins, and the bill became law. As one of the president's advisors admitted, "To oppose the bill would mean being labeled pro-Communist."[6]

Indeed, the charge that the president was "soft on communism" would play a major role in the midterm elections of 1950, and the GOP made substantial gains in both houses of Congress. Throughout the remainder of Truman's presidency, McCarthy in the Senate and HUAC in the House directed a constant stream of abuse toward the Democrats in general and the administration in particular. The 1951 conviction of Julius and Ethel Rosenberg for stealing atomic secrets added even more fuel to the fire, so that by 1952, McCarthy was even accusing former secretary of state George C. Marshall of being a part of the conspiracy. The president tried repeatedly to fight back, but public opinion polls showed general approval of McCarthy's tactics. The Wisconsin senator would continue his assault until 1954, when the Senate voted to censure him.

The first document in this section is an address by McCarthy himself, explaining the nature of the communist threat to the United States. The second is Truman's message informing Congress of his veto of the McCarran Internal Security Act, which he claims would be of more help than harm to communism.

NOTES

1. David McCullough, *Truman* (New York: Simon & Schuster, 1992), 652.
2. Donald R. McCoy, *The Presidency of Harry S. Truman* (Lawrence: University Press of Kansas, 1984), 217.
3. *Congressional Record*, 81st Cong., 2d sess., vol. 3, pt. 2 (February 20, 1950): 1956–57.
4. Alonzo L. Hamby, *Man of the People: A Life of Harry S. Truman* (New York: Oxford University Press, 1995), 530.
5. McCoy, *Presidency*, 234–35.
6. Ibid., 234.

SENATOR JOSEPH MCCARTHY (R-WISCONSIN) EXPLAINS THE COMMUNIST THREAT

Fellow Americans, thank you very much for the opportunity to be with you tonight to discuss a subject which, in my opinion, towers in importance above all others. It is the subject of international atheistic communism. It deals with the problem of destroying the conspiracy against the people of America and free men everywhere. . . .

. . . [M]any of you have been engaged in this all-out fight against communism long before I came on the scene. You have been engaged in what may well be that final Armageddon foretold in the Bible—that struggle between good and evil, between life and death, if you please.

At the start, let me make clear that in my opinion no special credit is due those of us who are making an all-out fight against this Godless force—a force which seeks to destroy all the honesty and decency that every Protestant, Jew and Catholic has been taught at his mother's knee. It is a task for which we can claim no special credit for doing. It is one which we are obligated to perform. It is one of the tasks for which we were brought into this world—for which we were born. If we fail to use all the powers of mind and body which God gave us, then I am sure our mothers, wherever they are tonight, may well sorrow for the day of our birth. . . .

We know that the major aim of communism, as stated by its atheistic leaders more than 30 years ago, is to create a Red China, thence a Red Asia, wash it with a Red Pacific—and then enslave America.

In this connection let us take a look at the magnitude of Russian success and the enormity of our disaster in China. This is the disaster to which Mr. Acheson refers as the dawning of a new day; the disaster to which Mr. [Owen] Lattimore [an East Asia scholar at Johns Hopkins University] refers as a "limitless horizon of hope."

For whom is Mr. Acheson's new day dawning? Who faces Lattimore's limitless horizon of hope? Not China. Not the forces of democracy in America, but the military masters of the Soviet Union.

The question in the mind of a man elected to represent the people of this Nation and indirectly the people of the world is, Why is this so?

Is it because we are less intelligent than the Communists? Is it because we can't match them in courage? Is it because their devotion to atheism is greater than our devotion to God? Is it because we are less willing to stand up and fight for what we think is right? Ladies and gentlemen, the answer to all those questions is "No." Then what is the answer? Is it in our leadership? To that my answer is "Yes," and I challenge anyone to find another answer.

I have been naming and presenting evidence against those leaders who have been responsible for selling into Communist slavery 400,000,000 people—those leaders responsible for the creation of Communist steppingstones to the American shores.

Those in power in Washington say that this is not so; that those are not the men. Now if I have named the wrong men, then the American people are entitled to know who is responsible for the tremendous Communist victory in Asia and the dismal American defeat—the greatest defeat any nation has suffered in war or peace.

It is essential, therefore, that we put the spotlight of exposure on those who are responsible for this disaster. This is important, not for the purpose of exposing past failures, but because those same men are now doing America's planning for the future. Unfortunately they have become so deeply entrenched that almost every power of the Government is used to sabotage any attempt to expose and root them out. . . .

. . . I have tried to give you the highlights of a difficult and dangerous situation that exists. You have as a flaming backdrop to my remarks the facts of the world as you find them today. Communism is no longer a creeping threat to America. It is a racing doom that comes closer to our shore each day. To resist it we must be intelligently strong.

Such strength will come only from men and women dedicated to the wholehearted defense of democracy. The average American who constitutes the heart and soul of this Nation is so dedicated. We must be sure that those who seek to lead up today are equally dedicated. We cannot survive on half loyalties any more than we can find the facts of Communist conspiracy with half-truths.

Congressional Record. 81st Cong., 2d sess., vol. 96, pt. 15 (June 2, 1950): A4159–62.

TRUMAN VETOES THE MCCARRAN INTERNAL SECURITY ACT

[. . .] This is an omnibus bill containing many different legislative proposals with only one thing in common: they are all represented to be "anticommunist." But when the many complicated pieces of the bill are analyzed in detail, a startling result appears.

H.R. 9490 would not hurt the Communists. Instead, it would help them.

It has been claimed over and over that this is an "anticommunist" bill—a "Communist control" bill. But in actual operation the bill would have results exactly the opposite of those intended. . . .

It would help the Communists in their efforts to create dissension and confusion within our borders.

It would help the Communist propagandists throughout the world who are trying to undermine freedom by discrediting as hypocrisy the efforts of the United States on behalf of freedom.

Specifically, some of the principal objections to the bill are as follows:

1. It would aid potential enemies by requiring the publication of a complete list of vital defense plants, laboratories, and other installations.

2. It would require the Department of Justice and its Federal Bureau of Investigation to waste immense amounts of time and energy attempting to carry out its unworkable registration provisions.

3. It would deprive us of the great assistance of many aliens in intelligence matters.

4. It would antagonize friendly governments.

5. It would put the Government of the United States in the thought-control business.

6. It would make it easier for subversive aliens to become naturalized as U.S. citizens.

7. It would give Government officials vast powers to harass all of our citizens in the exercise of their right of free speech.

Legislation with these consequences is not necessary to meet the real dangers which communism presents to our free society. Those dangers are serious and must be met. But this bill would hinder us, not help us, in meeting them. Fortunately, we already have on the books strong laws which give us most of the protection we need from the real dangers of treason, espionage, sabotage, and actions looking to the overthrow of our Government by force and violence. Most of the provisions of this bill have no relation to these real dangers. . . .

The idea of requiring Communist organizations to divulge information about themselves is a simple and attractive one. But it is about as practical as requiring thieves to register with the sheriff. Obviously, no such organization as the Communist Party is likely to register itself voluntarily. . . .

There is no more fundamental axiom of American freedom than the familiar statement: In a free country, we punish men for the crimes they commit, but never for the opinions they have. And the reason this is so fundamental to freedom is not, as many suppose, that it protects the few unorthodox from suppression by the majority. To permit freedom of expression is primarily for the benefit of the majority because it protects criticism, and criticism leads to progress.

We can and we will prevent espionage, sabotage, or other actions endangering our national security. But we would betray our finest traditions if we attempted, as this bill would attempt, to curb the simple expression of opinion. This we should never do, no matter how distasteful the opinion may be to the vast majority of our people. The course proposed by this bill would delight the Communists, for it would make a mockery of the Bill of Rights and of our claims to stand for freedom in the world. . . .

We need not fear the expression of ideas—we do need to fear their suppression.

Our position in the vanguard of freedom rests largely on our demonstration that the free expression of opinion, coupled with government by popular consent, leads to national strength and human advancement. Let us not, in cowering and foolish fear, throw away the ideals which are the fundamental basis of our free society. . . .

I do not undertake lightly the responsibility of differing with the majority in both Houses of Congress who have voted for this bill. We are all Americans; we all wish to safeguard and preserve our constitutional liberties against internal and external enemies. But I cannot approve this legislation, which instead of accomplishing its avowed purpose would actually interfere with our liberties and help the Communists against whom the bill was aimed.

This is a time when we must marshal all of our resources and all the moral strength of our free system in self-defense against the threat of Communist aggression. We will fail in this, and we will destroy all that we seek to preserve, if we sacrifice the liberties of our citizens in a misguided attempt to achieve national security. . . .

No considerations of expediency can justify the enactment of such a bill as this, a bill which would so greatly weaken our liberties and give aid and comfort to those who would destroy us. I have, therefore, no alternative but to return this bill without my approval, and I earnestly request the Congress to reconsider its action.

Congressional Record. 81st Cong., 2d sess., vol. 96, pt. 11 (September 22, 1950): 15629–32.

THE DISMISSAL OF GENERAL DOUGLAS MacARTHUR (1951)

It did not take long for tensions to develop between Truman and his top military commander in Asia, General Douglas MacArthur. Already well-known for his conduct of the war in the Pacific, MacArthur had been named supreme commander of the occupation forces in postwar Japan. He became even more famous in September 1950, when he orchestrated an amphibious landing at Inchon that outflanked the North Korean Army and immediately turned the tide of the war. An arrogant, headstrong man, he disliked taking orders from Washington, and when he disagreed with his superiors, he tended to complain about it in public. Given MacArthur's vast popularity in 1950 and 1951, this was a very dangerous situation for the president.

Part of the problem was the sheer magnitude of the victory at Inchon. Within days, the North Korean army had been virtually destroyed, its shattered remnants in full retreat toward the thirty-eighth parallel, which formed the border between North and South Korea. MacArthur sent his United Nations army after them, despite warnings from the Chinese that they would come to the assistance of the North Koreans if UN forces crossed the border. At a meeting between the general and Truman on Wake Island on October 15, MacArthur assured the president that the Chinese were bluffing, and promised an end to the fighting by Thanksgiving.

As it turned out, the Chinese were not bluffing. On October 26, as UN troops were nearing the Manchurian border, Chinese troops launched an attack that turned the tide of war once again. MacArthur called it an "entirely new war," as his army fell into retreat.[1] By Christmas they had been pushed back to the thirty-eighth parallel, and it began to look as though they might be forced off the Korean peninsula altogether. Americans at home began demanding the use of the atomic bomb, or alternatively that all U.S. troops be withdrawn. Truman quickly denied that he was considering either course; instead he asked Congress for nearly $17 billion in extra military spending to finance the war.

By March 1951 the Chinese advance had been halted, and the war settled into what appeared to be a stalemate. At this point the president hoped to sound out the enemy for possible peace terms, preparing a note proposing that both sides return to the situation that had existed before the North Korean attack—the peninsula would remain divided along the thirty-eighth parallel. However, after MacArthur received a copy of the draft proposal, he issued his own statement on March 24, in which he ridiculed the fighting power of the Chinese army and threatened to expand the war. His words effectively sabotaged the administration's diplomatic efforts, and Truman demanded that the general make no further public pronouncements on the matter.

MacArthur, however, was not finished. By this time many Republicans had begun to question the administration's handling of the war. House Republican leader Joseph W. Martin, Jr., noted that the Chinese nationalists on Taiwan had 800,000 soldiers, and that they were looking for an opportunity to avenge their 1949 defeat by the Chinese communists. Why not bring them to Korea? The administration, however, feared that this might lead to Soviet intervention, resulting in a Third World War. The Korean conflict would remain a "limited war" aimed at bringing China and North Korea to the bargaining table.

This answer did not satisfy Martin, who chose to sound out MacArthur for his views on the subject. Always eager for publicity, the general responded in a blunt letter that Martin promptly read aloud on the floor of the House. The general claimed that in Korea "Communist conspirators have elected to make their play for global conquest." The fall of Korea would lead to the loss of all Asia, and the collapse of Europe would soon follow. He concluded, in a now-famous phrase, "There is no substitute for victory."[2]

For Truman, this was the final straw, and the president issued an order dismissing MacArthur from command. On April 11, 1951, he gave a radio address explaining his policy in Korea, as well as his reasons for sacking the popular general. Nevertheless, the public outcry was tremendous. One southern senator described the mood in his home state as "almost hysterical." The press attacked Truman for removing the only man who seemed to offer a way out of the Korean mess—proof that the president was, in the words of the *Chicago Tribune*, "unfit, morally and mentally, for his high office."[3] Republicans in Congress echoed this line, and demanded hearings to investigate the controversy. Some even began to speak of impeaching the president.

Upon his return to the United States, MacArthur was treated to a hero's welcome, and was invited to make speeches throughout the country, including before Congress. Many began to speak of the general as a possible presidential candidate for 1952. Meanwhile, Truman's popularity sank to its lowest point ever—one public opinion poll showed his approval rating at 24 percent. Yet public opinion can be fickle, and nowhere was this more obvious than in the aftermath of the MacArthur controversy. After a few weeks of speeches and ticker tape parades the American people seemed to grow tired of the bombastic general. The congressional hearings on the dismissal attracted little attention, and after two months of testimony the investigating subcommittee adjourned with precious little to show for its efforts. Meanwhile Truman's approval rating began to bounce back—by the time the hearings ended, it had reached 31 percent. MacArthur eventually entered the primary contest for the Republican nomination for president; however, he attracted little support, and was easily swept aside by the front-runner, Dwight D. Eisenhower.

In many ways, the Truman-MacArthur controversy was more important for its symbolism than for its merits. After all, MacArthur had been clearly insubordinate, and in the end even the general's supporters had to admit that the president was within his constitutional rights to dismiss him from command. More importantly, the public and congressional outcry represented a widespread sense of frustration over the course of the war in Korea. Americans were not accustomed to "limited war"; they expected massive intervention, followed by the enemy's unconditional surrender—just as had happened in World War II. When the Korean War failed to develop in this way, the public blamed the president. Indeed, the continuing stalemate in Asia was the primary motive behind Truman's decision in 1952 not to seek another term in the White House.

The documents in this section include a public statement by Truman explaining MacArthur's dismissal, and excerpts from an address by Senator Alexander Wiley (R-Wisconsin), who faults the administration for the firing of the "great soldier."

NOTES

1. Donald R. McCoy, *The Presidency of Harry S. Truman* (Lawrence: University Press of Kansas, 1984), 244.
2. U.S. Department of State, *Foreign Relations of the United States*, 1950, 7: 826.
3. David McCullough, *Truman* (New York: Simon & Schuster, 1992), 844–45.

TRUMAN EXPLAINS HIS FIRING OF MACARTHUR

[. . .] In the simplest terms, what we are doing in Korea is this: We are trying to prevent a third world war.

I think most people in this country recognized that fact last June. And they warmly supported the decision of the Government to help the Republic of Korea against the Communist aggressors. Now, many persons, even some who applauded our decision to defend Korea, have forgotten the basic reason for our action.

It is right for us to be in Korea. It was right last June. It is right today. . . .

The question we have had to face is whether the Communist plan of conquest can be stopped without general war. Our Government and other countries associated with us in the United Nations believe that the best chance of stopping it without general war is to meet the attack in Korea and defeat it there.

That is what we have been doing. It is a difficult and bitter task.

But so far it has been successful. . . .

So far, by fighting a limited war in Korea, we have prevented aggression from succeeding, and bringing on a general war. And the ability of the whole free world to resist Communist aggression has been greatly improved.

We have taught the enemy a lesson. He has found out that aggression is not cheap or easy. Moreover, men all over the world who want to remain free have been given new courage and new hope. They know now that the champions of freedom can stand up and fight and that they will stand up and fight. . . .

We do not want to see the conflict in Korea extended. We are trying to prevent a world war—not to start one. The best way to do that is to make it plain that we and the other free countries will continue to resist the attack.

But you may ask, why can't we take other steps to punish the aggressor. Why don't we bomb Manchuria and China itself? Why don't we assist Chinese Nationalist troops to land on the mainland of China?

If we were to do these things we would be running a very grave risk of starting a general war. If that were to happen, we would have brought about the exact situation we are trying to prevent.

If we were to do these things, we would become entangled in a vast conflict on the continent of Asia and our task would become immeasurably more difficult all over the world.

What would suit the ambitions of the Kremlin better than for our military forces to be committed to a full-scale war with Red China? [. . .]

I believe that we must try to limit the war in Korea for these vital reasons: to make sure that the precious lives of our fighting men are not wasted; to see that the security of our country and the free world is not jeopardized; and to prevent a third world war.

A number of events have made it evident that General MacArthur did not agree with that policy. I have therefore considered it essential to relieve General MacArthur so that there would be no doubt or confusion as to the real purpose and aim of our policy.

It was with the deepest personal regret that I found myself compelled to take this action. General MacArthur is one of our greatest military commanders. But the cause of world peace is more important than any individual.

The change in commands in the Far East means no change whatever in the policy of the United States. We will carry on the fight in Korea with vigor and determination in an effort to bring the war to a speedy and successful conclusion.

We are ready, at any time, to negotiate for a restoration of peace in the area. But we will not engage in appeasement. We are only interested in real peace. . . .

In the hard fighting in Korea, we are proving that collective action among nations is not only a high principle but a workable means of resisting aggression. Defeat of aggression in Korea may be the turning point in the world's search for a practical way of achieving peace and security.

The struggle of the United Nations in Korea is a struggle for peace.

The free nations have united their strength in an effort to prevent a third world war.

That war can come if the Communist rulers want it to come. But this Nation and its allies will not be responsible for its coming.

We do not want to widen the conflict. We will use every effort to prevent that disaster. And, in so doing, we know that we are following the great principles of peace, freedom, and justice.

Congressional Record. 82nd Cong., 1st sess., vol. 97, pt. 3 (April 13, 1951): 3842–43.

SENATOR ALEXANDER WILEY (R-WISCONSIN) DENOUNCES THE FIRING OF MACARTHUR

[. . .] A great crisis in American and world politics has arisen. It has been precipitated by the Chief Executive of our country in his firing of a great soldier, statesman, administrator, patriot—Douglas MacArthur. . . .

When Harry Truman sacked this great leader he was not simply removing a brigadier general or a captain down the line, he was removing a man who has become the world-wide symbol of America's fighting greatness, of our strength and courage, a man . . . who has carved for himself a niche in American history which is virtually unique. He removed a man who was not only the commander of our forces, but those of 52 other nations.

Surely, if the President felt that his differences were so intensely strong with MacArthur and that some decision was necessary, surely a better way could have been found. Further consultation could have taken place between our Chief Executive and the United Nations commander. Instead, the President chose to take an action whose repercussions are so staggering that we can only barely perceive them now. . . .

. . . [T]here has been a great deal of bunk and baloney put out by the administration within the last 4 or 5 days in its puny attempt to justify the dismissal action. I want to analyze point by point some of the smears and phony inferences that have been made; some of the innuendoes that have been cast against General MacArthur; some of the misinterpretations that have been made of his position.

Now, first, is it true as administration supporters say, that MacArthur has willfully flouted higher authority? I say "No."

As has been documented from MacArthur headquarters in Tokyo, the general is firmly convinced that he complied with the letter and spirit of the directives sent to him by Mr. Truman and by the Joint Chiefs of Staff. As a soldier, as former Chief of Staff, as a man who has been subject to discipline all his life and who has necessarily imposed discipline, MacArthur knows the necessity for obedience to one's superiors. He is not a man who lightly dismisses higher authority. . . .

Second, I want to point out that the administration's supporters would have us erroneously believe that MacArthur was lightly toying with a third world war in Asia. I think that such a charge is absurd. Douglas MacArthur has seen the horrible results of war. He carries the scars of battle on his body. He has seen enough combat to know that war is a bloody, sickening affair. He knows that war, of itself, solves nothing.

Third, the administration's supporters contend that Douglas MacArthur by urging the bombing of Manchurian bases would bring on a full-scale war with Red China. Well, my friends, according to the latest reports, there are over a half million Red Chinese troops posed for a spring offensive against the some three hundred thousand UN troops. If that is not a full-scale war, what is? [. . .]

. . . [T]here are those who contend that MacArthur wants us to fight endlessly on the Asiatic continent. Well, we seem to be fighting endlessly on the Korean Peninsula and, according to geographers, that is still a part of the Asiatic continent.

But let me further point out this, my friends: Earlier this week the question was asked in the Senate, Has General MacArthur ever stated that he wants to land an American army on the Asiatic continent? No supporter of the administration could answer that question by proving that MacArthur ever made any such a recommendation. . . .

But I ask you . . . what would you do if you were in MacArthur's shoes and you saw the Red Chinese forces building up for their spring offensive? Would you keep your hands tied behind your back, so to speak, or would you want to send bomber formations up so as to stop the Red offensive before it started?

What I am driving at is this, my friends: Douglas MacArthur with all his years of military background knows that the best time to stop an attack is to hit it before it is in a position to hit you. What's wrong with that policy? Nothing.

And so, we could go on, answering point by point the smears against MacArthur. The situation boils down to the fact that the American people have faith in Douglas MacArthur, just as they lack faith in the Democratic administration. On the other hand, the administration lacks faith in Douglas MacArthur just as it lacks faith in the American people.

It is quite clear that the Democratic Party has been handling this MacArthur situation with the November 1952 election in mind. I say that it is up to the Republican Party to realize that to a tremendous extent the 1952 decision is at stake in how the MacArthur situation is handled. But I want to make myself perfectly clear.

I don't feel that we can become so exclusively absorbed in partisan politics and angles that we forget that infinitely more important than the welfare of our party is the welfare of our country. In this instance it is my firm judgment that a victory for the Republican Party in November 1952 is imperatively necessary for the future peace, prosperity, and freedom of America.

Congressional Record. 82nd Cong., 1st sess., vol. 97, pt. 3 (April 17, 1951): 3957–58.

RECOMMENDED READINGS

Berman, William C. *The Politics of Civil Rights in the Truman Administration.* Columbus: Ohio State University Press, 1970.

Davies, Richard O. *Housing Reform during the Truman Administration.* Columbia: University of Missouri Press, 1966.

Ferrell, Robert E. *Harry S. Truman: A Life.* Columbia: University of Missouri Press, 1994.

Freeland, Richard M. *The Truman Doctrine and the Origins of McCarthyism: Foreign Policy, Domestic Politics, and Internal Security, 1946–1948.* New York: Knopf, 1972.

Hamby, Alonzo L. *Man of the People: A Life of Harry S. Truman.* New York: Oxford University Press, 1998.

Hartmann, Susan M. *Truman and the 80th Congress.* Columbia: University of Missouri Press, 1971.

Hogan, Michael J. *The Marshall Plan: America, Britain, and the Reconstruction of Western Europe, 1947–1952.* New York: Cambridge University Press, 1987.

————. *A Cross of Iron: Harry S. Truman and the Origins of the National Security State, 1945–1954*. New York: Cambridge University Press, 1998.

Ireland, Timothy P. *Creating the Entangling Alliance: The Origins of the North Atlantic Treaty Organization*. Westport, Conn.: Greenwood Press, 1981.

Karabell, Zachary. *The Last Campaign: How Harry Truman Won the 1948 Election*. New York: Alfred A. Knopf, 2000.

Kaufman, Burton. *The Korean War: Challenges in Crisis, Credibility, and Command*. New York: Alfred A. Knopf, 1986.

Lee, R. Alton. *Truman and Taft-Hartley: A Question of Mandate*. Lexington: University of Kentucky Press, 1966.

Lowitt, Richard, ed. *The Truman-MacArthur Controversy*. Chicago: Rand McNally, 1967.

McCoy, Donald. *The Presidency of Harry S. Truman*. Lawrence: University Press of Kansas, 1984.

Miller, Merle. *Plain Speaking: An Oral Biography of Harry S. Truman*. New York: Putnam, 1974.

Poen, Monte M. *Harry S. Truman versus the Medical Lobby: The Genesis of Medicare*. Columbia: University of Missouri Press, 1979.

Stueck, William. *The Korean War: An International History*. Princeton, N.J.: Princeton University Press, 1995.

Thompson, Francis H. *The Frustration of Politics: Truman, Congress, and the Loyalty Issue, 1945–1953*. Rutherford, N.J.: Fairleigh Dickinson University Press, 1979.

Wainstock, Dennis D. *The Decision to Drop the Atomic Bomb*. Westport, Conn.: Greenwood Press, 1996.

Internet Sources

Harry S. Truman Library and Museum—http://trumanlibrary.org/.

Project Whistlestop—Harry S. Truman digital archive on the web—http://www.whistlestop.org/.

BIBLIOGRAPHY

PRINT SOURCES

Achenbaum, Andrew. *Social Security: Visions and Revisions.* New York: Cambridge University Press, 1986.

Adams, Michael C. *The Best War Ever.* Baltimore: Johns Hopkins University Press, 1994.

Badger, Anthony J. *The New Deal.* New York: Farrar, Straus and Giroux, 1989.

Bellush, Bernard. *The Failure of the NRA.* New York: Norton, 1975.

Berman, William C. *The Politics of Civil Rights in the Truman Administration.* Columbus: Ohio State University Press, 1970.

Best, Gary Dean. *Pride, Prejudice and Politics: Roosevelt versus Recovery, 1933–1938.* Westport, Conn.: Greenwood Press, 1991.

Brinkley, Alan. *The End of Reform: New Deal Liberalism in Depression and War.* New York: Alfred A. Knopf, 1995.

Burner, David. *Herbert Hoover: A Public Life.* New York: Alfred A. Knopf, 1979.

Cole, Wayne S. *Roosevelt and the Isolationists, 1932–45.* Lincoln: University of Nebraska Press, 1983.

Dallek, Robert. *Franklin D. Roosevelt and American Foreign Policy, 1932–1945.* New York: Oxford University Press, 1979.

Divine, Robert A. *The Reluctant Belligerent: American Entry into World War II.* New York: John Wiley & Sons, 1965.

Fausold, Martin L. *The Presidency of Herbert C. Hoover.* Lawrence: University Press of Kansas, 1985.

Ferrell, Robert H. *American Diplomacy in the Great Depression: Hoover-Stimson Diplomacy, 1929–1933.* New Haven, Conn.: Yale University Press, 1957.

———. *Harry S. Truman: A Life.* Columbia: University of Missouri Press, 1994.

Freidel, Frank. *Franklin D. Roosevelt: A Rendezvous with Destiny.* Boston: Little, Brown, 1990.

Gaddis, John L. *The United States and the Origins of the Cold War, 1941–1947*. New York: Columbia University Press, 1972.

Hamby, Alonzo L. *Man of the People: A Life of Harry S. Truman*. New York: Oxford University Press, 1998.

Hartmann, Susan M. *Truman and the 80th Congress*. Columbia: University of Missouri Press, 1971.

Haynes, John E. *Red Scare or Red Menace? American Communism and Anticommunism in the Cold War Era*. Chicago: Ivan R. Dee, 1996.

Heinrichs, Waldo, Jr. *Threshold of War*. New York: Oxford University Press, 1988.

Herman, Arthur. *Joseph McCarthy: Reexamining the Life and Legacy of America's Most Hated Senator*. New York: Free Press, 1999.

Hogan, Michael J. *The Marshall Plan: America, Britain, and the Reconstruction of Western Europe, 1947–1952*. New York: Cambridge University Press, 1987.

———. *A Cross of Iron: Harry S. Truman and the Origins of the National Security State, 1945–1954*. New York: Cambridge University Press, 1998.

Karabell, Zachary. *The Last Campaign: How Harry Truman Won the 1948 Election*. New York: Alfred A. Knopf, 2000.

Kaufman, Burton. *The Korean War: Challenges in Crisis, Credibility, and Command*. New York: Alfred A. Knopf, 1986.

Keegan, John. *The Second World War*. New York: Viking, 1990.

Kennedy, David M. *Freedom from Fear: The American People in Depression and War, 1929–1945*. New York and Oxford: Oxford University Press, 1999.

Leff, Mark H. *The Limits of Symbolic Reform: The New Deal and Taxation*. New York: Cambridge University Press, 1984.

Leuchtenburg, William E. *Franklin D. Roosevelt and the New Deal, 1932–1940*. New York: Harper Torchbooks, 1963.

———. *The Supreme Court Reborn: The Constitutional Revolution in the Age of Roosevelt*. New York: Oxford University Press, 1995.

Maney, Patrick J. *The Roosevelt Presence: A Biography of Franklin Delano Roosevelt*. New York: Twayne Publishers, 1992.

Marks, Frederick W. *Wind over Sand: The Diplomacy of Franklin Roosevelt*. Athens: University of Georgia Press, 1988.

McCoy, Donald. *The Presidency of Harry S. Truman*. Lawrence: University Press of Kansas, 1984.

McCraw, Thomas K. *TVA and the Power Fight, 1933–1939*. Philadelphia: Lippincott, 1971.

McCullough, David. *Truman*. New York: Simon & Schuster, 1992.

McElvaine, Robert. *The Great Depression: America, 1929–1941*. New York: Times Books, 1984.

Miller, Nathan. *FDR: An Intimate Biography*. Garden City, N.Y.: Doubleday, 1983.

Oshinsky, Michael. *A Conspiracy So Immense: The World of Joe McCarthy*. New York: Free Press, 1983.

Patterson, James T. *Congressional Conservatism and the New Deal*. Lexington: University Press of Kentucky, 1967.

Perrett, Geoffrey. *Days of Sadness, Years of Triumph: The American People, 1939–1945*. New York: Coward, McCann and Geoghegan, 1979.

Polenberg, Richard. *War and Society: The United States, 1941–1945*. Philadelphia: Lippincott, 1972.

Prange, Gordon. *At Dawn We Slept: The Untold Story of Pearl Harbor*. New York: Penguin, 1981.

Rhodes, Richard. *The Making of the Atomic Bomb*. New York: Simon & Schuster, 1986.

Romasco, Albert. *The Politics of Recovery: Roosevelt's New Deal*. New York: Oxford University Press, 1983.

Sherwin, Martin. *A World Destroyed: The Atomic Bomb and the Grand Alliance*. New York: Alfred A. Knopf, 1975.

Smith, Gaddis. *American Diplomacy During the Second World War, 1941–1945*. New York: John Wiley & Sons, 1965.

Sobel, Robert. *Panic on Wall Street*. New York: Macmillan, 1968.

Stueck, William. *The Korean War: An International History*. Princeton, N.J.: Princeton University Press, 1995.

Wainstock, Dennis D. *The Decision to Drop the Atomic Bomb*. Westport, Conn.: Greenwood Press, 1996.

Weed, Clyde P. *The Nemesis of Reform: The Republican Party during the New Deal*. New York: Columbia University Press, 1994.

Wilson, Joan H. *Herbert Hoover: Forgotten Progressive*. New York: HarperCollins, 1975.

Yergin, Daniel. *Shattered Peace: The Origins of the Cold War and the National Security State*. Boston: Houghton Mifflin, 1977.

INTERNET SOURCES

America's Great Depression—http://www.amatecon.com/greatdepression.html.

Center for New Deal Studies—http://www.roosevelt.edu:80/newdeal/.

Cold War International History Project—http://cwihp.si.edu/.

Fireside Chats of Franklin D. Roosevelt—http://www.mhrcc.org/fdr/fdr.html.

Franklin D. Roosevelt and the New Deal—http://www.geocities.com/Athens/4545.

Franklin D. Roosevelt Presidential Library and Museum—http://fdrlibrary.marist.edu/.

Harry S. Truman Library and Museum—http://trumanlibrary.org/.

Herbert Hoover Page, The—http://www.bayserve.net/~falkland/hoover/.

Herbert Hoover Presidential Library and Museum—http://www.hoover.nara.gov.

Herbert Hoover on the World Wide Web—http://www.cs.umb.edu/~rwhealan/jfk/hoover_links.html.

New Deal Network, The—http://newdeal.feri.org/.

Project Whistlestop—Harry S. Truman Digital Archive on the Web—http://www.whistlestop.org/.

World War II (1939–1945)—http://www.cfcsc.dnd.ca/links/milhist/wwii.html.

World War II: The Homefront—http://library.thinkquest.org/15511/.

World War II Timeline—http://history.acusd.edu/gen/WW2Timeline/start.html.

INDEX

Acheson, Dean: accused of communist sympathies, 206–7, 210–11, 212, 214; and Point Four, 200; and Truman Doctrine, 155–56; African Americans, 7, 8, 10, 69; civil rights for, 177–82; support for FDR by, 4–5, 60. *See also* Civil rights
Agricultural Adjustment Act (1933), 59, 60, 64–68, 94
Agricultural Adjustment Administration (AAA), x, 4, 59, 65–66, 127
Agricultural Marketing Act (1929), ix, 2, 12, 15–19, 64
Albania, 5, 157
Amerasia, 166
American Economics Association, 25
American Legion, 38
American Medical Association, 195
Argentina, 201
Atomic bomb, xii, 7, 140, 142, 144–50
Austria, 5, 61
Axis pact, 62–63. *See also* Germany; Italy; Japan

"Baby boom," 9, 140
Bailey, Josiah, 100, 103
Ball, Joseph H., 194
"Bank holiday," 58

Barbour, William W., 90, 92
Belgium, 61, 121, 188
Bennett, Henry G., 200
Berlin Airlift, xiii
Boileau, Gerald, 105
Bonus Army, 14, 35. *See also* Veterans' Bonus Bill (1931)
Borah, William E., 116, 117, 119
Braden, Spruille, 201, 203
Brandeis, Louis, 95
Bricker, John, 189
Brussels Pact, 188. *See also* North Atlantic Treaty Organization (NATO)
Bulgaria, 157
Burke, Edward, 121

Canada, 142, 155, 188
"Cash-and-carry," xi, 116–20, 126. *See also* Neutrality Acts (1935–37)
Chiang Kai-Shek, 171, 210. *See also* China
Chicago Defender, 178
Chicago Tribune, 218
China, 105, 130–31, 145, 171, 205; communist takeover of, xiii-xiv, 8, 142, 192, 212, 214; Japanese invasion of, 5, 6, 62; and Korean War, 142–43, 210, 217–23. *See also* Chiang

Kai-Shek; Japan; Korean War; Mao Tse-Tung

Churchill, Winston, xii, 126, 127, 144. *See also* Great Britain; Lend-Lease Act (1941)

Civil rights, 8, 141, 142, 177–82. *See also* African Americans

Civil War, 34, 99

Civilian Conservation Corps, x, 58, 68–72

Clayton Act (1914), 164

Cleveland, Grover, 98

Clifford, Clark, 200

Cold War, 8, 9, 141–43. *See also* Berlin Airlift; China; Korean War; Marshall Plan (1948); North Atlantic Treaty Organization (NATO); Soviet Union; Truman Doctrine

Connally, Tom, 132

Coolidge, Calvin, 31, 39

"Court-packing" plan. *See* Judicial Procedures Reform Act (1937)

Cuba, 201

Currie, Lauchlin, 211

Czechoslovakia, 5, 61, 188

Denmark, 62, 188, 192

Dewey, Thomas E., xiii, 8, 64, 142

"Dixiecrats," 141, 178. *See also* Civil rights

Donnell, Forrest C., 194

Eastland, James, 178, 181

Economy Act (1932), 3

Eighteenth Amendment, 29, 30–34. *See also* Prohibition; Volstead Act (1919); Wickersham Commission

Eisenhower, Dwight D., xiv, 143, 219

Ellender, Allen J., 183

Emergency Relief Bill (1932), x, 3, 13, 50–54

European Coal and Steel Community, 173

European Recovery Program. *See* Marshall Plan (1948)

European Union, 173

Executive reorganization, xi, 61, 99–104

Faddis, Charles, 106, 108

"Fair Deal," xiii, 142, 178, 195, 200. *See also* Truman, Harry S.

Fair Employment Practices Commission, 178.

Fair Labor Standards Act (1938), xi, 61, 109–15

Federal Bureau of Investigation (FBI), 166–67, 215

Federal Farm Board. *See* Agricultural Marketing Act (1929)

Fordney-McCumber Tariff Bill. 24–25, 28

Foreign Assistance Act (1948), 172. *See also* Marshall Plan

Foreign Economic Assistance Act (1950), 200. *See also* Point Four

Fortune, 105

"Four Freedoms" speech by FDR (1941), 126

"Four Horsemen," 94, 99. *See also* Supreme Court of the United States

France, 115, 150, 171, 186–87; declaration of war on Germany by, 5, 61–62, 116–17; German conquest of, xi, 6, 121; and London Naval Treaty, 19–20; and North Atlantic Treaty Organization, 187–88; war debts of, 42–43. *See also* London Naval Treaty; Marshall Plan; North Atlantic Treaty Organization (NATO); War Debt Moratorium; World War II

Frazier, Lynn, 44, 45

Garner, John Nance, 50

Garrett, Garet, 16, 18

Geneva Conference of 1927, 20

Germany, 141, 144, 157, 187; reparations after World War I, 42–43; and World War II, xi-xii, 5, 6, 9, 57, 61–63, 115–16, 120–21, 126–27, 149. *See also* Hitler, Adolf; War Debt Moratorium (1931); World War II

GI Bill of 1944, 194

Glass, Carter, 96, 98

Gold standard, 4

Good Housekeeping, 105

Grand Army of the Republic, 34
Great Britain, 9, 10, 104, 119, 121, 150; declaration of war on Germany by, 5, 61, 115–17; interests in eastern Mediterranean of, 155, 157; and Lend-Lease Act, xi, 6, 62, 126–27, 130–31; and London Naval Conference, 2, 12, 19–24; and North Atlantic Treaty Organization, 187–88; war debts of, 42–43. *See also* Churchill, Winston; Lend-Lease Act (1941); London Naval Treaty; Mac-Donald, Ramsay; North Atlantic Treaty Organization (NATO); War Debt Moratorium; World War II
"Great Debate" of 1951, 189. *See also* North Atlantic Treaty Organization (NATO)
Greece, 130–31, 192; U.S. aid to, xiii, 8, 141, 155–60, 188. *See also* Truman Doctrine
Groves, Leslie, 144
Grundy, Joseph, 25
Guadalcanal, battle of, xii, 63

Hale, Frederick, 21, 23
Hamilton, Alexander, 24
Harding, Warren G., 11, 57, 65
Hardy, Benjamin, 200.
Harness, Forrest A., 133, 135
Hartley, Fred, 161
Hawley, Willis, 25
Hawley-Smoot Tariff Bill (1930), ix, 12, 24–29, 42
Hearst, William Randolph, 89
Hiroshima, atomic bombing of (1945), xii, 140, 145, 146–49. *See also* Atomic bomb
Hiss, Alger, 211–12
Hitler, Adolf, 43, 61–63, 121, 170. *See also* Germany; World War II
Holifield, Chester, 167, 169
Hoover Dam, 39
Hoover, Herbert, 9, 58, 100, 171,189; and Agricultural Marketing Act (1929), 15–19; and Emergency Relief Bill, 50–54; and Hawley-Smoot Tariff (1930), 24–29; and London Naval

Treaty (1930), 19–24; and Muscle Shoals Joint Resolution, 38–42; opposition to NRA by, 74, 76; presidency of, ix-x, 1–3, 11–15; and Reconstruction Finance Corporation, 46–50; and Veterans' Bonus Bill (1931), 34–38; and War Debt Moratorium, 42–46; and Wickersham Commission, 29–34
Hoover, J. Edgar, 166. *See also* Federal Bureau of Investigation (FBI)
House Un-American Activities Committee (HUAC), 211, 213
Housing Act of 1949, xiii, 182–87
Hughes, Charles Evans, 95. *See also* Supreme Court of the United States
Human Events, 145, 148

Iceland, 188
Inchon, amphibious landing at (1950), 206–7, 217
Indochina, xii, 6, 62
"island-hopping," 63
Israel, xiii
Italy, 3, 171; and London Naval Treaty, 19–20; and World War II, xii, 5, 6, 62–63. *See also* London Naval Treaty (1930); Marshall Plan; Mussolini, Benito; World War II

James, William, 160
Japan, 157; atomic bombing of, 144–49; bombing of U.S.S. *Panay* by, 105; and London Naval Conference, 2, 12, 19–21; and World War II, xi-xiii, 5, 6, 57, 62–63, 132, 205. *See also* Atomic bomb; Hiroshima, atomic bombing of; London Naval Treaty; Nagasaki, atomic bombing of; *Panay*, U.S.S.; Pearl Harbor
Japanese Americans, internment of, xii
Jefferson, Thomas, 120
Johnson Act (1934), 105
Johnson, Hugh S., 59, 73–74
Johnson, Lyndon B., 195
Judicial Procedures Reform Act

(1937), xi, 94–99, 110. *See also* Supreme Court of the United States

Kennedy, John F., 143
Kim Il-Sung, 206. *See also* Korean War; North Korea
Kitchens, Wade, 111, 113
Knowland, William F., 189
Korean War, xiv, 142–43, 189, 195, 205–11, 212, 217–23. *See also* Kim Il-Sung; MacArthur, Douglas; North Korea; South Korea; Syngman Rhee

LaGuardia, Fiorello, 49
Lamont, Thomas, 25, 43
Land o' Lakes Creameries, 18
Landon, Alfred M., xi, 5, 60
Lattimore, Owen, 214
"leap-frogging," 63
Lend-Lease Act (1941), xi, 6, 62, 125–32, 155. *See also* Great Britain; World War II
Lewis, John L., 84, 132–33, 160–61
Lincoln, Abraham, 99, 200
Lindbergh, Charles, 116
Lippmann, Walter, 25
London Naval Treaty (1930), ix, 2, 12, 19–24
Long, Huey P., 89–90
Loyalty-Security Program, xiii, 166–71, 211
Ludlow Amendment (1938), 104–9
Ludlow, Louis, 105–6
Luxembourg, 61, 121, 88

MacArthur, Douglas, xiv, 8, 35, 142, 206, 210, 217–23. *See also* Inchon, amphibious landing at (1950); Korean War
MacDonald, Ramsay, ix, 12, 20. *See also* London Naval Treaty (1930)
Manchuria, 145, 205, 220
Manhattan Project, 4, 144. *See also* Atomic bomb
Mao Tse-Tung, xiii. *See also* China
Marshall, George C., 155, 172, 213
Marshall Plan (1948), xiii, 8, 141, 171–77, 187–88, 199

Martin, Joseph W., Jr., 218
McCarran Internal Security Act (1950), xiv, 143, 213
McCarran, Patrick, 212
McCarthy, Joseph, xiii, 8, 143, 207, 209, 212–13
Medicaid, 195
Medicare, 195
Mexico, 192
Meyer, Herbert A., 184, 186
Midway, battle of (1942), xii, 63
Miller, A.L., 195, 197
Milligan, Jacob, 26, 27
Molotov, Vyacheslav, 172
Monroe Doctrine, 191–92
Morgenthau, Henry, 78, 90
Morley, Felix, 145, 148
Murray, James E., 194
Muscle Shoals Joint Resolution, x, 3, 13, 38–42, 58
Mussolini, Benito, 170. *See also* Italy

Nagasaki, atomic bombing of (1945), xii, 140, 145. *See also* Atomic bomb
Nation, The, 40, 41
National health insurance, 8, 142, 192–99
National Industrial Recovery Act (1933), 59, 60, 72–78; Section 7(a) of, 84, 85, 87. *See also* National Recovery Administration (NRA)
National Labor Relations Act (1935), x, 4, 59, 84–88, 94, 132, 162, 164. *See also* National Labor Relations Board (NLRB); Taft-Hartley Act (1947); War Labor Disputes Act (1943)
National Labor Relations Board (NLRB), 84, 134, 135. *See also* National Labor Relations Act (1935)
National Recovery Administration (NRA), x, 4, 59, 73–74, 76–77, 99. *See also* National Industrial Recovery Act (1933)
Netherlands, 62, 121, 188
Neutrality Acts (1935–37), 5, 61–62, 105, 115–20
Normandy, Allied invasion of (1944), 63

Norris, George, 38–39, 43
Norris-LaGuardia Act (1931), 164
North Atlantic Treaty Organization (NATO), xiii, 142, 187–93, 199
North Korea, xiv, 8, 142–43, 205–11, 217–21. *See also* Korean War; Syngman Rhee
Norway, 62, 188, 192
Nye, Gerald P., 122, 124

Office of Price Administration (OPA), 150–51, 153–54, 193, 197–99. *See also* Wage and Price controls
Old Age Revolving Pensions, Limited, 78.

Panay, U.S.S., 105
Peace Corps, 201
Pearl Harbor, xii, 6, 63, 132, 145, 146, 148. *See also* Japan
Perkins, Frances, 73, 78
"Phony war," 120. *See also* World War II
Pittman, Key, 115
Point Four, xiii, 8, 199–205
Poland, xi, 5, 61, 116, 121. *See also* World War II
Portugal, 188
Potsdam Conference (1945), 144, 147
President's Committee on Administrative Management, 99–100
Price Controls. *See* Wage and price controls
Progressive Party, 172, 177. *See also* Wallace, Henry
Prohibition, x, 29–34

Rayburn, Sam, 200
Reconstruction Finance Corporation (RFC), x, 3, 12, 13, 46–50, 50–51, 53–54
Reed, David A., 66, 67
Relief and Reconstruction Act (1932), 51
Revenue Act of 1935. *See* "Wealth tax"
Rich, Robert, 85, 87
Richardson, Seth, 167

Rockefeller, John D., 90
Roosevelt, Franklin D., 11, 13, 14, 30, 140, 142, 177, 200; and Agricultural Adjustment Act (1933), 64–68; and Civilian Conservation Corps (1933), 68–72; and Executive Reorganization, 99–104; and Fair Labor Standards Act (1938), 109–15; and Lend-Lease (1941), 125–32; and Ludlow Amendment (1938); 104–9; and National Industrial Recovery Act (1933), 72–78; and National Labor Relations Act (1935), 84–85; and Neutrality Revision (1939), 115–20; presidency of, ix-xii, 3–7, 57–64; and Selective Service Act (1940), 120–25; and Social Security Act (1935), 78–84; and Supreme Court Reorganization (1937), 94–99; and War Labor Disputes Act (1943); and Wealth Tax (1935), 89–94
Roosevelt, Theodore, 57, 200
Rosenberg, Julius and Ethel, 213
Russia. *See* Soviet Union

Saturday Evening Post, The, 16
Schechter Poultry Corp. v. United States (1935), x, 74. *See also* National Industrial Recovery Act (1933); National Recovery Administration (NRA)
Section 7(a). *See* National Industrial Recovery Act
Selective Service Act (1940), xi, 120–25, 134
Share Our Wealth Society, 89. *See also* Long, Huey P.
Smith, Alfred E., ix
Smith, Howard W., 132
Smith-Connally War Labor Disputes Act. *See* War Labor Disputes Act (1943)
Smoot, Reid, 25
Social Security Act (1935), x, 4, 8, 59, 78–84, 94
South Korea, xiv, 8, 9, 10, 142–43, 205–11, 212, 217–21. *See also* Kim Il-Sung, Korean War

Soviet Union, 3, 9, 61, 140, 214; detonation of atomic bomb by, 8, 9, 142; espionage by, 166, 212; postwar expansion by, 155–56, 187–89, 205; relations between U.S. and, 7–8, 141, 159, 172, 175–77, 191–92; and World War II, xii-xiii, 6, 62–63, 127, 145. *See also* Cold War; Stalin, Joseph

Special Committee to Investigate the National Defense Program, xi, 139

Stalin, Joseph, xii, 7, 61, 140, 144, 170, 206. *See also* Soviet Union

State Department, 201, 205; accusations of communist infiltration of, 8, 143, 166, 192, 207, 210–11, 212. *See also* Acheson, Dean; McCarthy, Joseph

States' Rights Party. *See* "Dixiecrats"

Stevenson, Adlai, xiv, 143

Stimson, Henry, 144

Stock market crash. *See* Wall Street Crash of 1929

Supreme Court of the United States, 65, 74, 104; attempt by FDR to "pack," x, 5, 60, 74, 94–99, 110. *See also* Judicial Procedures Reform Act (1937); *Schechter Poultry Corp. v. United States* (1935); *United States v. Butler* (1936)

Syngman Rhee, 206. *See also* Korean War; South Korea

Taber, John, 70, 71

Taft, Robert A., 194, 206; and Marshall Plan, 172; and North Atlantic Treaty Organization, 188; and public housing, 183, 184–86; and Taft-Hartley Act, 161, 164–66; and Truman Doctrine, 156; and Wage and Price Controls, 151–55

Taft-Hartley Act (1947), xiii, 8, 141, 160–66

Taylor, Glen, 156

Teheran Conference (1943), xii

Tennessee Valley Authority (TVA), 4, 39–40, 58. *See also* Muscle Shoals Joint Resolution

Thurmond, Strom, 141, 178. *See also* "Dixiecrats"

Time, 139

Townsend, Francis 78. *See also* Old Age Revolving Pensions, Limited

Truman Doctrine, xiii, 8, 141, 155–60

Truman, Harry S., x, xi, 14, 64; and civil rights, 177–82; and decision to intervene in Korea, 205–11; and decision to use the atomic bomb, 144–50; dismissal of MacArthur by, 217–23; and Loyalty-Security Program, 166–71; and Marshall Plan (1948), 171–77; and McCarthyism, 211–17; and national health insurance, 193–99; and North Atlantic Treaty Organization (1949), 187–93; and Point Four program, 199–205; presidency of, xii-xiv, 7–9, 139–44; and public housing, 182–87; and Taft-Hartley Act (1947), 160–66; and Truman Doctrine, 155–60; and Wage and Price Controls, 150–55

Turkey, 192; U.S. aid to, xiii, 8, 141, 155–59. *See also* Truman Doctrine

Twenty-First Amendment, 30. *See also* Prohibition

United Mine Workers, 84, 132, 134. *See also* Lewis, John L.

United Nations, 140, 158, 173, 193, 199; and Korean War, 142, 190–91, 206, 207–9

United States v. Butler (1936), x. *See also* Agricultural Adjustment Act (1933); Supreme Court of the United States

Vandenberg, Arthur, 35, 37, 155–56, 172, 188

Vandenberg Resolution (1948), 188. *See also* North Atlantic Treaty Organization (NATO)

Veterans' Bonus Bill (1931), x, 3, 13, 34–38

Volstead Act (1919), 29, 32. *See also* Prohibition

Voltaire, 171
Vursell, Charles, 173

Wadsworth, James, 80, 82, 121
Wage and Price Controls, xiii, 140–41, 150–55, 193
"Wages and hours" bill. *See* Fair Labor Standards Act (1938)
Wagner, Robert F., 73, 100, 183, 194; and Emergency Relief Bill (1931), 50, 51; and National Labor Relations Act (1935), 84–85
Wagner Act. *See* National Labor Relations Act (1935)
Wall Street Crash of 1929, ix, 2, 12, 64
Wallace, Henry, 78, 140, 141, 172, 177, 188; and Agricultural Adjustment Act (1933), 64–5, 67; and Truman Doctrine, 156, 159
Walsh, David I., 100
War Debt Moratorium (1931), x, 3, 12, 42–46
War Finance Corporation, 46
War Labor Disputes Act (1943), xii, 7, 64, 132–36, 161
Washington, George, 120
"Wealth Tax" (1935), x, 59, 89–94
Wheeler, Burton K., 121, 127
Wherry, Kenneth, 189
White, Harry Dexter, 211
Wickersham, George W., 29. *See also* Wickersham Commission

Wiley, Alexander, 219, 221
Willkie, Wendell, xi, 6, 62, 122, 127
Wilson, Woodrow, 3, 57, 125–26, 200
Wolcott, Jesse P., 183
World War I, 5, 46, 73, 132, 139, 152, 186; bonus for veterans of, 34–35; foreign debts arising from, x, 3, 12, 42; U.S. intervention in, 104, 115. *See also* Veterans' Bonus Bill (1931); War Debt Moratorium (1931)
World War II, xi–xiii, 5–7, 61–64, 166, 192, 193, 211, 219; aftermath of, 9, 140, 150, 205; and American neutrality, 115–32; labor disputes during, 132–36. *See also* Atomic bomb; Axis pact; "Cash-and-carry"; GI Bill of 1944; Guadalcanal, battle of; Hiroshima, atomic bombing of (1945); Hitler, Adolf; Lend-Lease Act (1941); Midway, battle of (1942); Nagasaki, atomic bombing of (1945); Neutrality Acts (1935–37); Normandy, Allied invasion of (1944); Pearl Harbor; "Phony war"; Potsdam Conference (1945); Selective Service Act (1940); Teheran Conference (1943); War Labor Disputes Act (1943); Yalta Conference (1945)

Yalta Conference (1945), xii
Yugoslavia, 157

About the Author

JOHN E. MOSER is Assistant Professor of History at Ashland University in Ohio. He is also author of *Twisting the Lion's Tail: American Anglophobia between the World Wars* (1999).

WARNER MEMORIAL LIBRARY
EASTERN UNIVERSITY
ST. DAVIDS, 19087-3696